ANCIENT ROME

IN

SO MANY WORDS

ANCIENT ROME

IN
SO MANY WORDS

CHRISTOPHER FRANCESE

HIPPOCRENE BOOKS, INC.
New York

Design and composition by K & P Publishing, Conshohocken, PA

For information, address:
HIPPOCRENE BOOKS, INC.
171 Madison Ave.
New York, NY 10016
www.hippocrenebooks.com

Cataloging-in-Publication Data available from the Library of Congress.

ISBN-13: 978-0-7818-1153-8
ISBN-10: 0-7818-1153-8

Printed in the United States of America.

CONTENTS

5

INTRODUCTION

THE BRIEF WORD HISTORIES in this book are meant to provide background on some words that everyone learns when they study Latin, as well as some rarer terms that tell interesting stories about Roman culture. The initial inspiration came from Allan Metcalf and David K. Barhart's *America in So Many Words: Words That Have Shaped America*. This enjoyable book lists a new word or phrase that came into American English every year from 1751 to 1998, with a selection of early additions from 1497 to 1750, and discusses the history behind the adoption of each, from *buffalo* (1633), and *cruller* (1818), to *jambalaya* (1872), *dude* (1877), *blues* (1911), and "go postal" (1994). It struck me that nothing existed for Latin that similarly combined history and philology in a relatively lighthearted and accessible way. I also remembered that the most successful parts of my own Latin classes are not my spellbinding explanations of the ablative absolute but the stories I tell to try to make the new vocabulary more memorable. I hope that all teachers and students of Latin can benefit from the slightly more formal, but still anecdotal, approach taken here to some key words in the Latin lexicon.

It was immediately clear that the chronological presentation of Metcalf and Barnhart was impractical for Latin. The evidence does not permit it, since only in rare cases (as with *paganus* or *fornix*) do we know anything about exactly when a new word, or a new sense of an old word, came into the language. Secondly, Latin, or written Latin at least, which is all we have to go on, is far more conservative than English in its adoption of new words. The vocabulary and grammar of written Latin is recognizably consistent, with some interesting changes, over a period of seven hundred years or more, from (to take very approximate dates) around 200 BC to AD 500. Read some English from even two hundred years ago and the extent of Latin's stasis will become clear. New words could crash the gated community of written Latin only when given approval by poets and scholars, who were generally in no mood to innovate. While this is convenient for us trying to read Latin now, it is an obstacle to seeing the kind of historical development that is so clear in the case of the much better documented and much more porous language of American English.

How, then, to proceed? Advances in scholarship on Roman social history, which have added much to our understanding of ancient Rome in the last thirty years, seemed to recommend a presentation by areas of social life, rather than by chronology or by letters of the alphabet. One of the strengths of classical scholarship has always been its careful attention to language in its social aspects. I have been able to draw on a large body of earlier studies that discuss the cultural implications of distinctive Latin terms in law, poetry, politics, economics, religion, and daily life. Many of the words in this book have had, or probably will one day have, entire books devoted to them. All studies of, say, Roman religion, include information on the precise meanings and implications of key Latin religious terms. Since I have no pretense to completeness, I have simply included a reference or two to some recent or seminal publications that will send the curious in the right directions. Similarly, I have not attempted to provide complete data on all the known meanings of a particular word, something better pursued through the two best Latin dictionaries—the *Oxford Latin Dictionary* and the *Thesaurus Linguae Latinae*. Where appropriate I have included exact references to the *Thesaurus* and other comprehensive reference works that I have consulted.

What I have tried to do is single out the aspects of these words that, while perhaps buried in the dictionaries and specialist literature, might effectively tell some of the central stories of Roman history and culture. I am not, however, under the illusion that these words provide unique keys to understanding the Romans. Indeed quite a few of them show how shifty, deceptive, and downright misleading vocabulary can be. And of course, as the Roman philosopher Seneca points out, "There are a vast number of things that have no name" (*Ingens copia est rerum sine nomine*). Language is an interesting vantage point from which to look, but it hardly provides a complete or unambiguously reliable view of anything but itself.

My method has been to provide several quotations, in English, that illustrate some key senses of a word or phrase, and then a brief discussion. I hope the quotations are vivid enough to be interesting in themselves. On a few occasions, when the quotation seemed sufficiently pithy or memorable in Latin, I have included the original version as well. But I did not think it necessary to cite full Latin texts for everything, when for the present purpose I am interested in the sense of single words and phrases. For those who want to look up the Latin text of a particular quotation, either to explore the context or to check my translation, I have included exact references. Many of the source texts can be found in the widely available Loeb Classical Library, and I have generally tried to cite those editions. Fronto's *Letters* for example, are cited by Haines's Loeb, though Van Den Hout's Teubner edition (1988) is the scholarly standard, and I have used this text to translate from. For those without access to a large library, many of the texts, even fairly obscure ones, can be found in electronic form at the well-maintained Web site The Latin Library (www.thelatinlibrary.com). Some Christian and other post-classical texts not found there can be browsed at a rich site called Bibliotheca Augustana, maintained by Ulrich Harsch (www.fh-augsburg.de/~harsch/a_chron.html). Finally,

Latin inscriptions are being comprehensively collected at the online Epigraphische Datenbank Heidelberg, by a team under the direction of Christian Witschel (www.uni-heidelberg.de/institute/sonst/adw/edh/index.html.en).

I have tried to choose quotations that are striking, that come from a variety of eras and authors, and that illustrate as concretely and unambiguously as possible the various important senses of each word. Again, I have not aimed at a comprehensive treatment of all senses, nor a scientific or chronological presentation of material, as in a dictionary. Nor was it my intention, in the beginning, that Seneca the Younger turn up as often as he does in the final result; but he is just extremely quotable. When I refer to Seneca without further qualification, I mean the essayist and philosopher who was Nero's tutor. His father, the writer on rhetoric, is here called Seneca the Elder. I have appended a list of authors quoted with their dates, so far as those can be determined; further information on just about everyone quoted can be found in the *Oxford Classical Dictionary*.

My policy in translating has been to go for the sense, as I perceive it, rather than trying to keep the style of the original; though if a text comes from, say, a comedy of Plautus, I have not been afraid to be colloquial. My aim has been to capture the meaning of the Latin, even if the result is slightly wordy, rather than always choosing a single English word for a single Latin one. While devoted to sense, I feel no such loyalty to Latin syntax, grammar, and word order, which are quite different from those of English. So I often have broken up sentences that in English would have seemed interminable, confusing, or weak; I have not hesitated to convert passive verbs to active ones and relative pronouns to demonstratives, since not doing so often yields maddeningly confused English. So my translations are often not what would be called "literal," but a translation that turned beautiful Latin into miserable English seemed to me like a worse sin.

The brief discussions that follow the quotations attempt to sketch in some of the background and context for the quotations. Despite the caveats about chronology above, many of my comments involve putting the Latin terms in a historical setting and charting some of their changes in nuance and use over time. Several historical terms and chronological labels, many of them vague and unfamiliar to the general reader, are unavoidable. When I refer to the "Republic" or "Republican times" I mean the era after the end of the monarchy and before the accession of the first emperor, Augustus (i.e., 510/509–31 BC), when Rome was governed primarily by the Senate, with magistrates elected and laws passed by assemblies of the Roman people. The late Republic is a key period, with abundant texts, great writers like Cicero and Caesar, and an eventful, turbulent history.

The term *late Republic* covers a period from about 130 to 31 BC, the date of the battle of Actium. That battle concluded the recurrent civil wars of the late Republic and clinched the ascendancy of Octavian (later called Augustus), warlord, boy genius, and shaper of a newly modified Roman constitution. This new dispensation made room for an emperor (Augustus himself, naturally) amid the old institutions, and the emperor was called, in Latin, *princeps*, or leading man. The

Augustan period (31 BC–AD 14) is another key era, one of in some ways even greater literature, by the likes of Horace, Vergil, and Ovid, names that will recur in this book. The Augustan period begins a longer era known as the Empire, or the Principate, after the Latin term used for emperor in Augustus's new dispensation. The term *Principate* refers to the constitutional arrangement of Augustus and his successors, as opposed to the absolute monarchy into which it developed at a later stage. In this period the authority of the *princeps* gradually grew, while that of the Senate receded, much to the consternation of the senators who wrote most of the history of the time. It was the age of emperors great and flamboyantly bad— Tiberius, Caligula, Nero, and Trajan—and the high-water mark of Roman imperial expansion. Literature, still relatively abundant in the Principate of the first and second centuries AD, falls off a cliff in the third century, which is virtually a mini–Dark Age of invasions, pandemics, and civil wars. At this point, somewhere around AD 250, we enter what is known as "late antiquity," or the "late Empire," the era that stands between the classical period and the Middle Ages. The vibrant civic life and secular intellectual ferment that characterized the late Republic and early Principate would not return in Europe until modern times.

By the end of the disastrous third century and the beginning of the economic revival in the fourth, Christianity had emerged as a major social force. This force begins to show itself in new, Christian Latin terminology, language, and thought, which we can now read in the writings of highly literate Christian bishops attempting to defend their faith against persecution and to convert non-Christians. "Early Christian" Latin, as it has since been called, means essentially treatises, sermons, and letters by Tertullian (late second and early third centuries), Lactantius (ca. AD 300), and the great writers of the late fourth and early fifth centuries, Saints Ambrose, Jerome, and Augustine, as well as the underrated poet Prudentius. This same "late antique" period sees the flowering of Roman legal writing, which summarized and codified many earlier laws, edicts, and legal opinions.

The compilers of the raw material for the great and comprehensive *Thesaurus Linguae Latinae* (begun in 1900, it has now reached the letter *P*) stopped making slips for texts dating after about AD 600. I too have not ventured much into the early Middle Ages, though I quote occasionally from the leading lights of the sixth century, Gregory of Tours and Gregory the Great. The term *classical Latin* is a modern one and refers to the norms of the language as they were regularized by writers and scholars of the first century BC, especially Cicero and (in poetry) Vergil. Stylistic norms changed, but such was the prestige of the classical authors of the late Republic and Augustan periods that they formed a canon of correctness to which all aspired, if few attained. The span of time I consider in this book is huge, but with a more or less unifying veneer of classical Latin literary culture. The Latinity of this culture was enforced by education amongst the *grammatici*, teachers whom one scholar has aptly called the "Guardians of Language." Significant changes can be traced in this classical Latinity, and we can see it pretty much broken down in the works of Gregory of Tours in the sixth century. He despairs of writing classical Latin (people had long since stopped speaking it), and his thought world has little to do with that of a Cicero or a Vergil.

Thus the term *classical Latin* in this book refers in the first instance to the works of the golden age of Latin literature (late Republic and early Principate), especially those by Julius Caesar, Cicero, Horace, and Vergil; but in an extended sense it refers to a canon of style that transcends that particular period and unifies, at least superficially, most of the authors quoted here.

The term *Caesar* may create confusion. This is the cognomen of the ill-fated dictator, Gaius Julius Caesar, who was killed at the height of his power by a group of senators in 44 BC. Octavian, his adopted heir, kept the cognomen when he became the first emperor Augustus. So he, too, might be called simply "Caesar," as could every other Roman emperor after him. Beginning as the proper name of an individual, *Caesar* became an imperial title, then a word, meaning emperor (whence it passed into Russian as *Tzar*). In this book, to avoid ambiguity, I refer to the dictator as Julius Caesar, and when quoting a writer who refers to a "Caesar," I specify, if possible, whether the dictator or some later emperor is meant. Occasionally it is necessary to express dates in the Principate imprecisely, by reign. The most important for our purposes are the reigns of the Julio-Claudian dynasty: Augustus (31 BC–AD 14); Tiberius (AD 14–37); Gaius, a.k.a. Caligula (37–41); Claudius (41–54); and Nero (54–68).

The selection of words has been difficult. Everyone who reads Latin will be annoyed at finding omissions and puzzled by some of my inclusions. It was an inevitably idiosyncratic set of choices, but one restricted to the parameters of contemporary scholarship and tempered by the knowledge that it had to stop somewhere. Traditionally, the study of culturally significant Latin terms has focused on the virtues that the Romans themselves loved to talk about, and some of which they actually treated as gods: *virtus, honos, fides, libertas, humanitas,* and the like. While this focus has yielded some extremely important insights, it has tended to make the Romans sound (as the centurions do in old movies) like wooden soldiers of virtue, without imagination, wit, or awareness of the real world. I find the Romans full of imagination, wit, and engagement with the real, so I have started with more concrete words and saved the virtues for the end. More recent scholarship has done much to clarify the vocabulary and dynamics of Roman social relations, in words like *amicitia, cliens,* and *nobilis*. This is reflected in my chapter on the "social contract" and in an emphasis throughout on the concepts of status, honor, and reciprocity. I have also made good use of the new interest (which I share) in the seamy underbelly of Roman life, be it magic, the punishment of slaves, the removal of unclaimed corpses from the city of Rome, or various unspeakable sexual practices. My own interest in economics, work, and technology goes somewhat against the grain of the sources, whose aristocratic authors usually disdained such things. By contrast, philosophical and rhetorical terms, which Latin authors discuss at length, did not seem readily treatable in a work of this scope.

The legacy of the transition from Latin to English is also naturally of interest, especially when the comparison of a Latin term with a related English one reveals something about how we and the Romans look at the world differently. So I have preferred words with English or Romance cognates where possible. The ideal word, from my perspective, was important or controversial to the Romans, revealed historical changes, and also provided a comparison or contrast with its descendants in English. In some cases I fixed on a word, like *caementum*, that was totally inconsequential for the Romans, whereas it looks very important to us in retrospect, so that its very insignificance is worth discussing. And a few words were chosen, I confess, simply because their peculiarity caught my fancy. In the process of researching and writing it emerged that many of the most interesting stories locked within the Latin lexicon derive from the great transition from pagan to Christian mores. The linguistic continuities and changes that make up an aspect of that transition presented an important theme. In the end, my own dissatisfaction with the many omissions must give way to the thought that my goal is not to write an encyclopedia but to stimulate people to learn and read more deeply in this amazing and still powerful language.

There are a vast number of things with no name.
(Seneca, *On Benefits* 2.34.2)

ABBREVIATIONS

AE *L'Année Épigraphique* (Paris: Presses Universitaires de France, 1888–). An annual journal that publishes newly discovered Latin inscriptions and reinterpretations of previously known ones. This is cited by the year and number of the inscription in that issue, rather than by page number.

CGL *Corpus Glossariorum Latinorum*, 7 vols., G. Goetz, ed. (Leipzig and Berlin: Teubner, 1888–1923). A compendium of late antique and early medieval glossaries, word lists and school books.

CIL *Corpus Inscriptionum Latinarum*, 17 vols. by various editors (Berlin: Walter de Gruyter, 1863–). The authoritative publication of most Latin inscriptions. Cited by volume and number of the inscription, rather than by page number.

CLE *Carmina Latina Epigraphica*, vol. 2 of *Anthologia Latina*, F. Bücheler and E. Lommatzsch, eds. (Stuttgart: Teubner, 1895–1926). The most comprehensive collection of Latin verse inscriptions, most of which also appear in *CIL*. Cited by number of the inscription, not page. Because *CLE*'s text often varies from that in *CIL*, I cite both.

ILS *Inscriptiones Latinae Selectae*, 3 vols. in 5. Hermann Dessau, ed. (repr. Chicago: Ares, 1975; orig. 1892). A standard collection of representative Latin inscriptions, including most of the more important ones, arranged by type of inscription.

New Pauly *Brill's New Pauly: Encyclopedia of the Ancient World*, H. Cancik and H. Schneider, eds. (Leiden: Brill, 2002–).

OCD[3] *The Oxford Classical Dictionary*, 3rd edition, S. Hornblower and A. Spawforth, eds. (Oxford: Oxford University Press, 1996).

Otto	A. Otto, *Sprichwörter und sprichwörtlichen Redensarten der Römer* (Leipzig: Teubner, 1890). A collection of Roman proverbs, arranged alphabetically by key words. Cited by key word and number of proverb within that entry.
PIR	*Prosopographia Imperii Romani Saec. I, II, III*, in several volumes by various eds. (Berlin: Teubner, 1897–1898) and the 2nd ed. in progress (Berlin: Walter De Gruyter, 1933–). The "Roman phone book," a comprehensive listing of known persons in the principate, with source citations for each. It is organized alphabetically by first letter of the family name (*nomen gentile*), and the entries are numbered sequentially within each letter; so it is cited here by the initial letter of the family name, and number.
PL	*Patrologiae Cursus Completus, Series Latina*, 221 vols., J.-P. Migne, ed. (Paris, 1844–1864). A comprehensive edition of the Latin Church fathers. Cited by volume and column number.
RE	*Paulys Real-Encyclopädie der classischen Altertumswissenschaft*, many vols. by various editors (Stuttgart: J.B. Metzler, 1893–1982), with the 15 volume Supplement (Stuttgart: J.B. Metzler, 1903–1978), and the *2nd Series* (Stuttgart: J.B. Metzler, 1914–) covering R–Z. The colossal dictionary of everything classical, named after its early architect August Friedrich (von) Pauly (1796–1845). Cited by volume number of the relevant series, and column.
SHA	*Scriptores Historiae Augustae*, 3 vols., D. Magie, trans. (Cambridge, MA: Harvard University Press, 1991). A collection of biographies of Roman emperors by pseudonymous authors, compiled in late antiquity. Cited by the name of the emperor and chapter number of his biography.
TLL	*Thesaurus Linguae Latinae*, many vols. by various editors (Leipzig: Teubner, 1900–). If ever completed, this will be the most comprehensive Latin dictionary. Cited by volume and column number.

CHILDHOOD

crepundia
liberi
paedagogus
bulla

CREPUNDIA: A CHILD'S TOY RATTLE, SOMETIMES USED FOR IDENTIFICATION; INFANCY

All too transitory and fragile, like the crepundia of childhood,
are the so-called power and wealth of human kind.

> (Valerius Maximus, *MemorableDeeds
> and Sayings* 6.9 ext. 7)

Now in here are the crepundia you had when that woman
brought you to me years ago. She gave them to me so as to make
it easier for your parents to recognize you.

> (The madam at a brothel, to one of her courtesans,
> in Plautus's comedy *Cistellaria*, 635-636)

Ebony comes from India and Ethiopia, and
when cut it becomes hard as stone ... it is
also attached to crepundia, so that the
sight of the color black will not scare the
infant.

> (Isidore of Seville, *Etymologies* 17.7.36)

From infancy [a crepundiis] he gave equal attention
to courage and to eloquence.

> (From an inscription honoring Flavius Merobaudes,
> an imperial official and writer of poetry of the
> fifth century, *CIL* 6.1724)

She had already given an indication that she was destined for
heaven and not for the couch of marriage: she had rejected
her very crepundia, a little girl who knew not how to play.
No interest in amber, she wept at roses, disdained aureate
bracelets, was sober of expression, modest of gate and,
though of all-too-tender years, her character imitated that of
gray-haired age.

> (Prudentius, on the twelve-year-old martyr Eulalia,
> killed in Merida, Spain in AD 304,
> *Crowns of the Martyrs* 3.16-25)

*crepundia** The noun *crepundia* derives from the verb meaning "to rattle" (*crepare*) and refers in the first instance to the metal charms jingled to try and calm fussing babies. From there *crepundia* comes to stand in as a symbol for early childhood itself, as in the comment of Valerius Maximus and the inscription quoted above. Unlike today, when such things are generally mass-produced, a Roman tot's *crepundia* were homemade and individualized. They might be inscribed with the name of the mother or father, or include some distinctive figurines. Archaeologists have found bells, clappers, letters of ivory, children's utensils for eating and drinking, and many other objects that served this purpose.

Since they were individualized, *crepundia* could be used to identify babies who got misplaced. Special *crepundia* could be given to children by mothers who were compelled by poverty to expose them or give them away, in hope that, when they had grown up in someone else's care, they might by some chance return and be recognized using the *crepundia*. Such improbable recognitions of lost or abandoned children, duly verified by *crepundia*, were a common plot device in Roman and Greek comedy, as in the line from Plautus quoted here.

But this does not mean it never happened in real life. The real rate of child abandonment in ancient Rome is unclear. By one estimate, impossible to verify, 20 to 40 percent of all urban children were abandoned in the third century AD. This is a very high figure, and probably not a normal situation, but it is well paralleled in pre-industrial Paris, Vienna, Milan, and Florence in the eighteenth and nineteenth centuries. The comparative evidence corroborates the impression we get from Roman sources, that the prototypical abandoner was an urban woman, perhaps from a peasant background, in the city as a domestic servant, for whom taking care of an infant interfered with the necessity of urban employment. The modern evidence suggests that, unlike the happy endings of Roman comedy, however, abandonment was often tantamount to infanticide. Eighty percent mortality and higher in the first year was regular, even when foundling homes were in place (which they were not in ancient Rome).

Just as *crepundia* were fragile and fleeting, childhood itself was seen as a time of immaturity and imperfection. Roman children were often praised by adults for not acting like children—that is, for being serious, responsible, and sober, like adults—the so-called *senex puer* or "old-man boy" phenomenon. Prudentius follows in this tradition when he praises the young martyr Eulalia for wanting to have nothing to do with her *crepundia*, and "not knowing how to play."

---

*Though singular in sense this word is grammatically plural and neuter.

TLL 4.1174-1175. J. Marquardt, *Das Privatleben der Römer* (repr. Darmstadt: Wissenschaftliche Buchgesellschaft, 1980) 1.120. Susan Dixon, *The Roman Family* (Baltimore: Johns Hopkins University Press, 1992) 98-132; David Kertzer et al., "Child Abandonment in European History: A Symposium," *Journal of Family History* 17 (1992) 1–23.

LIBERI: FREEBORN, LEGITIMATE CHILDREN (OF EITHER SEX)

I want you to take a wife to your house
so you can produce liberi.

(Plautus, *Aulularia* 148)

You had liberi not just for yourself but for the fatherland,
children who could be not just a source of pleasure for you
but also who would one day be useful to the state.

(Cicero, *Against Verres* 2.3.161)

Quite a few men are stingy in the raising of their liberi—which were
the original objectives of their marriages and prayers—nor do they tend
to their education or to the development of their physical faculties.

(Columella, *On Farming* 4.3.2)

You made a contract regarding the manner of your marriage. The writing of that
contract rings clear, "for the sake of bearing children" [liberi]. Therefore do not
approach her, if possible, unless for the purpose of bearing liberi. If you pass this
limit, you act against that agreement and that contract.

(Augustine, *Sermons* 278, PL 38.1272)

liberi Terms of affection for children are not as numerous in Latin as in English, but they include *pullus* ("chickadee"), *parvulus* and *putillus* ("little shaver"), and pupus ("puppet," "doll"). The most idiomatic and Roman of endearments is *pignus*. A *pignus* is whatever one gives as bond or security for a debt, or to assure appearance in court, good conduct, etc. By extension, a person who is a *pignus* can serve as a "collateral" or "hostage"—for example, in diplomacy between two states. When applied to children, as it sometimes is in epitaphs, in poetry and other emotive contexts, *pignora* casts them as "sureties" or "pledges" of the love of the parents, assuring the reality of their marriage. But in such contexts it has no legalistic flavor. Often the best translation is simply "dear ones" rather than something more literal, like "little guarantees."

Liberi is not a term of affection, but, like *pignora*, it has legalistic roots and lacks any real equivalent in English. It designates children born free (*liber*) from the legitimate union of a free man and woman. *Liberi* were the goal of marriage, and raising them properly was seen as a serious responsibility to the state, as Cicero reminds a courtroom adversary. For St. Augustine, they are the only possible reason for having sex. Not *spurii* (of unknown father), or "conceived promiscuously" (*vulgo concepti*) from a slave girl, concubine, or courtesan, they were instead certain (*certi*) and legitimate (*legitimi*) and provided an indisputable heir. Roman educational advice concerned itself exclusively with *liberi*, probably on the assumption that other children would be prevented by prejudice from pursuing a public career that was the point of education in the first place. As the Greek writer Plutarch says in this context, "I should advise those desirous of becoming fathers of notable offspring to abstain from random cohabitation with women; I mean with such women as courtesans and concubines. For those who are not well-born, whether on the father's side or mother's side, have an indelible disgrace in their low birth, which accompanies them throughout their lives, and offers to anyone desiring to use it a ready subject of reproach and insult."

The word *liberi* has a solemn tone that derives from its use in legal and ceremonial contexts, especially in the standard marriage contract. The words *liberi* and *filii* are often interchangeable; but in moments of high drama, such as when children were being threatened or dishonored, the solemnity of *liberi* might be used for emotional effect. "I myself have seen," says St. Ambrose, "the wretched spectacle of *liberi* being led off to the auction block to pay a father's debt, and being kept as heirs to his calamity, though they had no part in his success, and the creditor not even blushing to commit such an outrage." Another church father says, "You must work hard and take risks in order to keep your children [*pignora*], your home and your fortunes safe, and to enjoy all the good things of peace and victory. But if you prefer peace now to the hard work . . . your fields will be laid waste, your house plundered, your wife and children [*liberi*] will become the spoils of war, and you yourself will be captured or killed." In these passages *liberi*, with its connotations of legal legitimacy, honorable marriage, and secure inheritance, emphasizes the dastardliness of the moneylender and the threat posed by the enemy. On the other hand, when referring casually to one's children, it would not be necessary to use a word of such precision, and *nati* or *filii* would do.

Filii, as we can see from the French and Italian descendants (*figlio* and *fils*), won out in the long run. *Liberi* seems to have gone out of currency in later Latin, and it left no trace in the Romance languages. Writing in the early seventh century, Isidore of Seville seems not quite to understand it fully when he says, "In the laws, *filii* are called *liberi* to distinguish them from slaves." But of course one could be freeborn without necessarily being a *liber* in this sense, provided that one's mother was free. To be a true *liber* was to be free and also not a bastard.

Given the care with which classical Latin defines the legal status of children, a curious gap in the lexicon is an insult meaning "bastard." Of the recorded terms, *spurius* was a rare legalism referring to any child conceived out of lawful wedlock, or one whose father was not known; *nothus* was the insulting ancient Greek word for bastard, and it is occasionally borrowed by Roman writers. But neither *spurius* nor *nothus* ever became a common insult. *Illegitimi*, while a theoretically possible formation in Latin, is not recorded. Quintilian notes the lack of a good word for bastard in Latin and says that when necessary Romans used the Greek term, *nothus*. One would think, prone to invective and obsessed with birth and lineage as the Romans were, that *spurius* would have been a handy stone to throw.

At some point now impossible to determine, *bastardus* emerged. This mysterious but fertile Romance root yielded Italian, Portuguese, and Spanish *bastardo*, French *bâtard*, and passed into all the continental Germanic languages, including English, by the late thirteenth century. But it has no recorded existence in Latin. One theory of the etymology of this nonclassical insult says that it comes from the French word *bast*, as in *fils de bast*, meaning "son of the packsaddle." This compares with the British English usage of someone being "born the wrong side of the blanket" or being "the son of a gun" (as in a "shotgun wedding").

TLL 7.1301-1304. Plutarch: *On the Education of Children* 2. Ambrose: *On Tobias* 8.29. Another church father: Lactantius, *Divine Institutes* 6.4.15. Isidore of Seville, *Etymologies* 9.5.17. Quintilian: *On the Orator's Education* 3.6.97.

PAEDAGOGUS: TUTOR, CHILD MINDER

A paedagogus is assigned to the young so that the rowdiness of youth might be restrained and their hearts prone to sin be held in check ... by the fear of punishment.

(Jerome, *Commentary on Paul's Letter to the Galatians* 2.3.24)

For he removed that area of philosophy which has to do with admonitions, and said that it was the business of the paedagogus, not the philosopher. As if the wise man is something other than a paedagogus for the human race.

(Seneca, speaking of the philosopher Ariston of Chios, *Letters* 89.13)

I will say this much further about paedagogi: that they should either be educated, which would be my preference, or else they should know that they are not educated.

(Quintilian, *On the Orator's Education* 1.1.8)

How she used to cling to her father's embrace! How lovingly and modestly she used to hug us, her father's friends! How she loved her nurses, her paedagogi, her teachers, each appropriately according to their roles!

(Pliny the Younger, from a letter describing the death of a young girl, *Letters* 5.16.3)

paedagogus Well-to-do Roman children spent most of their time under the direct care not of their parents but of tutors, usually older and trusted male slaves, called often by the Greek term *paedagogus* ("child leader"). Other Latin terms exist: *comes* ("companion") and *custos* ("guardian"). But the foreign word presumably sounded more elegant, much as in English an *au pair* sounds more sophisticated than a nanny or babysitter. The custom was so general by Augustus's day that when that emperor was making regulations for theater seating, he assigned a section to boys (*praetextati*) right next to a section for their *paedagogi*, no doubt so the boys would be less unruly. *Paedagogi* were charged with constantly monitoring a youth's public behavior, in the streets, at meals, at shows, or in the atria of important men. The emperor Galba had three corrupt cronies who never left his side in public, and they were jokingly referred to as his *paedagogi*.

The use of corporal punishment was widely endured but criticized by enlightened educationalists such as Quintilian. Like primary teachers, they used a rod made of giant fennel, the *ferula*, because it left few scars. The poet Martial calls it "the sinister rod, sceptre of the *paedagogus*." When the young man was of the imperial house, however, more subtle methods might have to be used. The twelve-year-old future emperor Commodus once demanded, when his bathing room was too cool, that the bath slave in charge be thrown into the furnace. His *paedagogus* discretely had a sheep skin thrown into the furnace, the acrid smell of which convinced Commodus that his order had been carried out. Traditionally humorless, the *paedagogus* had as his job not so much education as behavioral control. Some might earn the affection of their charges, but as a type, they were not loved. Nero had the respected senator and devotee of Stoic philosophy Thrasea Paetus executed, by one account, "because he wore the miserable expression of a *paedagogus*."

An educated Greek, who could teach the boy how to speak proper Greek, was the best sort of *paedagogus* to have, but this of course was not always possible. Nero, who grew up in relative poverty, was said to have had two *paedagogi* as a young boy, a barber and a dancer. Augustus punished the corrupt *paedagogus* of his son Gaius for a serious offence by having him thrown into a river with weights around his neck. Claudius complained in his memoirs about being assigned a cruel barbarian for a tutor, who was given specific instructions to beat him with the slightest provocation.

The word dies out in the Middle Ages, because the custom itself faded with the prosperity of the high empire. But in the meantime it made an interesting detour in Christian Greek. St. Paul compared the law of the Jews to a *paedagogus* who disciplines us and shows us how to act, until the higher instruction of Christian faith gives us independent moral agency. Picking up on this idea, St. Clement of Alexandria in the late second century wrote an entire treatise called *Paedagogus*, which gives instructions on a Christian lifestyle for those who, though they have committed to a Christian life, have not advanced all the way to perfect Christian wisdom. It contains advice on what to wear, how to walk, how to kiss, and many other aspects of proper behavior for women and men.

In English, *pedagogue* resurfaced in the late 1300s, as a synonym for schoolmaster. It thus took a Roman rather than a Greek connotation, since while Roman *paedagogi* did do some language teaching, their Greek counterparts did not. The pedagogue has continued his rise up the educational ladder, until today *pedagogy* suggests not mere instruction but sophisticated teaching techniques based on some kind of scientific system—a vice of which the Roman *paedagogus* could not be accused.

TLL 10.31-34. RE 18.2375-2385. Theater seating: Suetonius, *Augustus* 44.2. Galba: Suetonius, *Galba* 14.2. Quintilian: *On the Orator's Education* 1.3.15. Martial, *Epigrams* 10.62.10. Commodus: *SHA, Commodus* 1.9. Thrasea Paetus: Suetonius, *Nero* 37.1. Nero's *paedagogi*: Suetonius, *Nero* 6.3. Thrown into a river: Suetonius, *Augustus* 67.2. Cruel barbarians: Suetonius, *Claudius* 2.2. Paul: *Letter to the Galatians* 3.24.

BULLA: AN AMULET (LEATHER POUCH OR METAL LOCKET) WORN BY FREEBORN CHILDREN UP TO THE AGE OF ABOUT FOURTEEN.

Authorities agree that a golden bulla was first given to his son by
Tarquinius Priscus [the sixth king of Rome] when in his early teens the
boy killed an enemy in battle. The custom of the bulla has lasted since
that time, so that the sons of those who have served in the cavalry
wear it as a distinguishing mark, while the rest wear a leather strap.

(Pliny the Elder, *Natural History* 33.10)

Like the toga praetexta worn by magistrates, so the
bulla was worn by generals in the triumph ceremony; they used to display it in the triumph with
certain things enclosed inside which they believed
were very potent remedies against ill-will [invidia].

(Macrobius, *Saturnalia* 1.6.9)

Later, when the gold bulla came off your young neck, and in
front of your mother's gods, you took the toga of manhood, then
Apollo started to teach you some of his poetry and forbade you
to thunder in the mad forum.

(Propertius, explaining his decision to become a poet
instead of a lawyer or orator, *Elegies* 4.1B.131–132)

As soon as my childhood chaperone left me and my
bulla hung as a gift to the Lares ... you took my tender
years in your Socratic embrace.

(Persius, speaking of his mentor, the philosopher
Cornutus, *Satires* 5.31)

bulla It is the custom in many societies to decorate babies and young people with amulets and charms to protect them from evil influences, natural and supernatural, such as the evil eye. Today in India, Hindu children often wear a black thread necklace with a silver piece representing the god Hunaman for just this purpose, and babies have their eyes outlined with charcoal. The Roman version was, characteristically, used as a way of distinguishing children by status. There would be many children on the Roman street, some free, some slave, some foster children, others children of a master and a slave, or children of freed, slave, and free parents in various combinations. The *bulla* was meant to mark out the freeborn child of free parents. Like the *toga praetexta*, with which it is often mentioned, it announced privilege and inviolability.

The gold *bulla*, in particular, was always seen as a privilege. We have somewhat confused reports about how it was given first by King Tarquin to his son (a sign of the custom's Etruscan origin). Then, at some later date, the gold *bulla* was worn by the children of the wealthy upper-classes; finally (supposedly in 217 BC) it was allowed to all freeborn children, even the relatively poor, while the children of freedmen were allowed to wear the leather *bulla*, previously worn by the free poor. The actual practice at any given date is unclear, as is the extent to which girls wore it. At any rate, archaeologists have found several actual *bullae*, one with the locket filled with hair. Macrobius implies that the content of the locket was often a phallus, a common protection against the evil eye. Its association with pagan magic made it uncongenial to the early Christians, and the custom seems to have died out—at least Christian authors do not mention it. The current Christian practice of wearing a cross for protection is obviously similar, however, and a distant historical link with the Spanish "bolo" tie is just possible.

As a mark of childhood, and a child's own possession, the *bulla* had sentimental value. Adults like Propertius and Persius looked back fondly at the day they put aside the *toga praetexta* and the *bulla*, hanging the amulet on the household shrine of the Lares. This was the first day of adulthood. At Julius Caesar's funeral, matrons threw their jewelry, and children threw their *bullae*, on his pyre, an extreme outpouring of grief.

TLL 2.2241-2242. *RE* 3.1048-1051. Sybille Haynes, *Etruscan Civilization* (London: British Museum, 2000) 282.

FAMILY

familia
> *pater familias*
> *coniunx*
> *noverca*
> *alumnus*

FAMILIA: HOUSEHOLD; GROUP OF SLAVES UNDER ONE OWNER; FAMILY

Orgetorix . . . gathered his entire familia from every
direction, about ten thousand men, and brought
together all his clients and debt-bondsmen.
  (Julius Caesar, on a Gallic chieftain, *The Gallic War* 1.4.2)

He was sent away into distant fields, so as not to
contaminate the familia.
  (Apuleius, referring to an epileptic slave, whose fellow
  slaves refused to eat or drink with him for fear of
  infection, *Apology* 44)

He obtained, I believe, a familia of gladiators—quite handsome,
distinguished and glorious; he knew what people like, he saw that
they would cheer and crowd around him.
  (Cicero, on his political adversary Vatinius, *Pro Sestio* 134)

I never had any doubt that the Roman people
would unanimously vote you consul, based
on your outstanding services to the state and
the great distinction of your familia.
  (Cicero to Lucius Aemilius Paulus, consul in 50 BC,
  Letters to His Friends 15.12.1)

Marriage ties long ago mixed many
famous and powerful familiae.
  (Livy, *Roman History* 23.4.7)

[Father:] "Am I to permit you to marry and become a wife without
a dowry?" [Daughter:] "You must, father; and by doing so you will
add to the fine reputation of our familia."
  (Plautus, *Trinummus* 378)

familia To define the family is a difficult and controversial enterprise. The "typical" or "ideal" family of two living parents with their biological children residing together has been the exception rather than the rule in human history, and any abstract legal definition is helpless to describe the variety of real life. It is certain, however, that Roman notions of *familia* differed strikingly from modern versions of that term.

For one thing, legally speaking, a *familia* was not restricted to people related by blood, marriage, or adoption; rather it comprised all under the protection and authority of a single *pater familias* ("head of household"). That includes slaves, freedmen, and foster children (*alumni*), and it might *exclude* the wife (in certain legal types of marriage) and any married daughters and sons emancipated from their father's control. But the legal definition was not the one in common use. *Familia* often meant a group or gang of slaves belonging to the same person—from a dozen to ten thousand. The word was said to derive from an old Oscan term for slave, *famel*. A troop of gladiators was a *familia*, as were the slave gangs that worked in the salt pits, maintaining the streets, sewers, baths, and temples.

The other main meaning of *familia* is closer to our use of the word, but it implies continuity over several generations, as in, "The Kennedys are a notable American family." It was a unit that transcended the occupants of any one house at any one time and took its identity from the distinctions of its most prominent members. The prologue to a comedy by Plautus illustrates this. It is spoken by the household god, the *Lar familiaris*, of a Roman *familia*: "I am the *Lar familiaris* of the *familia* from whose house I have just come. I have possessed this home for a long time now, keeping it safe for the grandfather and father of the man who has it now." The *familia* in this sense was a constellation surrounding its male head, deriving its shared status from the history of its *patres familiae*. It was a "consular" family if one of the past or current heads had been consul, "praetorian" if one had been a praetor, "equestrian" if he was of equestrian status, etc. One's *familia* was patrician, plebeian, noble, distinguished, or not. The assumption that a *familia* was a multigenerational succession of distinguished men made it natural to speak of a philosophical school as a *familia*. So Cicero speaks of the *familia* of Plato, or the Stoic *familia*.

Despite their stern, unemotional reputation, Roman spouses loved each other, children were doted on, spoiled, and grieved over in death, exactly as they are today. But because it included non-kin, and because it tended to be seen over the long term, *familia* itself as a concept lacks the sentimentalized associations of "family," as the idea developed in its modern form in the eighteenth century. *Familia* was sacred to the Romans as well; however, the sentiments involved were not the private ones of warmth and intimacy but the public ones of honor and pride. Contemplating marriage, the daughter in a Plautine comedy, quoted above, talks as much about the reputation of the *familia* as about her own desires.

TLL 6.234-246. Keith Bradley, *Discovering the Roman Family* (Oxford: Oxford University Press, 1991) 3-12. From an old Oscan term: Paulus Festus, *On the Significance of Words* 87, p. 77 ed. W. M. Lindsay. *Familia* of Plato: Cicero, *On the Laws* 1.55; *On the Orator* 3.61. I am the *Lar familiaris*: Plautus, *Aulularia* 2–5.

PATER FAMILIAS: HEAD OF HOUSEHOLD, ESTATE OWNER, LITERALLY "FATHER OF THE HOUSEHOLD"

He was considered just as good a pater familias as he was a citizen. For although he was rich, no one was less fond of buying, no one a less lavish builder. Nevertheless he did live extremely well, and everything he used was of the best.

(Cornelius Nepos, on Cicero's old friend and correspondent, T. Pomponius Atticus, *Life of Atticus* 13.1)

By this example [Horace] shows that one will never be believed in the future, even if he is telling the truth, if he has wasted his credibility in telling lies. Hence the proverb has arisen: "Once a scurra, never a pater familias." [A *scurra* is a fashionable city idler, a man-about-town.]

(Porphyrio, Commentary on Horace, *Letters* 1.17.58)

[Hadrian] had as deep a knowledge of all the public accounts as any diligent pater familias has of his private household.

(*SHA, Hadrian* 20.11)

I see how gently you treat your household, and will candidly confess to you with what indulgence I treat mine. I always keep in mind Homer's line, "he was as gentle as a father," and our own phrase "pater familias."

(Pliny the Younger to Valerius Paulinus, requesting help in providing a place for his freedman Zosimus to recuperate from a serious illness, *Letters* 5.19.1–2)

pater familias No Latin term evokes the old Roman family as well as *pater familias*. According to the stereotype, the Roman father was a rigid autocrat, endowed by law with power of life and death over his children and wife, the owner of all property, even that of his adult sons, exercising his authority with fierce discipline until his much-hoped-for (by everyone else) death. A commonly used modern textbook compares the powers of the *pater familias* to those of the Old Testament patriarchs, like Abraham or Jacob. "In the family circle these powers were equal to a king's, and included even the judgment of life and death." Discussions of the history of family institutions often refer to the *"pater familias* model," as a shorthand way to describe a whole system of patriarchal dominance.

While it is true that Roman fathers had what we consider extraordinary property rights, the tyrannical Roman *pater familias* is a modern myth that rests on a misreading of certain legal texts. Real cases show that while some fathers were stern, others were indulgent, and that *patria potestas* ("fathers' legal power") did not in practice prevent adult sons, daughters, and wives from leading an autonomous life. Moreover, the term *pater familias* means not father, but "head of household," and its most common meaning in the law codes, "estate owner," has no reference to familial relations at all. Indeed, fatherhood is optional. A young man without children could be one, as could a childless old man, provided he was a citizen and *sui iuris*—that is, in his own power, and not himself subject to a *pater familias*. In many legal contexts it is clear that the term is gender neutral, and that women are included, since women *sui iuris* could and did own substantial households. The "power of life and death" (*ius vitae necisque*) is an extremely rare legal formula expressing the ultimate limit encompassing the whole of *patria potestas*, rather than a sociological reality.

The essential aspect of being a *pater familias* was property management. The good *pater familias*, like Atticus, was thrifty and not prone to expensive and luxurious building. The most commonly applied terms of praise are "diligent" (*diligens*), "prudent" (*prudens*), and "fit, suitable" (*idoneus*). He was supposed to live up to his financial and legal obligations and to be trustworthy and solid—hence the proverb quoted by Porphyrio, "once a *scurra*, never a *pater familias*," and the comparison by a biographer of the financially literate emperor Hadrian to a diligent *pater familias*.

The associations of the word that does mean father, *pater*, always included kindness, as well as responsibility and authority. In so far as being a head of household meant owning and supervising slaves and freedmen, the Romans considered the *pater* part of the formulation *pater familias* to suggest gentleness. Unlike the harsher word *dominus* ("master"), *pater familias* implied that the ideal slave master should be indulgent and concerned, "like a father." Pliny says this explicitly in the letter quoted above, in which he tries to make sure that one of his freedmen gets adequate medical care. Not that all masters were as compassionate as Pliny (they weren't), but the point is that *pater familias* suggested to Latin speakers something very different from what the term has come to connote in modern usage.

Another point to keep in mind is the rarity of the term *pater familias* outside of legal contexts. It always retained its legalistic flavor and never occurs, for example, in epitaphs, where expressions like "dearest father" (*carissimus pater*) and the like are understandably common. The most famous case of a stern Roman father is Lucius Brutus, the first consul, founder of the Republic, and banisher of the last king. When Brutus's two sons were convicted of conspiring to reinstate the monarchy, he endured to see them executed under his own authority. A spectacular case of the "power of life and death" of the Roman father? No. As the author who tells the story says, Brutus "laid aside the role of *pater* so that he could play the role of consul." Severity is not the dominant connotation of *pater*, even in stereotyped depictions of the early Republic. A far better picture of the emotions typically surrounding Roman family life is given by *coniunx* ("husband," "wife") or *pietas* ("devotion," "loyalty"), discussed elsewhere in this book, than by *pater familias*, which has much more to do with a man's relationship to his property than to his family.

TLL 10.690-692. R. P. Saller, "*Pater Familias, Mater Familias,* and the Gendered Semantics of the Roman Household," *Classical Philology* 94 (1999) 182–197. H. A. Treble and K. M. King, *Everyday Life in Rome in the Time of Caesar and Cicero* (Oxford: Clarendon Press, 1930, repr. 1972). Laid aside the role of *pater*: Valerius Maximus, *Memorable Deeds and Sayings* 5.8.1.

CONIUNX: WIFE OR HUSBAND, SPOUSE

While alive I pleased my husband as his first and dearest coniunx.
Upon his mouth I bestowed my final cold kiss, and he, in tears,
closed my dying eyes. After death a woman finds sufficient distinc-
tion in this proud claim.

(Epitaph found in the family tomb of the Statilii
in Rome, *CIL 6.6593 = CLE 1030*)

Here I lie, the coniunx *of Cratius and*
[later] of Hilarus, called Asphale, a girl
worthy of her husbands in character
and life.

(Epitaph of Asphale Octavia, who died at
age 33, *CIL 6.7873 = CLE 1024*)

For his incomparable coniunx, *with whom he lived six-*
teen years and four months without any complaint.

(Epitaph of Iulia Chrysanthis, who died at age 31,
put up by her husband T. Lusidienus Nestor,
a successful freedman, *CIL 5.69*)

If these measures seem harsh and cruel, you ought to judge it far worse
for your children and coniuges *to be enslaved, and you yourselves to*
be killed, which is what inevitably befalls the conquered.

(Vercingetorix, the Gallic chieftain, arguing that Gallic towns and
farms should be burned, in order to starve out the invading
Roman army. Julius Caesar, *The Gallic War* 7.14)

I ask wedlock and the fulfillment of a solemn pledge, not crime;
I love you like a promised coniunx, *not like an adulterer.*

(Acontius wooing Cydippe in Ovid, *Heroides* 20.8)

coniunx This is an emotive and resonant word, quite unlike its nominal English equivalent, the legalistic *spouse*, or the bland English derivative of the Latin term *conjugal*. The verb *coniungo* means to join together, but the more popular etymology of *coniunx* and its stem *coniug-* would connect it with the word for yoke, *iugum*, as if the married couple were hooked together like oxen, hauling behind them their property and their posterity.

This distinctly unromantic view of marriage fits well with our conception of the Romans as serious-minded and unsentimental. But the actual use of the word *coniunx*, especially on gravestones, tells a different story. Even when we discount the usual hyperbole of the epitaph genre, the tone of the word suggests all the deep affection that we associate with modern ideals of marriage. Some of the adjectives commonly used with it are *carissima* ("dearest"), *castissima* ("most chaste"), *dulcissima* ("sweetest"), and *incomparabilis* ("incomparable"); *amantissima* ("most loving"), however, is rare, *amor* being an intractable and irrational emotion, not something the Romans usually associated with marriage. So when Ovid's eager young lover Acontius protests "I love you like a *coniunx*," the expression is slightly paradoxical.

Uxor was the normal word for wife in everyday speech, and *vir* or *maritus* was probably the most common word for husband; but neither of these has the sentimental charge of *coniunx*. *Coniunx* is not a word so much for conversation or for law codes as for poetry. The coolly objective Julius Caesar avoids *coniunx* completely in his writings, except for the single instance quoted above, significantly from a highly emotional speech. To breathe one's last while kissing one's *coniunx* was among the best kinds of death, boasted about in one epitaph quoted above, and also attributed to the fortunate emperor Augustus, whose biographer Suetonius says that he died suddenly amidst the kisses of Livia and making the remark, "Live mindful of our marriage [*coniugium*], Livia, and farewell."

TLL 4.341-344. Susan Treggiari, *Roman Marriage* (Oxford: Oxford University Press, 1991) 5–7. Popular etymology: Isidore of Seville, *Etymologies* 9.7.9. Live mindful of our marriage: Suetonius, *Augustus* 99.1.

NOVERCA: STEPMOTHER

But if a man who has a child from a previous marriage takes you into
his home, even if you have a heart of gold, you will be the savage
noverca that every comic playwright, every mime-writer, every
declaimer inveighs against. If your stepson gets sick or has a headache
you will be defamed as a poisoner; if you deny him food you will be
called cruel, if you give it you will be said to have bewitched him.
> (Jerome, counseling a widow against remarriage, *Letters* 54.15)

For a noverca, a stepson can never be killed enough.
> (Cestius Pius, from a hypothetical legal case,
> quoted by Seneca the Elder, *Controversiae* 7.1.9)

To each kind of plant, shade is either a nurse or
a noverca—in any case the shadow of a walnut
tree or a stone pine or a spruce or a silver fir is
undoubtedly poison when it touches any plant
whatever.
> (Pliny the Elder, *Natural History* 17.91)

Why are you looking at me like a noverca, or like a beast
who has been attacked with a spear?
> (An anonymous boy to a witch who is about to torture
> him to death and turn parts of him into a love potion;
> Horace, *Epodes* 5.9-10)

noverca The wicked stepmother is a familiar figure in folklore all over the world, most famously in the stories of Cinderella and Hansel and Gretel. She haunts the Romans primarily as a villainous poisoner, both in the practice speeches of the declaiming teachers and also in classical poetry. Confirmed historical cases of lethal stepmothers are not numerous, though it seems that Agrippina did have a hand in poisoning her stepson Britannicus to make way in the imperial succession for her natural son, Nero. The inbuilt tension between stepmothers and stepchildren caused the emperor Marcus Aurelius to take a concubine (rather than a new wife) after the death of his wife Faustina. It was a gesture of kindness to his many children, to avoid putting a stepmother over them.

One puts a stepmother "over" one's children in Latin (the common phrase is *novercam liberis superducere*) and they live "under" her, as if under some kind of tyrant. The proverbial expression "complain to your stepmother" (*apud novercam queri*) means to tell your troubles to someone who is not only unsympathetic but is likely to rejoice in them. Soldiers used the term *noverca* for places unsuitable for pitching camp, either because the terrain was uneven so the enemy could spy into the camp or near a forest where enemies could lurk, or because of some other vulnerability or hazard. The stereotypical stepmother is *iniusta* ("unfair"), *saeva* ("harsh"), or *dira* ("dreadful"), and eventually in later Latin the verb *novercor* arises, meaning simply "to be mean."

Otto 245-246. Agrippina: Tacitus, *Annals* 13.16.4. Marcus Aurelius: *SHA, Marcus Aurelius* 29. Complain to your stepmother: Plautus, *Pseudolus* 313. Soldiers: ps.-Hyginus, *The Fortification of the Camp* 57.

ALUMNUS: NURSLING, FOSTER CHILD; PROTÉGÉ, WARD, FAVORITE

It is more suitable for women to manumit alumni; but it is also sufficiently accepted for men that the manumission of a slave is permitted in whose rearing they have taken a special interest.

(Marcian, in Justinian's Digest of Roman Law 40.2.14)

Often do new and freely adopted children work their way into our hearts more deeply than our own kin. To beget sons is an obligation, to choose them is a joy. . . . Old Peleus did not accompany his son (Achilles) to the Trojan war, but Phoenix stuck close by his famous alumnus.

(From a lament written for Atedius Melior on the death of his
alumnus, Glaucias; Statius, Silvae 2.1.86–91)

In memory of Julia Almyrda, nurse.
She lived 63 years. Her alumnus
Gaius Julius Quintianus, centurion
[put up the monument].

(Gravestone from Roman North
Africa, CIL 8.2917)

He was met by a dense and joyful throng who called him, in addition to other well-omened names, their "star," their "chick," their "baby," and their alumnum.

(The crowd greeting the young Caligula at
the time of his accession in AD 37;
Suetonius, Caligula 13)

[Christian offerings go] to feed the poor and to bury them, and to boys and girls lacking means and parents, now to slaves grown old, likewise to the shipwrecked. If any are captive in the mines, or on islands or in a prison house, provided they became prisoners by reason of the way of God, all these become alumni of their faith.

(Tertullian, Apology 39.6)

alumnus A Roman foster child was typically a slave singled out for preferential treatment by the master or mistress, or else an abandoned child, or perhaps the child of another family member who could not raise it. Foster parents took on *alumni* in addition to natural children, or because they could not produce children, or could not produce any more. Foster children were usually slave or freed in status. This explains why the adoptive parents were called *patronus* or *patrona*, not *pater* or *mater*. The natural child of one slave and one free or freed parent was also called an *alumnus* (not *liber*, which implies free parents).

Given the servile associations of foster children, one would expect them to have a second-class status within the family. But in fact the sources show the opposite—that *alumni* were favored and sometimes doted on. Their tombstones use the same highly emotive adjectives—especially *dulcissimus, carissimus, pientissimus*—as those of *liberi*. The rich had a special class of *alumnus* called the *puer delicatus* or *amatus*, kept as a kind of favored child companion. The *puer delicatus* was like a son whom one did not have to discipline (their forwardness was encouraged), to whom one did not have to deny luxuries and indulgences (they were given fine clothing, jewelry, and parties), and to whom one could openly express affection (they were showered in hugs and kisses). Statius's poem on the death of Atedius Melior's *alumnus* Glaucias dwells on all these themes and also mentions that, even though he was a slave born on Melior's estates, Glaucias was educated enough to speak Greek without an accent. Throughout, Statius emphasizes the pleasure Glaucias gave to Melior and the aged Melior's inconsolable grief at Glaucias's death.

The modern child-welfare bureaucracy, and the fact that foster children now are usually older and often troubled, has given the term *foster child* a tinge of pity, implying that the foster parent has made a considerable altruistic sacrifice. *Alumnus*, by contrast, means favorite, as when Seneca calls his hero Cato the Younger the *alumnus* of the gods. It is even a term of endearment, as in the case of Germanicus's young son, the heir to the throne, Caligula, in whom people had great hopes. The word actually covered, and in a sense dignified and elevated, a wide variety of non-kin relationships, such as that of a freeman and his freed slave nurse (like the centurion Quintianus and his nurse Julia Almyrda, whose tombstone is quoted above), a favored manumitted slave and his master or mistress, an abandoned child and his foster parents, and also a young person taken in as an apprentice or student. We have tombstones of *alumni*-protégés belonging to doctors, to carpenters, and athletes; and in the Syrian desert, St. Jerome had *alumni*-students "devoted to the art of copying manuscripts"—perhaps the first recorded interns. Used in an extended way, *alumnus* could refer to the protégé of a politician or the followers of a philosophical school. Tertullian, quoted above, calls the poor and destitute who are supported by the church the "nurslings of their faith" (*alumni confessionis suae*), attributing a measure of dignity to some thoroughly despised groups.

The connecting thread in all these contexts is that *alumni* are profoundly shaped for the better by their benevolent environment and generously given nurture—the word itself derives from the verb *alere*, "to nourish." This is something that every college graduate's *alma mater* (nourishing mother) hopes they remember when the annual *alumni* giving campaign comes around.

TLL 1.1793-1799. B. Rawson, "Children in the Roman *Familia*," in B. Rawson, ed. *The Family in Ancient Rome: New Perspectives* (Ithaca, NY: Cornell University Press, 1986) 170–200. Tombstones of *alumni*: E. Ruggiero, *Dizionario Epigrafico di Antichità Romane* (repr. Rome: L'Erma, 1961) 1.437–440. Cato the *alumnus* of the gods: Seneca, *On Providence* 2.12. Jerome's interns: *Letters* 5.2.

EDUCATION

exemplum
ferula
grammaticus
artes liberales

EXEMPLUM: A MODEL OF CONDUCT TO BE TAKEN FOR EMULATION

Life must be equipped with illustrious exempla.
(Seneca, *Letters* 83.13)

Literature, philosophy and history are full of exempla ... writers have left us many images of the bravest men, created not just for our contemplation, but also for imitation.
(Cicero, *Pro Archia* 14)

Could there be any better teachers of courage, justice, loyalty, self-control, frugality, or contempt for pain and death than men like Fabricius, Curius, Regulus, Decius, Mucius, and countless others? Rome is as strong in exempla as Greece is in precepts; and exempla are more important.
(Quintilian, *On the Orator's Education* 12.2.30)

By new laws passed at my proposal, many exempla of our ancestors, now fallen out of use in our time, were brought back into use; and in many areas I myself handed down exempla to posterity for their imitation.
(Augustus, *Res Gestae* 8.5)

They are instantly wise, instantly omniscient, they revere no one, imitate no one, and they themselves are their own exempla.
(Pliny the Younger on the youth of his day, *Letters* 8.23.3)

exemplum Roman education had a strong moral element. It was assumed that learning was meant to foster good *mores*, or character, as well as to provide practical advantages. How was this attempted? Through philosophers' precepts? Hardly. Philosophy, obviously out of the question for the poor, was the pursuit of the bookish few and generally considered an eccentricity unsuitable for Romans intent on a publicly useful career. Through religious instruction? No. Roman paganism had no bible, no memorized creed, no list of commandments, even if the gods were felt to expect and reward honesty and virtue. The primary Roman vehicle of moral teaching was the *exemplum*, a concrete instance or story taken from history, fable, or daily life that shows a vice to be avoided or a virtue to be emulated.

In the somewhat idealized pictures we have of ancient instruction by *exemplum*, parents, teachers, and books work hand in hand. A poet praises an upper-class girl about to marry an emperor: "But she, safe on her bed and not knowing that marriage is in the offing, enjoys the conversation of her divine mother, and drinks in her mother's good character [*mores*] and learns about old time *exempla* of chastity, unceasingly unrolling scrolls both Latin and Greek, with her own mother as the teacher." Horace's father likewise had real respect for book learning, but he made sure to hammer plenty of concrete *exempla* into his son's brain: "The best of fathers taught me thus, to shun the various vices by pointing them out with examples. When he was urging me to live sparingly, frugally, content with what he had saved for me, he would say, 'You see how badly Albius' son lives, and old broke Baius? A loud warning not to squander your father's fortune.' When warning me off a disgraceful affair with a courtesan, he would say, 'Don't be like Scetanus.'" A good *exemplum* was clear and well-known (*illustris*), the unambiguous product of lived experience. Through the *exemplum*, a life could become a lesson, a fable, a parable. "My bereft old age should be added to the *exempla* to show that sterile wives can experience true joy," says a lady's gravestone. Another says, with typical directness, "My advice to you is to live and be happy. Death waits for all. You who read this, learn an *exemplum* from me."

Exempla were not just for private moral education. The habit of exemplary thinking had a pervasive effect on all education and intellectual life. Higher education revolved around public speaking and the training of orators and advocates, and one of the most important things a good speaker needs is a ready stock of illustrations. What history the Roman student got was typically in the form of *exempla*—pre-digested anecdotes about famous historical personages that could be turned rhetorically in various ways to make a point. The more diligent student, like the eighteen-year-old Pliny the Younger, might go to the effort of reading through Livy's monumental history of Rome, copying out *exempla* for later use—this is what he was doing in an effort to calm his mother with a show of normalcy during the terrible earthquakes that preceded the eruption of Mt. Vesuvius in AD 79. The less diligent would rely on compilations of *exempla* by others, a literary genre that arose in the late Republic and culminated in Valerius Maximus's *Memorable Deeds and Sayings*, compiled in AD 31. Valerius read Livy and Cicero and drew from his reading historical anecdotes that illustrated abstract categories such as "Friendship," or "Luxury and Lust," or "Cruelty," or "Illustrious Men Who Dressed Somewhat Outlandishly." Once excerpted from their context and recast as moral lessons, historical *exempla* lost most of what accuracy and analysis they might ever have had, and became not so much history proper as Chicken Soup for the Roman Soul.

One of the reasons that a more scientific historiography never developed in the ancient world is that teachers and schools did not feel the need. Whether for elementary moral instruction or the training of effective public speakers who would administer the state and the empire, the Roman educated class wanted not a balanced and thorough understanding of the past, but *exempla*. This tyranny of the moralizing anecdote endured through the Middle Ages and Renaissance. More manuscripts of Valerius Maximus's *Memorable Deeds and Sayings* survive than of any other Latin prose text, save the Bible.

TLL 5.1326-1350. W. Martin Bloomer, *Valerius Maximus and the Rhetoric of the New Nobility* (Chapel Hill: University of North Carolina Press, 1992). An upper-class girl: Claudian, *Epithalamium on the Wedding of Honorius and Maria* 229–233. The best of fathers: Horace, *Satires* 1.4.105-112. My bereft old age: epitaph of Papiria Tertia, from Ferrara, *CIL 5.2435 = CLE 369*. Live and be happy: *CIL 5.3403 = CLE 1004*. Pliny the Younger: *Letters* 6.20.5.

FERULA: GIANT FENNEL; FERULE, ROD, CANE

Then they are led into the schools to learn their letters, crying under the blows of the straps, ferulae, and rods, the varieties of their mental abilities matched by the variety of the punishments distributed.

(One of the arguments against having children, as listed by Augustine, *Against Julian* 3.154 ed. Zelzer)

[The ferulae speak:] Most hateful to boys and pleasing to teachers, we are the rods made famous by the gift of Prometheus. [Prometheus hid fire inside the pith of the giant fennel and gave it to mankind.]

(Martial, *Epigrams* 14.80.)

Be not afraid. We are your fathers, we do not have the ferulae and rods of the grammar teachers. If anyone mistakes a word, he will not err in faith.

(Augustine, *Sermons* 213, p. 449 ed. Morin.)

So, was it for nothing that I studied all that time, and often pulled my hand out from under the ferula?

(Jerome, *Letters* 57.12)

Some people say that ferula derives from ferio, "to strike." [The derivation is not historically correct.]

(Isidore of Seville, *Etymologies* 17.9.95.)

ferula Of the several instruments of corporal punishment used in Roman schools, the *ferula*, the stalk of the giant fennel plant, was the most characteristic, favored because it did not leave bruises. "To have snatched one's hands away from under the *ferula*" was a proverbial way of saying one had been to school and learned the ABCs. It was much used, both in the *ludus litterarum*, which provided general utilitarian literacy for the masses, and in the school of the *grammaticus*, who taught poetry and proper diction to the elite. It became the very symbol of primary school and was apparently also the main pedagogical tool, or at least the thing adults remembered. "Let the *ferulae* rest," says a satirical poet to a schoolmaster in July. "If boys stay healthy in the hot summer months, they learn well enough."

The somewhat callous attitude of adults toward this childhood suffering is recalled with bitterness by Augustine: "Though I was only a small child, there was great feeling when I pleaded with you [God] that I might not be caned at school. And when you did not hear me . . . adult people, including my parents, who wished no evil to come upon me, used to laugh at my stripes, which were at that time a great and painful evil to me." Once in a while the students might take horrible revenge, as in the case of the martyrdom of St. Cassian of Imola. A Christian schoolmaster, he refused to make pagan sacrifice and was handed over to his students for punishment (probably after the emperor Julian's edict of AD 362 against Christian schoolmasters). According to Prudentius, who tells this story, they stabbed him to death with their writing styluses.

Such methods of instruction were not of course confined to ancient Roman schools, nor to far distant times. Many live who suffered under similar methods. My own predecessor as Latin teacher at Dickinson College, Professor James Ross (1744–1827), is described by a biographer as genial on the street but terrible in the schoolroom. He carried a cat-o'-nine-tails, attached by a ring to his little finger, and was so absentminded that he sometimes forgot to remove the implement of torture when he took his dinner.

TLL 6.598–599. Let the *ferulae* rest: Martial, *Epigrams* 10.62.10–12. Augustine: *Confessions* 1.9.14, trans. Chadwick. St. Cassian of Imola: Prudentius, *Crowns of Martyrdom* 9. James Ross: "James Ross, Latinist," *Papers Read before the Lancaster County Historical Society* 9.2 (1904) 29-36.

GRAMMATICUS: TEACHER OR SCHOLAR OF GRAMMAR, LANGUAGE, AND LITERATURE

He was already shouldering the boyhood yoke on his tender neck, subject to the harsh commands of the grammaticus, and to the teacher's amazement, the noble boy absorbed his lessons with talent and aptitude.

(From an elegy for a boy named Celsus, who died at age 8;
Paulinus of Nola, *Poems* 31.23-25 ed. Hartel.)

Some have judged that the question we should ask of liberal studies is this: do they make a man good? They do not even promise this or pretend knowledge of it. Grammatica *has to do with careful speech and, in a wider sense, with* historia *[history and mythology] and, at its furthest extent, with poetry. Which of these paves the way to virtue?*

(Seneca, *Letters* 88.3)

And so this discipline, though it has a single name, acquired an endless multiplicity of subject matter, more filled with study than with pleasure or truth, since history and mythology [historia] provides as much work for grammatici *as it does to the historians themselves. For it is maddening that a man seems to be ignorant if he has not heard of the flight of Daedalus, but that he is not called a liar if he invented it, a fool if he believed it, and impudent if he questioned someone about it—or, to take an example of the kind of thing I am often sorry to see happen to my friends, if one cannot answer what Euryalus' mother was called, he is accused of ignorance, while those very experts who are asked about such matters dare to call their questioners empty-headed and foolish, instead of curious.*

(Augustine, *De ordine* 2.12)

grammaticus The typical method of the *grammaticus* was to ask questions about poetry. He might read out, say, a line of Vergil and ask, "Do you understand this line?" "Yes." "How many words are in it?" "Eight." "Define each one." There would follow an attempt at definition, with correction by the *grammaticus*. He posed questions about grammar, history, or mythology as well—anything relevant to understanding the language of the poet, line by line, word by word. This could easily degenerate into a humiliating game of trivial pursuit, and *grammatici* notoriously made their students miserable by correcting their pronunciation, their use of improper or nonstandard Latin (the standard being set by the poets), and generally making them feel ignorant. While he offered a spot on the island of literacy in a sea of illiteracy, the price the *grammaticus* exacted was a regimen of crushing pedantry, "filled more with study than pleasure or truth," as Augustine says.

Despite their pedantry, *grammatici* enjoyed considerable prestige. Roman emperors, even if they did not know much about the problems of the empire, were expected to have impeccably pure Latin, and several knew enough *grammatica* to turn semi-pro. Julius Caesar wrote a grammatical treatise on proper word formation. Augustus had strong, contrarian opinions about usage, hated archaism, and used several low expressions from common speech. His successor, Tiberius, had listened to *grammatici* to pass the time during his period of exile on Rhodes; as emperor he enjoyed their company, and used to test their knowledge of mythological minutiae, asking, "Who was Hecuba's mother, what was Achilles' name when he was among the maidens on Scyros, what song did the Sirens sing?" Claudius' forays into this area were radical and eccentric. Before ascending to the throne he wrote a treatise arguing that the Latin alphabet needed three more letters. When he became emperor he ran into no obstacles in getting them adopted, and they were used—at least until his death, after which they were abandoned.

Rigorous training in the rules of grammar and linguistic nicety was the basis of all education for the literate elite in the ancient world, and until recently the same could be said of modern times as well. So thoroughly have the tables turned against grammar in the United States that it has virtually disappeared from American primary schools. No less a body than the National Council of Teachers of English has adopted resolutions and issued reports arguing that the study of traditional school grammar does students a "gross disservice"; so it is only symptomatic of a wider cultural trend that recent American presidents are as known for their grammatical gaffes as the Roman emperors were for their meticulous correctness.

Grammatica, however, encompassed a larger field than our "grammar," including familiarity with canonical poetry and the special vocabulary, myths, and stories that could be found there. This is so because the scientific study of language and grammar grew up in Greece in the context of the study of the poets, who were taken as authoritative on these matters. The Greek forerunners of Roman *grammatici* were expected to be encyclopedically informed experts on this most important and prestigious of art forms. The Greek adjective *grammatikos* could mean either "literate" in an elementary sense, or "literate" in a broader sense, designating an educated person, man of letters, or a literary scholar. The specialized, occupational sense, "teacher of grammar," is a late development in Greek, for the reason that in the classical period of Greek literature no such profession existed. But later, when the Romans conquered Greek-speaking lands in the second and first centuries BC, literary scholarship and the study of grammar and language were flourishing at such centers as Athens, Pergamon, and Alexandria. There followed a brain drain of scholars to the center of power. Roman officers brought back learned Greeks as prisoners of war and employed them as teachers for their children; distinguished literary scholars also visited Rome on their own, such as Crates of Mallos, who fell down and broke his leg in a sewer hole in the neighborhood of the Palatine and spent the whole time of his convalescence giving lectures. Inspired by Crates and others, Romans began to systematize Latin as they had previously systematized Greek, adopting their codification of the parts of speech, purifying and rationalizing Latin poetic texts, and setting up schools. By the time the word *grammaticus* arrives in Latin for the first recorded time, in the first century BC, it has lost the general sense of "learned man" and has the specialized, occupational sense of scholar/teacher. Once the profession of the *grammaticus* as teacher established itself at Rome, it spread to the rest of the empire, bequeathing its distinctive and arduous methods of grammar-through-poetry to the Middle Ages and beyond.

TLL 6.2170-2174. R.A. Kaster, *Guardians of Language: The Grammarian and Society in Late Antiquity* (Berkeley: University of California Press, 1988), and his edition of Suetonius, *De Grammaticis et Rhetoribus* (Oxford: Oxford University Press, 1995). Who was Hecuba's mother?: Suetonius, *Tiberius* 70. Gross disservice: quoted by David Mulroy, *The War Against Grammar* (Portsmouth, NH: Boynton/Cook, 2003) 6.

ARTES LIBERALES: THE LIBERAL ARTS

Hippias of Elis, when he had come to Olympia during the famous celebration of the great quinquennial* games there, boasted in earshot of practically all of Greece that there was nothing in any of the fields of study which he did not know. Not only those arts which comprise the liberal and gentlemanly studies, geometry, music, literature and poetry, and those which deal with natural science, ethical philosophy and politics; he also said that he had made with his own hands the ring he was wearing, the cloak on his back and the shoes on his feet.

(Cicero, *On the Orator* 3.127)

---

* The Olympic games occurred every fourth year, but the Romans counted inclusively, hence "quinquennial," or five-yearly.

That excessive pursuit of the artes liberales makes men troublesome, wordy, tactless, self-satisfied bores.

(Seneca, *Letters* 88.37)

The fields of the artes liberales are seven. First is grammar, that is knowledge of proper speech. Second is rhetoric, which, because of the elegance and power of expression it imparts, is considered especially necessary in matters of state. Third is dialectic, also known as logic, which in subtle disputations separates the true from the false. Fourth is arithmetic, which comprises the principles of numbers and their classification. Fifth is music, which consists in songs and instrumental music. Sixth is geometry, which embraces the system of measurement of land. Seventh is astronomy, which comprises the laws pertaining to the heavenly bodies.

(Isidore of Seville, *Etymologies* 1.2.1)

Although all those artes liberales are studied in part for practical application, and in part for the understanding and contemplation of things, acquiring them is a very difficult task except for those with great natural talent who expend vigorous and constant effort from early youth.

(Augustine, *De ordine* 2.16)

The artes liberales should indeed be studied, but only up to the point that through instruction in them the divine eloquence [of the scriptures] is understood more exactly.

(Gregory the Great, *Commentary on First Kings* 5.84)

artes liberales In theory and etymologically, the liberal arts are simply what a free-born person (*liber*) ought to know and be able to do. Cicero specifies geometry, music, literature, and poetry, subjects that were preparatory to natural philosophy, ethical philosophy, and politics. The canon of seven liberal arts described by Isidore had become fixed as a basic curriculum for upper-class youngsters by later antiquity. It was followed, at least as a blueprint, by educationists throughout the Middle Ages.

Ingrained class prejudice excluded from elite education anything that smelled of handicraft, industry, or entertainment. These were the *vulgares artes* (such as construction, cooking, baking, or litter* bearing) or the *ludicrae artes* (acting and theatrical production, also highly developed). "I am not persuaded," says Seneca, "to include painters among the practitioners of the liberal arts, any more than I would include sculptors or marble-masons or the other ministers to luxury." They therefore excluded some arts that are considered quintessentially liberal today. In the case of the "free," "gentlemanly," "humane," or simply the "good" arts, the Romans adopted the Greek practice of privileging grammar and language (learned through study of the poets), logic, and the art of speech making, as well as scientific subjects that were felt to be "higher." In practice, the elite curriculum was even more narrow than it at first appears, since the first three liberal arts relating to grammar and logic (the *trivium*) were far more important than the last four (the *quadrivium*). St. Augustine understandably complains about the difficulty of the liberal arts of his day. Rather than learning anything "useful," he and his friends were reading very abstruse texts like Aristotle's *Categories*, in Greek, at age 20.

Were the liberal arts therefore useless? Only if precise language, clear thought, and effective argument are unimportant. The Roman elite's obsession with these things may have held back scientific progress (this is debated), but it did secure Latin's place as the best language for law, philosophy, literature, science, and government, well into the Renaissance. Even in late antiquity, Christians who were otherwise hostile to pagan institutions admitted that the old language- and logic-based liberal arts were indispensable to any educated person, though (as Gregory the Great advises) to be taken in moderation.

---

*A couch shut in by curtains and carried on two or more persons' shoulders.

TLL 2.656–673. *New Pauly* 2.71–73. Seneca: *Letters* 88.18.

STATUS AND CLASS

vulgus

   plebs

      eques

         latus clavus

            imagines (maiorum)

              nobilis

VULGUS: THE COMMON PEOPLE, THE MOB, THE RABBLE

I loved you, not as the vulgus loves its girlfriend,
but as a father loves his sons and sons-in-law.
(Catullus to his mistress Lesbia, 72.3–4)

In the vulgus there is no reason, no
discrimination, no diligence. Wise men
have considered that we must always
endure what the people have done. But
we do not always have to praise it.
(Cicero, *Pro Plancio* 9)

Barbarians rush into sword-fighting, the
vulgus rushes into brawls. [Barbari in
ferrum ruunt, vulgus in rixas.]
(Ambrose, discussing the effects of alcohol,
On Elias and Fasting 12.43)

The vulgus ... rejoices in empty pomp and looks at everything
with childlike minds, delights in worthless trifles and is captivated
by the show of images, and is incapable of judging the importance
of each thing so as to realize that nothing should be worshipped
that can be perceived with mortal eyes, because it must itself be
something mortal.
(Lactantius, *Divine Institutes* 2.3.7)

I shun the vulgus, and I keep them at a distance.
(Horace, adopting vaguely sacral language to
speak about his own stance as a "priest"-poet,
Odes 3.1.1)

The vulgus also calls places in which bee-hives are
located apiaria; but I can recall practically no one
who uses the language in an uncorrupted way who
has written or said this.
(Aulus Gellius, *Attic Nights* 2.20.8)

vulgus The *vulgus* is that portion of humanity whose persistent ignorance and infi-
nitely varied foolishness restore faith in one's own wisdom and solid judgment. The
throngs that make up the *vulgus* are "without name" (*sine nomine*); they are "ignoble"
(*ignobilis*), literally "not known." The *vulgus* is unlearned (*indoctum*), it uses the wrong
terms; it holds false opinions and superstitions. Its likes and dislikes are as fickle as the
breeze. Its love is shallow and physical, its grief misplaced. It jumps to conclusions, it
works on supposition and rumor. It is incapable of judging the true value of things. It

makes the life of the office seeker difficult by its inconsistency and its ruthless demands for flattery. It is "profane" (*profanum*), literally outside the temple or *fanum*, uninitiated, uncomprehending of the true religion. It worships idols, is captivated by vain display and empty entertainment. Its skills are common, not "liberal"—cooking, baking, litter bearing, and other things that do not require book learning. Its grasp on proper Latin is shaky, its characteristic vocabulary is "sordid" (*sordidus*)—that is to say, unwashed like themselves.

In English, the primary meaning of *vulgar* was long similar to the Latin *vulgaris*, "common, ordinary." Only recently has the sense "coarse, obscene" come to predominate. Vulgar Latin, then, is simply that used by the common people. Latin grammarians, endeavoring (with no dictionaries) to invent the rules of grammar, typically spoke not of correct and incorrect usage but of correct usage as distinguished from that of the *vulgus*. The proper Latin used for public speaking and writing was an elite language, the mastering of which took time and study and set one off from the common herd. The creation of the rules of classical Latin in the second and first centuries BC was a process not just of regularization but of wholesale purging of vulgar vocabulary. Some complaints of the second-century scholar Aulus Gellius about vulgar Latin include the inability of the *vulgus* to distinguish between the near-synonyms *levitas* and *nequitia*, to decline the word *praecox*, and to use the word *humanitas* properly. He also criticizes their insistence on using words like *apiaria* (bee-house), which are not witnessed by any classical authors. It was not the general consensus of usage by Latin speakers, but the approved canonical authors (coincidentally inaccessible to the illiterate *vulgus*) who set the ultimate standard of proper usage.

The Christians were not quite so hard on the language of the *vulgus*, who in the beginning at least formed the church's primary constituency. Inspired by the example of Jesus, the writers of the Greek New Testament adopted simple, common language as a vehicle for moral teaching. St. Augustine in the fourth century simplified certain aspects of Latin grammar in his sermons. In the same century it was St. Jerome who translated the Bible from Hebrew and Greek into simple Latin that most people in the Western Empire could understand, the so-called Vulgate version of the Bible that became standard in the Latin church. But this, too, eventually became unintelligible to any but the clergy, as vulgar Latin moved on, gradually sliding toward Italian, Spanish, and French. We cannot date the final linguistic departure of the *vulgus* from classical Latin with any precision, and the process no doubt varied considerably from region to region. But evidence suggests that classical Latin had lost its aural intelligibility in the early eighth century, when an anonymous author of a saint's life says that he eschewed grammatical correctness deliberately, "so that certain rustics and illiterate people might understand this work when they hear it."

Otto 378, s.v. *vulgus*. Aulus Gellius: *Attic Nights* 6.11, 10.11, 13.17, 2.20.8. Certain rustics and illiterate people: *Monumenta Germaniae Historica, Scriptores Rerum Merovingicarum* vol. 5, p. 324, cited by József Herman, "La conscience linguistique de Grégoire de Tours," in H. Petersmann and R. Kettemann, eds., *Latin vulgaire, latin tardif* vol. 5 (Heidelberg, Germany: Winter Verlag, 1999) 31–39.

PLEBS: THE GENERAL BODY OF ROMAN CITIZENS, AS DISTINCT FROM THE PATRICIANS; THE COMMON PEOPLE, THE RANK AND FILE; THE LAITY

There were four secessions of the plebs from the fathers [i.e., the Senate]: the first secession because of the abuses of the moneylenders, when the plebs withdrew under arms to the Sacred Hill; the second because of the abuses of the Board of Ten when, after the murder of his daughter, Verginius surrounded Appius and his whole faction on the Aventine Hill and brought it about that Appius abdicated his magistracy and that those accused and condemned were punished by various penalties; the third was because of marriage, that plebeians be allowed to marry patricians, which Canuleius incited on the Janiculum Hill; the fourth secession, which Sulpicius Stolo incited, was in the forum because of magistracies, so that plebeians could become consuls.

(Lucius Ampelius, *Liber Memorialis* 25, referring to events of 494–493, 449, 445, and 376–367 BC. "Sulpicius Stolo" is an error for Licinius Stolo.)

[In Gaul] the plebs is held in a condition of near-slavery; they dare nothing on their own initiative, and are included in no decision-making. Most of them, oppressed as they are either by debt or heavy taxation or by the injustices inflicted by the powerful, consign themselves to servitude, and the nobles exercise over them all the rights of masters over slaves.

(Julius Caesar, *The Gallic War* 6.13)

I don't go hunting for votes cast by the fickle plebs, paying for their dinners and giving them used clothes.

(Horace, expressing lack of interest in a political career, *Letters* 1.19.37–38.)

*plebs** Open class struggle was endemic to the early Roman Republic. The poorer citizens, or *plebs*, seeing itself shut out of priesthoods and magistracies by the wealthier cast of patricians, and overwhelmed with debt held by wealthy landowners, responded by politicizing itself and forming its own organization. It was a phenomenon unparalleled in ancient history. Through strikes, demonstrations, and its trademark gesture of departing in a body to a hill and refusing to fight in the army (*secessio*), the *plebs*, over the course of two hundred years of constant conflict with the Senate, achieved an end to debt slavery, won official recognition for its representatives (the *tribuni plebis*, "tribunes of the *plebs*"), created its own assembly (the *comitia tributa*, whose laws were made binding

---

*Note that *plebs* is a group singular. There is no such thing as a "*pleb*."

on everyone), and gained access to all the most coveted magistracies, even the consulship. Historians and political theorists have found all this class-based hostility and dissension deplorable and out of place in a well-ordered state. But Machiavelli, in his great commentary on the early books of Livy, disagreed. The lesson he drew from the Roman "struggle of the orders" was that in every Republic there are two opposed factions, that of the people and that of the rich, "and that all the laws made in favor of liberty result from their discord." The place of the *plebs* in the Roman constitution was not as dominant as that of the Athenian *demos* in their democracy, but it was significant. Caesar draws an implicit contrast with the Roman way when he describes the supine condition of the *plebs* in Gaul.

As a result of this early history of political struggle and success, the word *plebs* never had the inbuilt sneer of other words for the non-rich, like *turba* ("mob"), *multitudo* ("rabble"), or *vulgus* ("the common herd"). Livy, who tells the story of the early struggles, speaks of the *plebs* with considerable respect. And even through the much more violent clashes of the late Republic, rhetorical invective against the *plebs* itself (as opposed to their self-appointed elite representatives, the *populares*) is rare. The main criticism we hear is that the *plebs* is fickle, *mobilis*, or in the unusual phrase of Horace, *ventosa*, "windy"—that is, turned by every breeze. Orators and candidates had to cater to the *plebs* to get elected, and this naturally rankled the aristocrats. An orator is supposed to have said to a military man, when the two were competing for office of consul, that the military man's chances were slim, "especially because—a thing which above all offends the minds of the *plebs*—you do not know how to beg."

Under the Principate things changed substantially. The Roman *plebs* lost its right to elect magistrates and started receiving occasional distributions of grain. The emperors took a decidedly paternalistic attitude. The story goes that when an inventor offered the emperor Vespasian a device that would allow him to raise large columns with much less expense and manpower than the usual labor-intensive methods, he gave the man a reward for the invention, but decided not to use it, allegedly saying, "Let me feed my little *plebs*." It is at this point that we start to hear denunciations of the *plebs* as a lazy urban rabble, addicted to free grain and chariot races (bread and circuses), the amenities provided by, or some would say extorted from, the government. In the writings of the later imperial historians, the meaning of *plebs* becomes indistinguishable from that of *turba* or *vulgus*. To believe them, the disciplined political force of the early Republic had become a gawking mob. At the same time, Roman law was delimiting an ever-stricter barrier between elite and commons, so that the *plebs* was subject to certain "plebeian" punishments (flogging, torture, consignment to the mines) from which the upper classes were legally exempt. A late Roman compendium of law, the *Codex Theodosianus*, uses the word *plebs* to refer to the serfs irrevocably assigned to North African estates in the fourth century. This kind of wretched *plebs* was a long, long way from the fighting *plebs* of the early Roman Republic, eight hundred years earlier.

Still, the essential dignity of the word made it appropriate, in the first Latin translations in the Hebrew Bible, for *amo*, the "people" of God—i.e., the Jews—and (from the fourth century on) an apt word for the Christian faithful (*plebs Domini*), and finally for a Christian "congregation," the "laity," as opposed to the clergy (*clerus*).

New Pauly, s.v. "plebs." Z. Yavetz, "Plebs Sordida," *Athenaeum* 43 (1965) 295-311.
Machiavelli: *Discourses on the First Decade of Titus Livius* 1.4, trans. Allan Gilbert.
You do not know how to beg: Calpurnius Flaccus, *Declamations* 47.
Let me feed my little *plebs*: Suetonius, *Vespasian* 18.

EQUES: HORSEMAN; A MEMBER OF THE EQUESTRIAN ORDER; "KNIGHT"

Just as in great cities the population is divided up, and the senatorial class [patres] keeps the leading position, and the equestrian class has the second place, and the commons [populus] comes after the equites, and below the commons you see the idle mob [iners vulgus], and finally the nameless throng [sine nomine turbam], so also there is a kind of Republic in the great Universe, made by nature, which has established a city in the heavens.

(Manilius, explaining the different stellar magnitudes, *Astronomica* 5.734-739)

I had already issued the poem [The Art of Love] when I passed by in review so many times, a blameless eques, as you [Augustus] were registering misdeeds.

(Ovid, protesting after his banishment by the emperor Augustus that he had earlier passed the moral review associated with the equestrian census carried out by that very emperor; *Tristia* 2.541–542)

Or [my father] would urge me to do something, saying, "You have a model for this behavior," and point out one of the [equestrian] select jurors.

(Horace, *Satires* 1.4.121–123)

For the equites.

(An inscription from the Colosseum, designating certain sections of seats, *CIL* 6.1796.5)

eques The leading senatorial class was called the *patres*, suggesting their fatherly concern for the whole state. The second class was the "equestrian," a reference to their primitive role in the cavalry, at a level both physically and economically above that of the foot soldier. *Knight* is a technically accurate but very inadequate translation of *eques*, because it implies the existence of some kind of mounted, militarized aristocracy, as though the *equites* went around jousting with each other. In fact, being an *eques* in the central period of Roman history had nothing to do with prowess in the saddle. It was all a matter of money and social status. Though originally *equites* were classed together in voting assemblies based on service in the cavalry, in the course of the Republic they became a rather heterogeneous social class united only by extreme wealth (since at least 67 BC membership in this class was determined by the ability to prove at census time that one possessed 400,000 sesterces of capital, enough to live comfortably off the proceeds) and by lack of aspiration to the Senate and the offices traditionally assigned to its members. They were the non-senatorial rich, numbering perhaps 5,000 men in the reign of Augustus. There would be more who had the property but were not officially listed in the census rolls and did not receive the special grant of a horse from the state.

There was slightly more involved than the property qualification, however, and we can see from Horace's father's advice, quoted above, that they were supposed to be pillars of the community. Indeed they were expected to pass an inspection before the censor every so often and could be ejected from the order by the censor or the emperor for crimes or moral turpitude—a fact that is the basis of a strained appeal by Ovid for clemency after his exile. The *equites* were highly visible in public, not just because of the identifying gold ring and dress but because they served as the primary jury pool, appeared together in an annual parade on horseback (July 15), and sat together in the first fourteen rows at the theater. They were also assigned as a class to special sections at the amphitheater—not skyboxes, but down front: the poor, slaves, and women were relegated to the upper seats at the Colosseum. Their informal titles emphasize this sense of social prominence and visibility. On their tombstones, Roman knights were given various epithets that amount to informal titles for the order: *splendidus* or *splendidissimus* ("most distinguished"), *ornatissimus* ("most decorated"), *honestissimus* ("most honorable")—never *clarissimus* ("most illustrious") or *nobilissimus* ("most noble"), though. Those words were deemed appropriate only for men of the senatorial class. The adjectives that attach themselves to knights emphasize their wealth (*locuples* and *lautus*, both meaning "wealthy," are common), but also their honor.

Equestrian status could be inherited (as Ovid's was), or earned (like Horace's) through military service or financial success. Though it was always relatively small, the equestrian class did provide an important avenue for upward mobility, both for soldiers and for those with business acumen, but no distinguished ancestors. Horace is the classic example of a new *eques*, son of a financially successful ex-slave, who grabbed the brass (actually gold) ring by service as an army officer as a young man. In his writings, Horace is modest about his spectacular rise, but one of his contemporaries, a certain Appuleius, was not. A military tribune and son of two ex-slaves named Asclepiades and Sophanuba, Appuleius is depicted on their common tombstone sporting on the fourth finger of his left hand a disproportionately oversize equestrian ring, which was probably gilded on the monument for extra display.

The equestrian order comes to its highest prominence in the third century AD, when it, rather than the old senatorial aristocracy, supplied much of the military and administrative leadership in that time of ceaseless warfare. But in the fourth century the *equites* as a distinct class went into eclipse, absorbed into the senatorial class, and the word *eques* went back to meaning only what it always had: a man who rides a horse (*equus*). Thus there is no historical or linguistic continuity between the Roman *eques* and the French *chevalier* or the English word *knight*. The last is a Germanic term dating only to around 1100, whose original sense was apparently "boy," then a boy employed as a servant to a person of high rank.

TLL 5.708-717. T. P. Wiseman, "The Definition of 'Eques Romanus,'" *Historia* 19 (1970) 67–83. On Horace's equestrian status and the monument of Appuleius: David Armstrong, "*Horatius Eques et Scriba: Satires* 1.6 and 2.7," *Transactions of the American Philological Society* 116 (1986) 255-288.

LATUS CLAVUS: THE "WIDE STRIPE" OF PURPLE CLOTH SEWN ON THE TUNIC WORN BY SENATORS AND THEIR CHILDREN.

For those without the right of wearing the latus clavus, the belt should be worn [when delivering a speech] so that the tunic falls just below the knees in front, and just at mid-knee in the back. Lower is for women, higher for centurions. Making the purple fall straight is a minor concern . . . . The length for those having the latus clavus is a bit lower.

(Quintilian, *The Orator's Education* 11.3.138–139)

When [Octavian, the young Augustus] was putting on the toga of manhood, his tunic that was adorned with the latus clavus came unstitched and fell to his feet on both sides. There were those who interpreted this omen to mean that the order whose insignia this is would one day be subjected to him.

(Suetonius, *Augustus* 94.10)

Gellia, while you were telling us about the great names of your grandparents, and their grandparents, and calling knights such as me a degrading match, and saying you couldn't marry anything but a latus clavus, you married . . . a police captain!

(Martial, *Epigrams* 5.17)

Afterwards Septimius Severus came to Rome to study; he sought the latus clavus from the emperor Marcus Aurelius, and received it thanks to the influence of a relative, who had twice been consul.

(*SHA, Septimius Severus* 1.5)

Caesar led the [conquered] Gauls in his triumphal procession, and the same man led them into the Senate house: the Gauls took off their pants and put on the latus clavus.

(From a taunting popular song about Julius Caesar, who had allowed some northern Italian Gauls into the Senate. Quoted by Suetonius, *Julius Caesar* 80.2.)

But your "upper class," your "magistracies," and your very Senate house is the Church of Christ. You belong to Him, for you have been enrolled [not in the Senate but] in the book of life. There the blood of the Lord serves for your purple robe, and your latus clavus is his own cross.

(Tertullian, *On the Crown* 13)

latus clavus While their old foes the Carthaginians sported gowns with bright colors and geometric patterns, and the Gauls wore multicolored pants, the Romans stuck to draping garments the color of untreated wool. In this austere sea of off-white, the bright purple stripes sewn onto the tunics of the two highest social classes, senators and *equites,* were instantly recognizable. It was also easy to tell the difference between the narrow stripe of the *equites* and the broad stripe of those in the Senate or of senatorial families, or of those who intended to pursue a career in the Senate. The cloth used in the late Republic was the color of violets and cost 100 denarii per pound; later the more brilliant "twice-dyed Tyrian" fabric came into fashion, which cost 1,000 denarii per pound, so that a single *tunica laticlava* was worth the equivalent of several years' salary for a soldier.

For the son of a senator, putting on the broad striped tunic when donning the toga of manhood was simply what was expected, the hopeful first step in a senatorial career. For those of lower status, or not from Rome itself, who wanted to move up, it was a risky and presumptuous act, inviting ridicule. Horace, who was from outside Rome and not extremely wealthy, says he declined to put on the *latus clavus* because he didn't want to hear the constant questions: "Who is this man? What was his father?" Under the Principate, one way to lower the risk of rejection was to apply to the emperor directly for the right to wear it. For those not born to the purple, being granted the privilege was an unforgettable moment of "making it." "I have never spent a happier day than that on which the *latus clavus* was offered to me," says a character in Tacitus's *Dialogue on Oratory.* The Christian preacher Tertullian ridicules such worldly pretensions but draws on the symbolism of Roman status clothing when he promises his flock that the cross of Christ is their "broad stripe."

TLL 3.1328-1351. B. Levick, "A Note on the *Latus Clavus,*"
Athenaeum 79 (1991) 239–244. Horace: *Satires* 1.6.27–28.
Tacitus: *Dialogue on Oratory* 7.

IMAGINES (MAIORUM): IMAGES OF THE ANCESTORS, WAX MASKS KEPT BY THE ROMAN NOBILITY

Not the cost, but the spectacle of the imagines is what makes
a great man's funeral a noble thing.
> (M. Aemilius Lepidus, giving instruction to his sons
> for his own funeral, held in 152 BC. Livy,
> *Roman History*, epitome of Book 48)

You slithered into office because men made a mistake, because of
the recommendation of your smoky imagines, which you
resemble only in your complexion.
> (Cicero to Lucius Calpurnius Piso Caesoninus,
> consul in 59 BC, at a meeting of the
> Senate in 55. *Against Piso* 1)

The people . . . are often stupid in giving elected
office to unworthy men and are silly in being
slaves to reputation . . . they are amazed at
labels and masks [tituli et imagines].
> (Horace, *Satires* 1.6.15–18)

What good are imagines if your life is going to ruin?
> (From a poem in praise of a certain Calpurnius Piso,
> first century AD. *Laus Pisonis* 8–10)

Even laying a false claim to the imagines of famous men
shows some love of moral excellence [virtus].
> (Pliny the Elder, *Natural History* 35.8)

imagines (maiorum) The nobles of England and Europe in the Middle Ages had their titles and charters, their seals and coats of arms. The Roman approach to the marks of inherited privilege was characteristically *exemplary*: the Roman noble displayed wax portrait masks of his noble ancestors, on whose achievements his own claim to hereditary nobility rested, as a daily encouragement to *virtus*. "The images" were kept in the atrium and brought out to be paraded at the funerals of family members. This makes them different from a mere portrait gallery kept in a hallway at home and gives them a public, ritual importance. But they had no religious function, so far as we know, nothing to do with ancestor worship per se. Rather they were both status symbols and educational tools, meant to impress and intimidate outsiders (both the lower orders and rival families within the elite) and also inculcate the younger generation with the duty to live up to the *exempla* of their distinguished forbears.

Since noble status rested ultimately on the holding of elected public office, it was essential to include a *titulus* explaining what the original owner of each grim visage had done, what offices he had held, what battles he had fought, what distinctions he had won in service to the state. This family lore was public knowledge and became an important part of the historical record. At funerals, actors were hired to wear the masks and, as far as possible, imitate the gait and gestures of the man. They processed through the city and sat at the ceremony as an implicitly judgmental audience, listening to the eulogy of the deceased. Did his life measure up? It is easy to imagine how a sense of pride in one's lineage could turn into one of shame, of dread of their constant ghostly presence in the atrium. While an atrium full of *imagines* could guarantee a young noble election over less well-born competitors, and could form the basis for a plea for leniency when convicted of a crime, it also meant exposure to the criticism of degeneracy. Castigating lazy nobles was a popular Roman pastime. A satirist asks, "Can you live badly in the presence of the Lepidi?" ("*Coram Lepidis male vivis?*")—that is, in the presence of their masks.

As with the word *nobilis*, the *imagines* attract the vocabulary of vision and light. Despite being physically smoky and sooty, they are said to shine (*fulgere* or *praefulgere*), and they are bright, clear, famous (*clarae*), illustrious (*illustres*), haughty (*superbae*), and beautiful (*pulchrae*); they ornament (*exornare*) the atrium and decorate (*decorare*) the funeral. By laziness or turpitude one can disgrace the masks and "turn the light received from one's ancestors into darkness," or bury one's masks in vice. They are meant above all to be displayed (*figere, exponere, aperire*), looked at (*conspicere, videre, intueri*), and paraded (*anteferre, ostentare*) at funerals. Their moral, hortatory function is constantly emphasized. The masks stirred the Romans to action (*suscitare*), urged them on (*adhortari*) or, for the less energetic, weighed them down (*onerare*).

TLL 7.404-414, esp. 406. Harriet I. Flower, *Ancestor Masks and Aristocratic Power in Roman Culture* (Oxford, UK: Oxford University Press, 1996). In the presence of the Lepidi: Juvenal, *Satires* 8.9. Turn the light into darkness: Valerius Maximus, *Memorable Deeds and Sayings* 3.3.7. Bury in vice: Seneca the Elder, *Controversiae* 1.6.3.

NOBILIS: RENOWNED, FAMOUS, NOTEWORTHY, DISTINGUISHED; NOBLE, WELL-BORN; HEROIC

I will give fame [nobilitas] to places now unknown.
(The ambition of Alexander the Great, according to
Curtius Rufus. *History of Alexander* 9.6.22)

*We see how great is the jealousy and
the hatred with which certain noble
men regard the talent and energy of
the new men.*
(Cicero, *Against Verres* 2.5.181)

*You are noble: so are those men, but
they are more noble in Christ.*
(Jerome to Julian, urging him to follow
the example set by Pammachius and
Paulinus, who gave up their riches to
become monks. *Letters* 118.5)

*To the most brave and most noble Caesar Flavius Valerius
Constantius: the commonwealth of the city of the Thimidia Bure
[set this up], eternally devoted to the divinity [of the Caesars].*
(The label from a statue or other dedication made
by a North African city to Constantius,
who was appointed one of the four Caesars by
the emperor Diocletian in AD 293. *ILS* 6791)

nobilis It is hard now to say the word *noble* without qualification, without an ironic tone, or without also using the word *but*, as in, "her plan to convert the landfill into a wildlife refuge was noble but doomed." The word has come to suggest unrealistic, naive high-mindedness. A noble experiment inevitably fails, noble aims are thwarted by practical difficulties, a noble profession is underpaid, noble deeds do not go unpunished, and a noble savage is nowhere to be found. Like its cousins *sublime* and *lofty*, *noble* is a term of high approval that seems to belong to a bygone era. Part of this anachronism and loss of credibility has to do with its blending of the social and the moral, the implied equation of high social class with virtue. The two things (as various Roman authors emphasize) do not always go together, and since the decline of power of the world's great aristocracies, we are more ready to admit this fact. The word has come to seem quaint or, if used sincerely, vaguely suspicious.

In Roman times, by contrast, when aristocracy ruled uncontested, the primary sense was always the objective, descriptive one, "belonging to the office-holding caste, aristocratic." A commentator on Horace says, "In the dark I pretend that that prostitute is some noble lady"—i.e., an authentic member of the nobility. Historians have variously defined the exact criteria for being considered *nobilis* in this sense in the Roman Republic: it seems that one had to have at least one direct ancestor who had been elected consul—quite an exclusive group. Among the elite, these old families were distinguished from the "new men," like Cicero or Marius, whose ancestors had not held high office in Rome. In a broader sense, and later in Roman history, *nobilis* referred to the office-holding elite in general. At any rate, it would be totally incorrect in the classical period to refer to a man of equestrian status in this way, no matter how rich or virtuous he was: a "noble knight" is a Latin contradiction in terms.

Second in popularity to this precise sociological meaning is the truly primary sense, "well-known, notable, famous, distinguished," cognate to the Germanic root in *known*. We very often hear of "noble" cities, like Troy or Capua, or "noble" poets, doctors, scholars, and philosophers. Epictetus is called a noble philosopher despite having been born a slave, and one can even speak of a "noble" gladiator or a "noble" courtesan. The common elements are fame and distinction above the competition in one's sphere. Material things that are noble are fine, high quality—a citron-wood table, a wine vintage, a fleece, even a particularly good cabbage. From there, *nobilis* is occasionally deployed in literary criticism, so that a noble speech or noble verses are simply excellent, well-known ones.

In a purely moral sense, the dominant one in our language, the word is comparatively rare in Latin. But when it does appear it is often associated with *virtus* in its most heroic guise. To have a "noble spirit" was to hold one's life cheap and to display remarkable courage on a matter of principle. Cato the Younger stabbed himself in the gut rather than submit to government under Caesar: a noble death (*nobile letum*), says Horace. On the other side, one of Caesar's centurions was captured, and when offered his life in return for going over to the side of Pompey, he is said to have replied, "I thank you, Scipio, but I have no need for life on those terms." Valerius Maximus, who tells the story, exclaims, "A noble spirit with no masks!"—i.e., with no aristocratic lineage. After Caesar's death, Cicero wrote to Cassius, the dictator's assassin, "nothing is more noble than your courage and your greatness of spirit."

An interesting area of *nobilis* applies to wild animals, where *nobiles ferae* are those that are dangerous, easily provoked, quick to anger, the ones you have to watch out for. The others, the ones that run away, are *ignobiles ferae*. In the *Aeneid*, Vergil refers to the serpents with flashing eyes who emerge from the sea to strangle Laocoon and his sons as *saevae* (savage), but the ancient commentator Servius explains to his late antique readers that Vergil means "powerful, or noble" (*fortis aut nobilis*). This attribution of nobility to beasts who are not to be tangled with perhaps provides a little window onto how the rest of the world viewed the nastier side of the Roman elite.

What we do *not* normally see in classical Latin is *nobilis* meaning high-minded, altruistic, or disinterested, the kind of *noblesse oblige* virtues we associate with nobility in its old-fashioned English guise. These virtues were part of the self-image of the English aristocracy, but not the Roman. Latin *nobilis* encodes how the Roman elite saw itself and how it was seen: as superior, renowned, principled, and formidable. Yet the roots of the nobility of self-abnegation can be found in the early church fathers. St. Jerome and others refer to many noble ladies and men who, becoming committed Christians, were made "more noble in Christ," especially by giving up their possessions (in ordinary times the very marks of their nobility) and devoting themselves entirely to the church. The idea that one could become more noble by becoming less wealthy was a significant innovation. The Biblical and early

Christian use of the word puts an unclassical stress on self-control as the mark of true nobility of character: the noble is one who does not abuse or flaunt his power and wealth. Yet this emphasis on charity and continence was really a shift of emphasis rather than a change of substance; Christianity comfortably incorporated traditional Roman notions of family, rank, and office in its hierarchy of values, and *nobilis* continued to refer to the rich and well-born.

Unlike the statesmen of the Republic, who knew the precise definition of *nobilis* and who qualified, the later emperors increasingly surrounded themselves with the word in formulaic titles and epithets. Superlatives like *nobilissimus* exemplify the kudzu-like growth of imperial nomenclature, seen in a small way in the inscription for Constantius quoted above. Stripped of real meaning, such superlatives acted simply like a spoken genuflection, the linguistic equivalent of the fawning formalities that characterized the court ceremonial of the later empire.

D.R. Shackleton Bailey, "*Nobiles* and *Novi* Reconsidered," *American Journal of Philology* 107 (1986) 255–260. Janet L. Nelson, "Nobility in the Ninth Century," in *Nobles and Nobility in Medieval Europe,* ed. A. Duggan (Woodbridge, Suffolk, England: Boydell Press, 2000) 43–51. Commentator on Horace: Poryphyrio on *Satires* 1.2.126, glossing Horace's line "I give whatever name I like to her." A noble death: Horace, *Odes* 1.12.36. Valerius Maximus: *Memorable Deeds and Sayings* 3.8.7. Cicero: *Letters to His Friends* 12.10.3. Vergil: *Aeneid* 2.226, with Servius's commentary on this passage.

PUBLIC PLACES

trivium
forum
balneum
basilica
atrium

TRIVIUM: A PLACE WHERE THREE ROADS MEET, CROSSROADS, "THE GUTTER"

Once, while he was eating lunch, a strange dog came in from the trivium bringing in a human hand, which it deposited under the table.

(An omen of the future power of the emperor Vespasian, recorded by Suetonius, *Vespasian* 5.4)

Some apply surprising remedies, and swear that when the fever comes one should seek out the playful gift of Venus; but first it is necessary to boil small frogs in oil in the trivia and rub the resulting oil on the limbs.

(A remedy for quartan fever. Quintus Serenus, *Liber medicinalis* 910–913)

If you've been fooled once you don't bother to pick up a man lying in the trivia with a broken leg, even if the fellow cries many tears and swears by holy Osiris and says, "Believe me, I'm not fooling. You heartless people, help a cripple." "Find a tourist," comes the rough reply of the locals.

(Horace, *Letters* 1.17.58–62)

Have you forgotten about our escapades in the late-night Subura,* and my window, worn down by nocturnal tricks when so many times I let down a rope to you and dangled in mid-air, coming to embrace you? Often we made love in the trivium, and our passionate battles, breast on breast, warmed the street beneath us.

(Cynthia to Propertius, appearing posthumously to the poet in a dream. *Elegies* 4.7.15–20)

---

*A neighborhood in Rome, often mentioned as a center of nightlife.

And then I saw my old friend Socrates. He was sitting on the ground, half-covered by a ripped cloak, almost unrecognizable in his pallor, pitiably deformed and shrunken, like those cast-offs of Fortune who beg for alms in the trivia.

(Apuleius, *Metamorphoses* 1.6)

trivium   This is a somewhat "low" word, avoided by classical historians, but for some reason permissible in elevated poetry such as the lines of Horace and Propertius quoted here. The related adjective *trivialis* is the ultimate origin of the English "trivial," but in Latin it does not mean pointless or negligible, so much as common, the kind of thing one meets every day in the streets. For that reason its use is revealing of the kind of things one met every day in the Roman streets. Beggars sat *in triviis* and asked for "street alms" (*trivialis stips*). Trivial players (*ludii triviales*) were street performers, for whom the emperor Augustus had an unusual affection—he would invite them in to perform at his dinner parties. Slapstick farces seem to have been common, as well as lots of bad street poetry (*triviale carmen*). Muck is *trivialis faex*. A character in Petronius's *Satyricon* asks the narrator "What piece of garbage or corpse did you tread on by night in the gutter?" an unlucky occurrence that might, she speculates, explain his impotence. The story about Vespasian in which a dog brought in a human hand *e trivio* suggests the deficiencies of Roman street cleaning.

The thing that is most commonly called "trivial," however, is speech. The language of the Roman street is impossible to reconstruct in any detail. We only know that educated writers found it almost as disgusting as the bits of corpses lying around. Horace says of those "native to the streets" (*innati triviis*) that they "rattle out foul and disgusting words." The verb he uses is the same one used for the sound of flatulation (*crepare*). St. Augustine says that he saw some allegedly religious men whistling at women in a public square in Carthage "with gestures so coarse as to surpass the raunchiness and rudeness of all the ordinary rascals [*omnium trivialium*]." St. Jerome, in attacking the degenerate style of one of his critics, cites the literary tastes of the mob on the street as an explanation of why the works of such an ignorant man could find an audience. A favorite work in that context was the supposedly side-splitting "Last Will and Testament of the Pig." In isolated vignettes like these, the Roman *trivium* can be glimpsed, through admittedly hostile eyes, as a noisy, bawdy, boisterous place, where people "collected in groups about the squares, crossings, streets, and other public places, engaged in heated argument on one side or the other of some question," as the historian Ammianus says derisively. One of the biggest criticisms leveled at the Christian Bible by educated pagans was that, since it was written for such people, its style was "trivial and sordid"—that is, rough and unrefined.

Augustus's affection for street performers: Suetonius, *Augustus* 74.1. Petronius, *Satyricon* 134. Foul and disgusting words: Horace, *Ars Poetica* 247. Augustine, *On the Character of the Catholic Church and the Manichaeans* 2.1374. Jerome, *Apologia against the Books of Rufinus* 1.17. Ammianus, *The Later Roman Empire* 28.4.29. Trivial and Sordid: Arnobius, *Against the Pagans* 1.58.

FORUM: A PUBLIC SQUARE IN THE CENTER OF TOWN

When you see the forum
packed with a crowd ... be sure
of this: there are as many vices
there as men.
(Seneca, *On Anger* 2.8)

When I speak in the forum, I feel I am
accomplishing something; when I declaim
[to a private audience] ... I seem to be
laboring in a dream.
(Seneca the Elder, *Controversiae* 3 pref)

 What could Cato [the Younger] do besides cry out in vain when
he was lifted up by the hands of the crowd and dragged, covered
in spit, out of the forum?
(Seneca, referring to the tumult of the late Republic. *Letters* 14.13)

One ought to choose dinner companions who are neither
chatter-boxes nor mutes, because the place for speeches is
in the forum and in the courts, but silence belongs not in
the dining room but in the bedroom.
(Varro, *Menippean Satires* 336.3, quoted by
Aulus Gellius, *Attic Nights* 13.11.3)

[Otho] made no secret of his view that
if he proved unable to become emperor,
it made no difference whether he was
killed by the enemy in battle, or in the
forum by his creditors.
(Suetonius, *Otho* 5.1)

I will see you on the 30th and, even if
I see you in the middle of the forum,
I will smother your eyes with kisses.
(Cicero to his freedman secretary Tiro, 44
BC. *Letters to His Friends* 16.27)

Why, jealous critics, do you reproach me with years of idleness and
call poetry the work of a lazy talent, [saying] that, unlike our ancestors, I do not pursue the rewards of dusty military service while in
the vigor of my youth; that I don't memorize the prolix legal code
and prostitute my voice in the ungrateful forum? The work you
demand is mortal and perishable; I am looking for eternal fame.
(Ovid, *Amores* 1.15.1–8)

forum For the lawyers, ex-officials, and town-bred idlers who wrote the majority of classical Latin literature, the *forum*—especially the *forum Romanum* in Rome—was the center of the action. It was the place where glory was to be had, where fortunes were won and lost, and the place from which poets like Ovid ostentatiously withdrew to pursue their quieter art. It was proverbially frantic and contentious. Seneca claims that, with the help of philosophy, it was possible to live calmly *even there*. The elder Seneca, who trained lawyers, compares it to a gladiatorial arena. Trials were held right in the open, so a successful speaker needed a good set of lungs. Though law and banking were the main activities, they were by no means the only ones. You might get married there, hire a wet-nurse, consult a freelance diviner, witness an imperial adoption, attend a rally, or even be cremated.

So central was the forum to public life that it became a synonym and symbol for public life itself. *In foro* could mean simply "in public," outside one's house; *forum attingere* ("to touch the forum") meant to take part in public life; and *in forum deducere* ("to lead into the forum") was to escort a young man to the forum on his assumption of the toga of manhood and formally introduce him to public life. In a more specialized sense, *forum* meant the Exchange, or financial center, and hence *foro cedere* ("to leave the forum") meant to go bankrupt. Alternatively, *forum* also meant the bar and the courts, and "to bring a matter to the forum" meant to litigate. Our derivative word *forensic*, as in forensic evidence, retains the legal association exclusively.

In the Middle Ages the *forum Romanum* became a field. Nothing evokes the loss of this vibrant center of Roman urbanism more poignantly than the many early modern engravings and paintings showing animals loitering among the ruins on the plot of ground that an anonymous author had once called "the temple of liberty and the arena of the litigators."

TLL 6.1198-1208. L. Richardson, *A New Topographical Dictionary of Ancient Rome* (Baltimore: Johns Hopkins University Press, 1992) 158–178. Even there: Seneca, *Letters* 28.6. Gladiatorial arena: Seneca the Elder, *Controversiae* 3 pr.13. The temple of liberty: *The Dialogue of Hadrian and Epictetus* 70.

BALNEUM: A BATHING ESTABLISHMENT

The name balnea derives from the fact that the Greeks
call them bala-neion, or "banishing from the mind,"
because the baths drive away anxiety from the mind.
[The etymology is not historically correct.]

(Augustine, *Confessions* 9.12.32)

The common people [of Campania, near Naples] suddenly
arrested them [officials and businessmen from Rome] and
ordered them to be locked in the balneae for detention,
where they suffocated in a wretched manner due to the heat.

(Livy, describing events of 216 BC, *Roman History* 23.7.3)

Baths and wine and sex destroy our
bodies—but balnea and wine and
sex are the essence of life.

(The tombstone of an imperial
freedman of the first
century AD, *ILS* 8157)

He built balnea in all neighborhoods
which by chance did not have one.

(*SHA, Alexander Severus* 39.3)

And now they consult a mirror to aid their beauty, they wear out their faces
grimly scrubbing, and perhaps they apply some cosmetics, toss their mantle
about them with an air, stuff their feet into multiform shoes, and start taking
more gear to the balneae.

(Tertullian, discussing the things that girls do to start acting
like grown women, *On the Veiling of Virgins* 12)

She never entered the balneae except when dangerously ill.

(Jerome, praising the asceticism of St. Paula after
her conversion to Christianity, *Letters* 108.15)

The bathing of the body and the use of balneae
should not be constant, but should be spaced out
at the customary interval, that is to say, once per
month.

(Augustine, instructions for a convent, *Letters* 211.13)

*balneum** Like the Russians, Turks, and Scandinavians, the Romans preferred to bathe in public, and a *balneum*, or bath building, was part of any self-respecting Roman city, just as essential as a forum or temples to the gods. Social bathing was mainly an urban comfort, however. A writer on military strategy, arguing that the toughest recruits come from the rural poor, notes approvingly that they are "ignorant of the baths, unfamiliar with creature comforts, and of simple minds." For the average town dweller, though, baths were cheap and readily available.

The *balneum* was a multipurpose facility where one could exercise, get reasonably clean, socialize, and have a snack. In size they varied from small neighborhood baths or private establishments to the vast complex provided for the city of Rome by the emperor Caracalla, the colossal shell of which survives. They were financed by entrepreneurs, by private philanthropy, or by local governments in the provinces. Civic pride sometimes led towns to build beyond their means and expertise, requiring an imperial bailout. But the biggest bath builders of all were the emperors, each of which tried to outdo his predecessors, a centuries-long competition that yielded stupendous engineering feats like the baths of Caracalla and Diocletian. Once they were built, maintenance was handled, it seems, by gangs of convicted criminals or publicly owned slaves.

It can fairly be said that the Romans were in love with the pleasure of the baths. The center of social life, a refuge from work and dust, a place of permissible self-indulgence with supposedly therapeutic benefit, bathing establishments were extolled in verse, described in lengthy letters, and built wherever anyone could afford it. Still, though thoroughly enjoyed by all classes, baths were not without their critics. One school of thought said that continual bathing made one weak and worn out, like a garment that is sent to the laundry too many times. Some Christians voluntarily abstained from hot baths, except when ill, as a self-imposed discipline; Augustine's once-a-month recommendation is indicative of the austerity of early monastic life. Early church fathers particularly condemned coed bathing and sex at baths. Such moralistic objections did not persuade most Christians to stay home, however, and before long popes and bishops were building *balnea* for their grateful flocks, just as the pagan authorities had. In fact, of all Roman customs, public bathing was one of the most persistent—in Western Europe, public baths lingered on until the sixteenth century, when a combination of church preaching and syphilis led to their demise.

---

*Normally neuter and singular, this noun is also frequently treated as feminine and plural, *balneae*, with no distinction in meaning.

TLL 2.1704-1708. Garret G. Fagan, *Bathing in Public in the Roman World* (Ann Arbor: University of Michigan Press, 1999). Ignorant of the baths: Vegetius, *On Military Science* 1.3.

BASILICA: A LARGE, OPEN HALL WITH A HIGH ROOF, AISLES CREATED BY COLUMNS, AND SOMETIMES AN INTERIOR BALCONY

The basilicae resound with the hubbub [fremitus] of trials.
(Seneca, *On Anger* 3.33.2)

Alfianus, a public slave at the Basilica Opimia.
(A tomb inscription of republican date, *CIL* 6.2338)

[Caligula] even threw coins, sizeable ones, from the upper gallery of the Basilica Julia for several days, scattering them among the common people.
(Suetonius, *Caligula* 37.1)

Perhaps you ask whom I consider the "overly busy"? There is no reason for you to think that I refer only to those whom the dogs which are let in can finally chase out of the basilica.
(Seneca, *On the Brevity of Life* 12.1)

The tribunal was also packed, and spectators of both sexes were leaning over from the gallery in the upper part of the basilica, straining to hear, which was difficult, and to see, which was easy.
(Pliny the Younger, *Letters* 6.33.4)

Those wretched, miserable people who neither fear nor blush to perform dances and pantomimes in front of the very basilicae of the saints, even if they go to church Christians, they return home pagans, because that kind of dancing is a holdover from pagan observance.
(Caesarius of Arles, *Sermons* 13.4)

Recently I saw the noblest Lady in Rome ... in the basilica of St. Peter, attended by her eunuchs, distributing single coins to the poor. She was doing it with her own hand, to increase her reputation for piety .... An old woman, full of years and dressed in rags, ran ahead to get another coin. When her turn came again she got a punch in the face instead of a denarius, paying for her great crime by the shedding of her blood.
(Jerome, *Letters* 22.32)

At Asna, where the priest is brother Argentius, the Circumcellions entered our basilica and smashed the altar.
(Augustine, *Letters* 29.12)

basilica The basilica is one of the most characteristic of Roman building types. Normally it was placed in a sunny spot along the forum, as a place of business. It sheltered moneylending and money changing, retail business, and, above all, public trials, sometimes several at once. Writers often speak of the crowds and the noise, specifically *fremitus*, which is the low rumbling created by voices of lawyers, businessmen, and bystanders echoing off the high ceiling. There were slave custodians (the grave monument of one is quoted above) who brought in dogs at night to chase out the workaholics and malingerers. The basilica was a crowded, chaotic venue for deal making, competitive display, and collective moral judgment: mall, courthouse, and bank all in one. This makes it a good symbol for Roman public life in general.

Christians, wanting to avoid the taint of pagan temple architecture, adopted the basilica as a church, modifying its plan into the shape of a cross (the Roman magistrate's tribunal, of which Pliny speaks, was traditionally at one end and became the site of the altar). Houses of worship, repositories of relics and (later) art, Christian basilicas were fought over fiercely by different sects in the age of the great heresies (roughly AD 300 to 500). Augustine describes a particularly nasty episode in these conflicts. The Christian basilica was doubtless normally a more decorous place than its pagan ancestor (note Caesarius's disapproval of dancing). But it remained a place of competition and display, as in Jerome's anecdote about the ostentatious Roman matron and her nasty eunuchs.

TLL 2.1761-1767. L. Richardson, *A New Topographical Dictionary of Ancient Rome* (Baltimore: Johns Hopkins University Press, 1992) 50–57.

ATRIUM: THE MAIN RECEPTION ROOM IN A LARGE ROMAN HOUSE

Already I seem to see your atria practically bursting with the
crowd, and people stepping on each other's toes for lack of space.
(Ovid to his friend Pompeius, recently elected consul,
Letters from Pontus 4.4.27–28.)

I will farm the atria of the great!
(Martial, proposing one way of
making a living in Rome,
Epigrams 3.38.9.)

How many men avoid leaving the house
through an atrium stuffed with clients,
and escape instead through an inconspic-
uous entrance of the house, as though it
were not more rude to deceive them
than to exclude them!
(Seneca, *On the Brevity of Life* 14.4)

In the atrium of his own house [Drusus]
was struck with a knife, which was left in his
side, and after a few hours he died.
(Velleius Paterculus, *Roman History* 2.14.1)

A friend is found in the heart,
not in the atrium. [In pectore
amicus, non in atrio quaeritur.]
(Seneca, *On Benefits* 6.34.5)

Finally they used force and broke down the door, toppling the
busts of [M. Aemilius Lepidus's] ancestors and smashing the couch
opposite, which belonged to his wife Cornelia, whose chastity was
considered exemplary. They also demolished fabric that was being
woven on looms in the atrium after the old fashion.
(Asconius, Commentary on Cicero, *Pro Milone* 38)

Cato, as a teenager, had come to Sulla's house for the purpose of
paying his respects, and had seen the heads of men killed in the
proscriptions brought into the atrium. Disturbed by the savagery
of these actions he asked his tutor, whose name was Sarpedon, why
no one could be found to kill such a cruel tyrant. . . . Cato asserted
that he could kill him easily, since he always sat on a couch. The
tutor both recognized Cato's spirit and was aghast at his proposal,
and thereafter frisked him first whenever he brought him to Sulla.
(Valerius Maximus, *Memorable Deeds and Sayings* 3.1.2)

atrium The first main room in the aristocratic Roman house, the atrium was dedicated to the reception of guests and callers, so in many ways it should be considered a public area. Its roof often had a large rectangular opening (*compluvium*) whose frame was supported by four columns. This let in air, sun, and occasionally rain, which was caught in a shallow basin set in the floor (*impluvium*). We hear little about furniture, apart from the *lectus genialis*, a ceremonial marriage bed placed across from the door. Cornelia (wife of M. Aemilius Lepidus whose house was invaded by a mob of political opponents in 52 BC) apparently used hers while working wool in the atrium like an old-fashioned Roman matron. But this was unusual. The atrium was primarily the place where the great Roman patrons and statesmen met their clients and friends who came en masse in the morning to pay their respects (*salutatio*). The degree of crowding in one's atrium was therefore a closely watched index of social importance. Seneca criticizes the artificiality of the morning reception, which would be attended by flattering clients in search of a handout, like Martial's would-be "atrium farmer." It is difficult, warns Seneca, to find a true friend among the denizens of one's atrium. It might be easier to find an enemy: because of its semipublic character, the atrium was a convenient venue for assassination, an act from which Julius Caesar's great opponent Cato, a tyrant hater even as a lad, had to be restrained by his slave tutor. A key feature of a proper atrium was the collection of ancestral portraits (*imagines*), usually wax, with inscriptions beneath listing the offices each had held and the honors he had received. This unambiguously advertised to visitors the distinction of one's family and in theory acted as a silent encouragement to live up to their example.

TLL 2.1101-1104. A. Wallace-Hadrill, *Houses and Society in Pompeii and Herculaneum* (Princeton, NJ: Princeton University Press, 1994) 82–87.

LIFE IN THE COUNTRY

colonus

nundinae

fundus

villa

COLONUS: FARMER, INHABITANT; TENANT FARMER; COLONIST; SERF

An excellent colonus, most thrifty, most
modest, most virtuous.

> (Cicero, speaking of a certain M. Antistius
> Pyrgensis, *On the Orator* 2.287)

After bestowing peace on the world, Augustus made coloni of both
the armies which had fought under Antony and Lepidus, as well as
soldiers from his own legions. Some he settled in Italy, others in the
provinces. He founded new cities on certain destroyed enemy com-
munities, and some men he settled in old towns and gave them the
title of coloni.

> (A Roman surveyor's manual, referring to the period around 30 BC.
> Hyginus Gromaticus, *On the Determination of Boundaries*,
> p.145 ed. Thulin)

Special care is demanded of the master in all things,
but especially in the matter of human laborers.
These can be either coloni or slaves, whether
unfettered or in chains. He should act courteously
with the coloni, and behave in an accommodating
way, and he should be more strict in demanding
work than in collecting rents, since this offends less
and is generally more helpful anyway.

> (Columella, *On Agriculture* 1.7.1)

We declare that coloni ... throughout Illyricum and the neighboring
regions cannot have the liberty of leaving the land on which they are found
to reside by virtue of their origin and descent. Let them be slaves of the land,
not by tie of tax, but under the name and title of coloni.

> (A law of Valentinian I, AD 371. *Codex Justinianus* 11.53.1)

colonus The cultivated part of the Roman countryside was a patchwork of estates and
plantations worked by slaves, smaller holdings worked by free farmers, and plots worked
by renters. The picture was always complex and subject to regional variations, but general trends can be observed. In the early Republic, small free-holders predominated. The
later Republic saw the growth of large plantations, tilled by slaves and/or sharecroppers;
in the Principate we know of huge imperial estates managed directly by the government

(for example, in North Africa) and worked by free tenant farmers. In the late Empire many tenant farmers were, it seems, reduced to the legal condition of serfs. The fortunes of the word *colonus* obliquely help us chart these changes.

The word originally applied to anyone who cultivates (*colere*) the land. An early farming manual claims that when the ancestors praised a man, they praised him as follows: "a good farmer [*agricola*], a good tiller of the soil [*colonus*]," language echoed by Cicero in the passage quoted here. Agriculture being so fundamental in a world dominated numerically by small farmers, this basic word for farmer continued throughout Roman history to mean simply "inhabitant." As large estates became more common, landowners were faced with the choice of employing slaves or tenant farmers, and in many circumstances they chose the latter. These sharecroppers, who paid rents in cash or in kind, were also called *coloni*. They were free, but very much dependent on the big man—the landlord, or *possessor*. In the civil war between Julius Caesar and Pompey, for example, a single ally of Pompey manned seven war ships and captured the city of Marseilles "with his own slaves, freedmen and tenants [*coloni*]." *Coloni* of this type tended to attract adjectives like poor (*pauperes*), destitute (*inopes*), and hairy (*hirsuti*).

At the same time as nominally free *coloni* tenant farmers were proliferating in the countryside, the Roman government was routinely compensating discharged soldiers by giving them land in conquered territories. These men too were styled "farmer inhabitants," though we would call them, using our version of the Latin term, colonists. Once these *coloni* had exchanged swords for plowshares, they were organized in *coloniae*, settlements that played an important role in the Romanization of Italy and the provinces. The German city of Cologne, for example, was once *Colonia Agrippinensis*.

The sharecropping *coloni* turn up in the law codes and in repeated imperial edicts of the fourth century and later. These measures attempted, unsuccessfully it seems, to tie the *coloni* to the land. Constant wars, devastations, famines, and plagues of the third century led in the late Empire to chronic shortages of agricultural labor (and of tax revenues that depended on agricultural production). The response of the imperial government, and the landlords whose interests it represented, was to create a class of hereditary serfs (*coloni originarii*), people who, once enrolled in a census of the late third century, were legally bound to the land, along with their descendants, in perpetuity. Laws of supply and demand being what they are, however, *coloni* tended to abscond in search of better terms under other landlords. On Judgment Day, says a contemporary Christian author, mankind will be summoned back by God to the cultivation of the Garden of Paradise, just like a *colonus originarius*, called back by the authorities to the cultivation of his ancestral plot.

TLL 3.1705–1712. P. W. De Neeve, *Colonus: Private Tenancy in Roman Italy during the Republic and the Early Principate* (Amsterdam: Gieben, 1984) 31–62. A. H. M. Jones, "The Roman Colonate," *Past and Present* 13 (1958) 1–13. The ancestors: Cato the Elder, *On Agriculture*, 1.2. Ally of Pompey: Julius Caesar, *The Civil War* 1.34. Judgment Day: Rufinus, *Apology* 1.45, paraphrasing, somewhat sarcastically, St. Jerome.

NUNDINAE: MARKET DAY; MARKET FAIR

The Romans instituted nundinae so that the peasants might do their work in the fields for eight days, but on the ninth leave the country and come to Rome for commerce and to accept legal rulings, and so that resolutions and decrees could be proposed when a large part of the people was present.

(P. Rutilius Rufus, consul 105 BC, quoted by Macrobius, *Saturnalia* 1.16.34)

Those who have handed down to us the early customs of the city say that people used to wash their legs and arms—which no doubt became dirty through work—every day, but they washed the whole body on nundinae.

(Seneca, *Letters* 86.12)

Because of such [unveiled] heads which are, as it were, put up for sale in the market [capita nundinaticia], holy virgins are dragged into the church, blushing because they are recognized in the crowd, trembling at being revealed, as if summoned to sex.

(Tertullian, *On the Veiling of Virgins* 3)

Well then, you worthless fools [lawyers], yes I mean you, you cattle of the courts, and you, you toga-wearing vultures, are you surprised that our modern judges now market [nundinantur] their verdicts for a price?

(Apuleius, *Metamorphoses* 10.33)

nundinae The periodic market is the centerpiece of rural life in many societies, and for the Romans it also gave structure to the week. On the eighth day, the Roman rested, except that, counting inclusively since the last one, they called it "the ninth day." This is the literal meaning of *nundinae*. Schools let out, and peasants gathered in the nearest town or village. This Roman "weekend" was a local event, falling on a different day in each area, and it never took on the iconic status of the modern secular counterpart. Nor did it have the religious sanctity of the Hebrew Sabbath. It differs from these in being dedicated to commerce and to public merrymaking (*communis laetitia*), rather than to prayer or private diversion. It was the kind of occasion where people could get into mischief, and farm manuals sternly advised not letting the slave farm manager (*vilicus*) go to the *nundinae* for any purpose other than buying or selling. The same strictures were placed on clerics by church authorities, who also had to issue repeated edicts against priests and bishops who abandoned their flocks and traveled around getting wealthy in the secular business of the *nundinae*.

When the Romans thought of leisure and entertainment they thought not of the *nundinae* but of the games and shows (*ludi*), which came around at various times of the year. The *nundinae* symbolized rather buying and selling, not wholesale but retail, with all the haggling and opportunities for fraud and venality that that involves. Cicero, in a speech, accuses Marc Antony of running "scandalous *nundinae* of lands, towns, exemptions, and revenues," using the papers of the dead dictator Julius Caesar. Here the word approaches the flavor of *bazaar*. The English *market* usually has positive connotations, though *marketing* is starting to take on the idea of deception when it involves the use of consumer data to push worthless products. Roman authors very often use *nundinae* and its derivatives negatively, not for anything to do with the exploiting of consumers but for the shameful buying and selling of things that should not be put up for sale: virginity, governmental decisions or judicial verdicts, medical services, education in eloquence. Thus in the passages of Tertullian and Apuleius quoted above, *market* suggests amoral vulgarity and prostitution. After the Semitic seven-day week came into use around the western Mediterranean in the late third century AD, this derogatory meaning endured, so that in legal contexts the noun *nundinatio*, literally "marketing," without further qualification, came to mean "corruption," especially the buying and selling of verdicts.

Brent D. Shaw, "Rural Markets in North Africa and the Political Economy of the Roman Empire," *Antiquités Africaines* 17 (1981) 37–83. Ramsay MacMullen, "Market-Days in the Roman Empire," *Phoenix* 24 (1970) 333–341. *Communis laetitia*: Gregory the Great, *Homilies on the Gospels* 1.14.6. Farm manuals: Columella, *On Farming* 1.6.8. Clerics: *Statuta ecclesiae antiquae* (ca. AD 475), in *Corpus Christianorum, Series Latina* vol. 148, p. 172. Bishops: Cyprian of Carthage, *De lapsis* 6 and Shaw, "Rural Markets," 69–70. A scandalous *nundinae* of lands: Cicero: *Philippics* 2.35. Corruption: see Cassiodorus, *Variae* 11.8.

FUNDUS: BOTTOM, BASE; FARM

One of the Christians, seeing that resistance was futile, went down to the fundus of the ship and punctured and broke through that fundus, so that the water came in from every direction, and when the ship was filled with water it sank to the fundus of the river with the Saracens and the Christians, where as many Saracens as Christians were drowned.

(Burchard of Worms, *Chronicon* p. 118)

He will have as much as he wants who wants but a little. And for this reason it is no better to judge wealth by fundi and money lent out at interest, than by a man's mind itself.

(Apuleius, *Apology* 20)

A fundus is so called because the family fortune is founded [fundatus] and established upon it.

(Isidore of Seville, *Etymologies* 15.13.4)

Certainly it is obvious that the world itself is more widely-cultivated every day, and better equipped than it originally was. Everything is accessible now, everything is known, everything is full of business: notorious wildernesses have been obliterated by beautiful fundi, tilled fields have conquered forests, herds have routed wild beasts.

(Tertullian, *On the Soul* 30.3)

fundus In most premodern societies land has been the main source and form of wealth. It is fitting, then, that Latin uses as its primary word for "farm" or "rural estate" a word that also means "bottom" or "base." Agricultural land was in every sense fundamental to Roman economic life, and in a way to political life as well, since only possession of a *fundus* as a source of food and income could free a man to have a public career in state service. A slave in a comedy by Plautus calls his young master's farm their "nurse" (*nutrix*); his master, when he acquires it, will be able to support the whole household and undertake *munera*, or public offices. Large-scale moneylending and *fundi* were the two most typical forms of investment held by Roman statesmen. But rather than having a single large plantation, like a landed gentleman of antebellum America, wealthy Romans of Cicero's day had many smaller *fundi* scattered all over Italy and even the provinces, each run by a slave or freed manager. And also unlike modern plantation owners, the members of the Roman aristocracy always had their primary residence in the city, visiting their *fundi* only occasionally.

Like Americans, the Romans idealized and romanticized the farmer-citizen-soldier and associated farming with political and moral virtue. History told of the heroic Cincinnatus, an early general who had to be summoned from the plow to defeat Rome's enemies, and who happily returned there after resigning the dictatorship. But as in American history, one of the inexorable trends of Roman history was the gradual displacement of small farms with larger estates, and the consolidation of farmland into fewer and fewer hands. Latin recognized this change by coining a new, somewhat derogatory term: *latifundium*, a compound of the adjective *latus* ("broad," "spacious") and *fundus*. It means essentially "plantation," but it has a bit of the flavor of the English compound "agribusiness," in that it symbolizes the decline of the idyllic family farm and its replacement by soulless industrial farming. Pliny the Elder famously intones, "To tell the truth, the *latifundia* destroyed Italy, and now they are destroying the provinces as well—half of Africa (i.e. the Roman province of Africa, including northern Libya, Tunisia and Algeria) was owned by six landlords when Nero put them to death."

Though it was an accurate description of the type of large-scale farming being done in many parts of the empire, the term *latifundium* did not catch on in Latin. At least, it is very rare in preserved texts. It did see a revival in Spanish, however. The re-conquest of Muslim territories on the Iberian peninsula provided the Christian kingdoms with huge areas of land, which they ceded to nobles and military officers to exploit as *latifundia*. Large feudal-like estates worked by landless peasants persisted in southern Spain and parts of Spanish South America well into the twentieth century. The overlords were called *latifundistas*—again, not a complimentary term.

The warmer term *fundus* continued to be used for all kinds of Roman farms, even very large consolidated estates. Many *fundi* in the provinces were created by government grants of captured territory to individual proprietors, whose names they bore. The land given to, say, Gaius Seius became known as the *fundus Seianus*, that of Bassus the *fundus Bassianus*, and the land kept these names long after it had passed to other owners. As parcels were combined through inheritance, marriage, and purchase, they tended to retain their original names. So we hear in one inscription from Italy of a farm called *fundus Antianus-Carellianus-Pullenianus-Sornianus*. In Celtic-speaking lands the Celtic suffix *-acus* was used as well as the Latin suffix *-anus*, so that Gaius Iulius's farm could be the *fundus Iuliacus*. After the decline in cities that accompanied the fall of the western Roman Empire, the *latifundia* became the centers of a fragmented Europe and arguably the basis for the European feudal system. Place names in part tell this story. As the Roman *latifundia* gave way to feudal estates in the Middle Ages, some of the baronial manors and medieval villages kept their old Roman farm names, and they in turn passed them on to the revived modern cities whose nuclei they provided. The Italian town of Bassano takes its name from the old Roman *fundus Bassianus*, Cornegliano from the *fundus Cornelianus*, Fleurac from a *fundus Floriacus*, Flavigny from a *fundus Flaviacus*, and Kessenich, near Bonn, recalls a *fundus Cassiniacus*.

TLL 6.1573–1580. RE 7.296-301. K. D. White, "Latifundia," *Bulletin of the Institute of Classical Studies of the University of London* 14 (1967) 62–79. Plautus: *Trinummus* 512. The *latifundia* destroyed Italy: Pliny the Elder, *Natural History* 18.35.

VILLA: A LARGE COUNTRY RESIDENCE, WHETHER THE HEADQUARTERS OF A PRODUCTIVE FARM OR A PLEASURE VILLA

When the pater familias arrives at the villa he should, after paying respects to the household shrine [lar familiaris], inspect the farm, on the same day if possible.

      (Cato the Elder, *On Agriculture* 2.1)

Smoke was rising everywhere from the burning not only of villae but also of many villages [vici] as well.

      (Livy, referring to events of 299 BC in Etruria, *Roman History* 10.11.6)

If the slave kiln attendant belonging to a tenant farmer falls asleep at the furnace and the villa burns down . . . .

      (A legal case imagined in Justinian's *Digest of Roman Law* 9.2.27.9)

So you get yourself another villa, because one country estate just isn't enough.

      (Juvenal, *Satires* 14.140–141)

He flies to his villa at a gallop, driving his ponies as though on his way to put out a fire; suddenly, on crossing the villa's threshold, he yawns, or seeks oblivion in rock-like sleep; or he even hurries to return to the city—in this way each man flees himself.

      (Lucretius, *On the Nature of the Universe* 3.1063–1068)

In the same villa, Antonia the wife of Drusus put earrings on her favorite eel; its fame spread, and some people decided to come to Bauli just to see it.

      (Pliny the Elder, *Natural History* 9.172)

Several people maintained they had seen serpents fall from a cloud. Others asserted that a villa had vanished in instant annihilation, along with its huts and the people in them.

      (Gregory of Tours, referring to events of AD 587, *History of the Franks* 9.5) *villa* What exactly makes a Roman villa architecturally is a subject of debate among archaeologists. But it is clear that, in comparison with the miscellaneous rectangular or round farm buildings favored in pre-Roman Gaul or Holland, the Roman villa was distinctive: a unified complex of rooms around a hall, garden, or courtyard, it normally had a dining room (often with a mosaic pavement), a bath complex, bedrooms, and servants' quarters. The façade usually included a south-facing portico, looking out over a fine view, for strolling at leisure or doing business. This characteristically Mediterranean house type, built for a sunny climate, transferred rather badly to rainy Bristol or Budapest, but no matter. Its prestige guaranteed its dominance all over the Roman empire for hundreds of years, and archaeologists have identified many examples from Belgium, the German frontier, Spain, to Hungary and the former Yugoslavia. Its spread is one of the tangible signs of Romanization in the provinces.

In the Italy of the first centuries BC and AD pleasure villas—country houses built for luxury, not working farmhouses—became common in high society. Horace lists "other people's villas" among common topics of gossip; as a young and ambitious politician trying to fit in, Cicero made it a point to memorize which country estates near Rome belonged to whom. These pleasure villas, gleaming on the top of hills, decorated with imported marbles, symbolized the retreat from business and politics toward leisure, relaxation, or (for some) reading and philosophy. The ultimate example of villa as retirement haven is the seaside palace built by the emperor Tiberius on Capri, where in later life he hid from the responsibilities of imperial power and was rumored to spend his time in unspeakable depravities. Many, like the philosopher Lucretius and the satirist Juvenal, quoted above, saw the pleasure villa phenomenon as a symptom of the decadence of the idle rich. By contrast, the productive villa as farmhouse was morally healthy, according to the Roman view of things. The good emperor Antoninus Pius liked to go to his working villa in the fall and participate in the vintage, much as American presidents have been known to vacation on a ranch and split wood.

The villa of either type was meant to provide in the country the features of the good life as the Romans saw it: dining rooms for a *cena*, a bathing establishment, courtyards, gardens, porticoes for strolling, and, what was especially prized, a beautiful view over land or sea. In late antiquity when the villa and its associated lifestyle were dying out, and the large estates of which the villas had been the headquarters were metamorphosing into towns, the word *villa* came to mean "village." It thus became the ancestor of the French *ville*. We can see this social and linguistic transition in the passage quoted here from the sixth-century author Gregory of Tours, where *villa* plainly means village.

J. T. Smith, *Roman Villas: A Study in Social Structure* (London: Routledge, 1997). J. Percival, "The Villa in Italy and the Provinces," in J. Wacher, ed., *The Roman World* (London: Routledge, 1987) 527–547. Horace: *Satires* 2.6.71. Plutarch: *Cicero* 7.

MONEY AND BUSINESS

faenerator

auctio

patrimonium

annona

stips

FAENERATOR: MONEYLENDER

He who gives a favor imitates the gods; he who
demands it back imitates the faeneratores.

(Seneca, On Benefits 3.15.4)

Octavius Ruso is said to have been a harsh faenerator.
He also wrote histories, to which he used to compel his
debtors to listen—no doubt listening to them was a bitter
punishment for them.

(Porphyrio, Commentary on Horace, Satires 1.3.86)

A dog barks and your heart pounds, you sweat and gasp,
you wrack your brain for a lie to put off the faenerator
and, when you find it, you rejoice.

(Ambrose, On Tobias 7.26)

None of us has been permitted to maintain our legal rights
according to ancestral custom, nor, once our patrimonies were
lost, could we keep our bodies free—so great was the savagery
of the faeneratores and of the praetor.

(Sallust, listing complaints of the revolutionaries of 63 BC,
The War with Catiline 33.1)

faenerator The Roman economy was cash-based but lacking in institutional banks, so the moneylender was an absolutely indispensable part of everyday life for the farmer and the city dweller alike. The polite word for a private banker was *argentarius* ("silver dealer"), but the more common and far more derogatory term was *faenerator* ("interest man"). Their favorite mode of operation was to attend auctions of property and land, advancing credit to buyers. Yet, despite its crucial role in the economy, moneylending was not an honorable profession. Cato the Elder equates it with theft; Cicero lists it among the "occupations which incur the hatred of mankind"; and St. Augustine groups moneylenders with liars, con men, adulterers, drunkards, and slave dealers—the undesirable types still welcome in the church.

The pitiless greed of the *faenerator* was proverbial. A particularly corrupt variety followed Roman magistrates in the provinces as they toured local market days, loaning money to provincials who wished to bribe Roman officials. Others tempted the sons of rich men whose fathers were too tightfisted, knowing that ultimately the father was liable for the debts of the son. Others simply victimized the poor, loaning in times of scarcity and enslaving those who could not pay. Flagrant abuses of this type led to open revolt by the poor and ultimately to the outlawing of debt slavery in 326 BC. But the *faenerator* remained a stock villain in comedy, and a ubiquitous and despised social type, right up through late antiquity. St. Ambrose in the fourth century claims often to have seen a dead man's corpse impounded by moneylenders and denied burial pending payment of his debts.

TLL 6.474-475. Jean Andreau, *Banking and Business in the Roman World*, trans. J. Lloyd (Cambridge: Cambridge University Press, 1999). Cato: *On Agriculture*, preface. Cicero: *On Duties* 1.150. Augustine: *On the Letter of John to the Parthians* 3.9, PL 35.2002.

AUCTIO: AUCTION

He should hold an auctio. Sell oil, if it fetches a good price;
sell wine, any remaining grain; sell old oxen, blemished
cattle, blemished sheep, wool, skins, an old wagon, old iron
implements, an old slave, a diseased slave, and if anything
else is surplus, sell it. [His advice to auction off old and sick
slaves was criticized as callous even in antiquity.]

(Cato the Elder, *On Agriculture* 2.7)

But when [Marcus Aurelius] had exhausted the entire treasury
for this war and he could not bring himself to impose any
extraordinary tax on the provincials, he held an auctio of
imperial furnishings in the Forum of Trajan, and he sold cups of
gold, crystal and jade [murra], as well as vessels made for kings,
his wife's robes of silk with gold embroidery, and even gems
which he had found in quantity in a special cabinet that had
belonged to Hadrian.

(*SHA, Marcus Aurelius* 17.4)

The most depraved of men, after they
have wasted their patrimony, hold
auctiones [of their possessions] in
the auctioneer's halls.

(Cicero, *On the Agrarian Law* 1.7)

Having declared an auctio, [Caligula] put on display and sold the
remains of all the spectacles, himself soliciting bids and exaggerating
them so much that certain men went bankrupt because of the
immense sums they had been forced to pay, and opened their veins.

(Suetonius, discussing the various unscrupulous measures
Caligula took to refill the treasury, *Caligula* 38.3)

auctio Auction was the primary mode of buying and selling of wholesale commodities in the Roman economy, as well as a very common way to dispose of personal property and effects. Anyone who has bid at an auction knows the panicky thrill that can be generated as the price rises. Auctions take the natural desire to possess and sharpen it with the natural desire to compete, a combination that has been making auctioneers rich for centuries. The Latin term *auctio* refers to the key feature, the rising of the prices; it derives from the verb *augeo*, "to increase."

Ever entrepreneurial and fond of public competition, the Romans loved auctions, and Roman historians have a surprising amount to say about them. There were "celebrity auctions." Tradition recorded in detail, for example, the items Marcus Aurelius sold to help finance the Marcomannic war, and the items of Commodus, which were auctioned off after his fall. These included a gladiator's toga and cups made in the shape of a phallus. Estate auctions held by bankrupt men (*decoctores*, those who "cooked away" their fortunes by luxurious living) were the subject of public scandal and also an opportunity, presumably, for the only moderately wealthy to own a piece of the life of privilege. The good *pater familias* was to auction off all surplus items, as Cato advises, and to be a seller more often than a buyer. Caligula was thus acting as a responsible steward of the public treasury, a veritable imperial *pater familias*, when he auctioned off the leftover furniture and supplies from the games and shows. But when the auctioneer is the emperor, it is hard to stop bidding, and Caligula characteristically took advantage of this to bankrupt some rich senators, supposedly driving them to suicide.

Auction was the customary way to dispose of war booty and property confiscated from enemies of the state. State auctions of confiscated goods were the special sphere of an unsavory brand of entrepreneurs called *sectores* ("slicers") who bought up such property and resold it. When the estate of the famous general Pompey, who had lost to Caesar in the civil war of 49 BC, was auctioned off in Rome, it took several days. To men like Cicero, who had been his supporters, it was one of the saddest spectacles of the war. Marc Antony played the *sector*, snatching up the property and giving it to his cronies. "Actors snatched this, actresses that . . . . You might see couches in slaves' quarters spread with Gnaeus Pompeius' purple coverlets," claims Cicero.

In addition to the snobbery here—the complaint that low-status individuals were pawing over Pompey's things—we can sense another level of bitterness. The first duty of the Roman *pater familias* was to protect his estate (*patrimonium*) and pass it down to his descendents. The auction of Pompey's effects under public auspices meant that the state was putting an effective end to the financial existence of his entire *familia*.

The Roman auction, then, was a very public form of commerce that was weighted with moral and sometimes political meaning. In addition to being a crucial way to move goods and capital around, auctions could also function as demonstrations of the emperor's self-sacrifice or tools of his rapacity, a venue for the public humiliation of disgraced debtors, and for the economic annihilation of enemies of the state.

TLL 1.1192-1194. J. B. Greenough, "Latin Etymologies," *Harvard Studies in Classical Philology* 4 (1893) 144-146. Auction of Commodus's effects: *SHA, Pertinax* 8. Cicero on the auction of Pompey's estate: *Philippics* 2.67.

PATRIMONIUM: THE PROPERTY OF A *PATER FAMILIAS*, PRIVATE ESTATE, FORTUNE

We say that a man is "devoured," whose patrimonium is used up.
(Quintilian, *On the Orator's Education* 8.6.25)

Aesopus the tragic actor left great wealth to his son Marcus Aesopus, who lived a luxurious lifestyle. This man, since he wanted in his heart to utterly defeat his patrimonium, is said to have conceived a desire to spend a million sesterces in an hour, and so he took some pearls from his wife Metella and dissolved them in vinegar.
(Porphyrio, Commentary on Horace, *Satires* 2.3.239)

To begin with, those who excelled anywhere in shamelessness and impudence, and others who had lost their patrimonia through disgraceful conduct, and finally all those whom wickedness and crime had forced to leave their homes, all these flowed into Rome like filth into a bilge.

(Sallust, explaining why the city populace especially favored the revolutionary designs of Catiline in 63 BC; *The War with Catiline* 37.5)

What have I done that is insane? As a young man I lived frugally, I increased my patrimonium, I took a wife, I raised a son, I love him.
(Lines spoken by a father, accused by his son of being insane, from a practice legal case, ps.-Quintilian, *Minor Declamations* 316.5)

patrimonium Patrimonium fuses the root for "father," *patr-*, with the fairly common abstract noun suffix *-monium*, which gives to English *acrimony, alimony, ceremony,* and *testimony*. The obvious counterpart of *patrimony* would be *matrimony,* combining the same suffix with the root for "mother." But in Latin, as in English, there is a striking asymmetry between the two. *Matrimonium* means marriage, but only for a woman. A man "leads" (*ducere*) his bride into *matrimonium,* which is literally the condition of being a mother, suggesting that childbearing is the true purpose of marriage for a woman. It would be absurd for a man to enter *matrimonium;* he "takes a wife into his matrimony" (*uxorem in matrimonium ducere*). *Patrimonium* means not marriage or fatherhood but inherited property and fortune, implying that fatherhood is a vehicle for passing down property. *Patrimonium* and *matrimonium* reflect the asymmetrical roles and duties of father and mother in the Roman patriarchal family.

The first duty of the Roman *pater familias* was to guard and, if possible, augment his *patrimonium.* Those who whittled down the principal through luxurious living fell under heavy moral, even official, censure. The verbs for spending down one's *patrimonium* use metaphors of eating, chewing, or devouring (*consumere, comedere, mordere, devorare*). Catullus writes a poem on this subject, addressed to Julius Caesar and criticizing one of Caesar's corrupt lieutenants: "Why the devil do you protect *him?* What is he good for besides devouring oily *patrimonia?*"—as though he were swallowing them at dinner. In fact, Seneca singles out the kitchen as the "disgraceful destroyer of *patrimonia,*" and there is a special verb that means to spend immoderately on eating: *helluor.* It was quite possible to spend fantastic sums on food, though Roman moralists exaggerate the prices in the same way that modern reformers use inflated statistics. In the first century AD two famous gourmets supposedly bid against each other for a particularly large fish, the winner paying five thousand sesterces—more than five times the annual salary of a Roman infantryman at the time. "What is more shameful than a dinner that consumes the census qualification even for a knight [i.e., 400,000 sesterces]?" asks Seneca.

A surprising number of anecdotes record the personal interest taken by the emperor in the *patrimonia* of individuals. Emperors sometimes augmented the fortunes of men who had fallen, through no fault of their own, below the property qualification for senatorial or equestrian status—a kind of charity for the rich. Emperors also felt free to publicly criticize those who had wasted *patrimonia.* Hadrian had such men flogged in the amphitheater. A certain *eques,* reproached by Augustus for having eaten up his *patrimonium,* is said to have replied saucily with two words, *meum putavi:* "I thought it was mine." Part of this imperial meddling was an extension of the traditional role of the censor, whose oversight of the property qualifications (*census*) of the upper classes the emperors assumed. But partly it was fear of what desperate debtors might do. Such men had often swelled the ranks of revolutionary movements, like Catiline's. In the Roman mind there was a direct line from luxurious dining to bankruptcy and unpayable debt, to anti-establishment rabble-rousing and revolution.

TLL 10.751-755. Caesar's lieutenant: Catullus 29.21-22. The kitchen: Seneca, *On Benefits* 1.10.2. A large fish: Seneca, *Letters* 95.42. Pay for a Roman infantryman: Tacitus, *Annals* 1.17. What is more shameful: Seneca, *Letters* 95.41. I thought it was mine: Quintilian, *On the Orator's Education* 6.3.74.

ANNONA: THE GRAIN HARVEST OR SUPPLY; THE PRICE OF GRAIN; A FREE DISTRIBUTION OF GRAIN

Speculators in particular tend to tamper with and manipulate the annona. Their greed has been countered both by imperial directives and by legislative enactments.

> (Ulpian, in Justinian's *Digest of Roman Law* 47.11.6 pref.3)

I ask that care be taken both for the health of the city's account books and for the well-being of the people, who are wholly subject to the annona.

> (From a letter to the ship owners' associations of Arles, from a certain Iulianus, perhaps the superintendent of the grain supply. *ILS* 6987)

When he was putting on the Games of Apollo, the low mob that had assembled was in such an uproar over the annona that all those who had sat in the theater to watch the games were driven out.

> (Asconius, on Lucius Caelius Rufus; the year was 57 BC. Commentary on Cicero, *Pro Milone* 43)

To the memory of Gaius Faesellius ... an excellent and most rare citizen, because he surpassed with his own deeds the examples set by his ancestors of generosity to his homeland and fellow-citizens. Among his other benefactions he often subvented the annona for the people.

> (An inscription from Ariminum, *ILS* 6664)

My father said I was born when grain was scarce [per caram annonam]. That must be why I'm so hungry now.

> (Lines spoken by a parasite in Plautus's comedy *Stichus* 179)

Aelius Vitalio, official grain measurer for life to the most worthy guild of bakers, dedicated this statue as a gift to the revered goddess Annona.

> (A statue base from Rome, *ILS* 3816)

annona Wheat for bread eaten in the huge city of Rome came mostly from North Africa, especially Egypt. Ensuring the supply was too difficult and important a task to be left solely to private merchants. Magistrates and emperors had to take an active role in regulating the trade, because the supply was unstable, corruption and manipulation by speculators common, and the danger of bread riots in case of scarcity ever-present. Beyond its importance as a commodity, *annona* was a key aspect of the customary system of public benefactions known as *euergetism*. This was the phenomenon whereby individual nobles made gifts that benefited the community, in return for personal prestige. Many civic functions handled today by local or state governments, such as public buildings, communal entertainments, and the control of trade in basic food commodities, were handled informally by way of euergetism. The emperor performed this function personally in Rome, and in a way he acted as a personal patron of the masses, in addition to being the head of state.

"The Roman people are held in check by two things especially," said the orator Fronto to Marcus Aurelius, "spectacles and *annona*"—by which he meant distributions of free grain, or simply the controlled price of grain and the ensuring of an adequate supply. All these were the concern of the government, and the object of private largesse, as we can see in the proud inscriptions set up by or for private donors. The upper class knew well that high grain prices led to desperation. For ordinary people, *annona*—the supply, the price—was the central fact of economic life. For politicians it was the magic key to popularity. Not without reason did Aelius Vitalio set up a statue to "the revered goddess Annona," and emperors put her image on coins.

TLL 2.110-113. Paul Veyne, *Bread and Circuses* (repr. London: Penguin, 1992). Fronto, *Preamble to History* 2.216 ed. Haines.

STIPS: SMALL COIN; ALMS; DONATION, CONTRIBUTION; WAGES

On the basis of a night vision [the emperor Augustus] used
to go about begging for stips from the people once a year,
offering a cupped hand to those who held out small coins.
(Suetonius, *Augustus* 91.2)

By imperial mandate it is ordered that provincial governors not permit
fraternal associations, or military clubs in the camps. But it is permitted
for the less fortunate to contribute a monthly stips, so long as they
meet only once per month, and so long as a prohibited association does
not meet under a pretext of this sort.
(An edict referring to the tradition of burial societies, in which people
contributed a small amount regularly in return for the assurance
of a proper burial from the common fund. Marcian,
in Justinian's *Digest of Roman Law* 47.22.1)

A good old age is the stips paid
for a clean life.
(Ambrose, *On Duties* 2.20.101)

All the other animals reach satiety in sexual coupling,
but for man alone there is practically none.
Messalina, the wife of the emperor Claudius, thinking
it quite a regal triumph, chose for a competition in
this activity the most notorious of the slave girls who
work as prostitutes for a hired wage [mercennariae
stipis], and beat her in a match lasting a whole day
and night, with a score of twenty-five.
(Pliny the Elder, *Natural History* 10.172)

stips Beggars congregated around bridges and on certain steep hills where the carriages of the wealthy would have to slow down enough so that the beggar could deliver his pitch. He asked for *stips* ("small coin"), a word of uncertain derivation, that through its association with free-will offerings came to have a much wider sphere of meaning than its literal English translation. The small monthly contributions collected by burial societies were called *stips*, as were the offerings placed on altars and in baskets at temples. Collections of *stips* were sometimes taken up to finance a statue, or even a temple or set of games. At sacred springs or wells people would throw in *stips* in honor of the god of the place. The ecstatic, self-castrating priests of the mother-goddess Cybele appeared periodically in the streets of Rome in noisy procession, asking everyone they met for *stips*. So *stips* took on the meanings of English "contribution," "religious free-will offering," as well as "alms" for the poor.

The meaning "wage" probably derives from the fact that some professions, notably lawyers and prostitutes, were paid not through set fees but by variable and negotiable contributions. Both professions are said to receive *stips* rather than *merces*, the kind of fixed wage a hired laborer gets. Soldiers similarly received in early times a *stipendium* ("*stips* payment," from the verb "to pay," *pendere*) at the conclusion of the year's campaign. This word was preferable to *merces*, with its demeaning associations of hired labor, and the implication it would have carried that the soldier was a mere mercenary (*mercennarius*, which means both "hired laborer" and "soldier of fortune"). From this military use of *stipendium*, for a somewhat more dignified kind of salary, comes our "stipend": a (seldom lavish) subsidy for somebody whose activities don't fit the traditional definition of work, such as clergymen, scholars, or public officials.

RE 2nd ser., 3.2538–2540.

JOBS AND PROFESSIONS

pistor

sutor

vespillo

parasitus

PISTOR: MILLER, BAKER

By day the schoolteachers make life impossible,
by night the pistores do.

> (Martial, complaining about noise pollution
> in Rome, *Epigrams* 12.57.5)

The pistores ask and desire,
along with their neighbors,
that you elect Gnaeus Helvius
Sabinus as aedile.

> (Electoral sign from Pompeii,
> CIL 4.7273)

[Julius Caesar] controlled the discipline
of his house so strictly that, when a
pistor supplied a different grade of
bread for his guests than for himself, he
threw the man in chains.

> (Suetonius, *Julius Caesar* 48)

After a period of five years has passed, the chief patron of the
guild of pistores should be given rest and leisure, so long as he
hands over and assigns to his successor the shop with its animals,
slaves, mills, and the farms belonging to the endowment—in
short all the equipment of bread making.

> (An edict of the emperors Valentinian and Valens, AD 364,
> *Theodosian Code* 14.3.7)

This [disgusting] man screws all kinds of girls and thinks he is quite
charming; why is he not handed over to the mill [pistrina] and the ass?

> (From a poem against an anonymous target, Catullus 97.9–10)

pistor Bakeries abound in the excavated neighborhoods of Pompeii and are easily identified by the tall conical millstones and by the large ovens, many with the emblem of a phallus above the opening (a *fascinum* to ward off evil magical influences during the risky enterprise of baking). Very few private houses there had baking ovens, and those that did lacked mills. Thus in Pompeii, as in the developed towns and cities of the Roman empire in general, people bought most of their bread in shops, rather than making it at home, a level of public convenience not seen again in Europe until the eighteenth century. The huge importance of bread to the Roman diet meant that the industry of the *pistores* was both lucrative and highly regulated. Their social status varied widely, and the trade had room both for skilled slaves (many in the employ of the imperial house), freedmen, and free entrepreneurs. A surprising number of them had money enough to afford inscribed tombs, on which they proudly announced their occupation. "To the departed shade of Marcus Orbius Princeps, freedman of Marcus, baker, member of the Board of Seven Priests of Augustus." The grandest example is the curious tomb of the commercial baker Marcus Vergilius Eurysaces, which still stands in Rome, complete with relief sculptures showing scenes of the operation of a large *pistrina*: grain sorting, milling, sifting the bran from the milled grain, kneading of the dough, the shaping of the loaves, baking in the oven, the weighing and counting of loaves on immense scales, and delivery of the finished product in large baskets. In the center of one panel stands the toga-clad Eurysaces delivering some kind of lecture to his subordinates, apparently a habit of bosses even in ancient times.

Pistor stems from the verb *pinsere*, "to pound," thus the central idea is that of crushing, the milling of the grain to remove the inedible husk. The same root is seen in the English *pestle* and *piston*. Slaves and donkeys did this work in the era before the wide adoption of water-powered mills. Being sent to the mill was a common fate for disobedient or difficult slaves, less severe a punishment than the mines, to be sure, but a life of very hard labor. This is the servile punishment Catullus wills upon his enemy in the lines quoted above. The edict from the Theodosian Code quoted here shows that the standard equipment of a *pistrina* could include slaves, donkeys, mills, and the farms that produced the grain, all of which shows that the usual translation of *pistrina* as "bakery" hardly gives an accurate impression.

A whole slew of laws in the Code relate to a time in the fourth century when bakers and their families had to be compelled by law to stay in the baking business to supply military and civilian needs. Men who married baker's daughters were to be forced to join the guild, and those who used accounting dodges to try to pretend to be too poor to carry on the work were to be punished. In normal times, however, *pistores* were simply subject to oversight by the prefect of the grain supply, who made sure that the weight and quality of the bread were adequate. In Rome, at least, it was a crucial political duty. Cassiodorus advises the prefect of the grain supply: "For if bread, as often happens, proves a source of complaints, you as the guarantor of abundance dissolve civic rebellions by satisfying the need in a moment, and through you it is made sure that public grumblings come to nothing." As we saw when discussing *annona*, bread riots were always a threat.

Commercial baking was made possible in the first place by the move from small domestic hand mills to large slave- and donkey-powered mills. Self-standing bakeries arise in Rome early in the third century BC. This is the situation we see in first century AD Pompeii, with its twenty or so neighborhood establishments, each with three or four mills. In time, however, especially with the coming of the water-driven mill in the Middle Ages, the two professions, milling and baking, split. Improved technology made it possible for a single mill to supply a great number of bakeries and households.

Written Latin, with its usual conservatism, refused to take account of this important change. It seems that by the sixth century, the spoken language, gradually dissolving into Spanish, Italian, and French, moved on to differentiate between the *molinarius* ("miller") and the *panificus* or *furnarius* ("baker"). These words, very rare in written Latin, are the apparent sources for the common Romance derivatives: Spanish *molinero*, Portuguese *moliero*, French *meunier*, Italian *mugnaio*; for bakers, Italian has both *fornaio* and *panifico*, Spanish *panadero*; the French *boulanger* comes from a borrowed Germanic root *bolla*, which is round bread. Change had rendered the classical vocabulary insufficient, and people filled the gap in various ways. Written Latin blithely ignored this well into the twelfth century, when the now sterile *pistor* and its derivatives were still in use. Meanwhile *molinarius*, fertile mother of half a dozen words in use today, left but a handful of attestations in surviving texts.

RE 20.1821-1831. B. J. Mayeske, "Bakers, Bakeshops, and Bread. A Social and Economic Study," in *Pompeii and the Vesuvian landscape* (Washington, DC: Archaeological Institute of America, 1979) 39–58. Europe in the eighteenth century: Fernand Braudel, *The Structures of Everyday Life*, vol. 1, trans. S. Reynolds (New York: Harper & Row, 1981) 139–142. Marcus Orbius Princeps: *CIL* 10.5346. Cassiodorus: *Variae* 6.18. For a large water-mill of the fourth century AD in France, see A. Trevor Hodge, "A Roman Factory," *Scientific American* (November, 1990) 106–111.

SUTOR: SHOEMAKER, COBBLER

Where are you coming from? Whose beans and rotgut have given you wind? What sutor have you been lounging with, scarfing leeks and boiled sheep's head? No answer? Speak, or feel my boot.

(Challenge issued by a mugger in Juvenal, *Satires* 3.292-295)

Peregrinus lies here, slave of Quintus Asinus, boot maker [sutor caligarius], Dacian by race, aged 20.

(Epitaph from Carnuntum in Austria. *AE* 1929, no. 217)

Lucius Vergilius Hilarus, freedman of Lucius, sutor, lies here. His wife and freedmen had the monument made.

(Epitaph from Carthago Nova in Spain. *CIL* 2.5125)

Julian also puts the case: a sutor, he says, struck with a last at the neck of a boy, a freeborn youngster, who was learning under him, because he had done badly what he had been teaching him, with the result that the boy's eye was knocked out.

(Ulpian, in Justinian's *Digest of Roman Law* 9.2.5.3)

sutor English seems to favor vagueness in job titles. What exactly are the duties of an "Administrative Assistant," a "Producer," a "Senior Vice President," or the increasingly popular and meaningless "Associate"? Only their immediate supervisors really know. Latin, by contrast, tends toward specificity. The various names for shoe specialists of which Latin happens to have a record include the *calceolarius* ("slipper maker"), *diabathrarius* (another kind of slipper maker), *solearius* ("sandal maker"), *caligarius* ("boot maker"), *crepidarius* (maker of a kind of thick-soled Greek sandal, the *crepida*), *gallicarius* (a maker of Gallic-style shoes), *sandalarius* (another kind of sandal maker), and *sutor veteramentarius* (cobbler dealing with old or worn-out shoes).

The more general word, *sutor*, has a prominent place in the lexicon of Latin snobbery. Cicero wrote a speech in defense of the manifestly guilty Valerius Flaccus, a governor prosecuted in 59 BC for provincial mismanagement. In it, Cicero discredits the resolution passed by the Greek city of Pergamon against Flaccus by calling it the work of a bunch of "cobblers and belt-makers" (*sutores et zonarii*), who were swayed, he claims, by a public meal and gifts provided by a malcontent local politician hostile to Flaccus. In painting this picture Cicero plays effectively on both the ethnic and class prejudices of the Roman jury. Fickle Greeks, with their direct democracy, are prone to impulsive, ill-advised, and impudent measures—unlike Roman assemblies, which are guided by the stable, wiser leadership of the Senate. And in contrast to the decisions of the Roman government, in the Greek assemblies important decisions were made by a rabble typified by the *sutores*, easily swayed by a good meal. Like Cicero (and presumably his audience, the jury), Juvenal's mugger also takes *sutor* as a synonym for "lowlife."

Tomb inscriptions like those quoted above show that *sutores* were actually of varied status—many slave, but some also freed or poor freeborn, like the free apprentice who lost his eye in the case imagined by the jurist Julian. They organized in guild associations, and occasionally one even rose to wealth and prominence, much to the disgust of the upper-class public. One of Nero's most favored courtiers, the formidable Vatinius, is described disdainfully by a historian as the "product of a cobbler's shop" (*alumnus sutrinae tabernae*).

RE 2nd ser., 4.989–994. The lexicon of snobbery: Ramsay MacMullen, *Roman Social Relations* (New Haven: Yale University Press, 1974) 138–141. Cicero: *Pro Flacco* 17. Disgust of the upper-class public: Martial, *Epigrams* 9.73. Historian: Tacitus, *Annals* 15.34.

VESPILLO: CORPSE CARRIER, A PALLBEARER FOR THE POOR AND INDIGENT

Q.: What is a vespillo?
A.: He whom many people avoid but no one escapes.

(From the anonymous *Dialogue of Hadrian and Epictetus* 27)

Until recently Diaulus was a doctor,
now he's a vespillo; what the vespillo
does now, the doctor used to do.

(Epigram against an incompetent physician, Martial 1.47)

As evening was coming on, he was snatched up
and carried home by his chair-bearers, slaves
more disgusting than the vespillones.

(Sidonius Apollinaris, on his enemy, a certain Paeonius. *Letters* 1.11.9)

[The emperor] Domitian was killed cruelly in the Palace by his
own attendants; his corpse was carried out in a pauper's coffin
by the vespillones, and was buried most disgracefully.

(Orosius, referring to events of AD 96, *Histories against the Pagans* 7.10.7)

At Oricum were Lucretius Vespillo and
Minucius Rufus with 18 ships ...

(Julius Caesar, *The Civil War* 3.7)

vespillo By one scholar's estimate, about 1,500 corpses turned up annually, unclaimed and unwanted, in the streets of early imperial Rome. The task of removing these anonymous bodies fell to the *vespillones*, whose appearance filled the Romans with disgust and dread. According to an ancient etymology, they were so called not because of any connection with wasps (*vespae*), but because they did their work in the evening (*vespertino tempore*). A modern theory, however, connects the name to *versipellis*, the Latin word for "werewolf," both figures being seen as despoilers of corpses.

In 133 BC the populist tribune of the plebs, Tiberius Gracchus, was clubbed to death by a group of senators whose interests were threatened by his attempts to assign public land to the poor. An aedile* in that year, Quintus Lucretius, ordered Gracchus's dead body cast into the Tiber River, and thus earned for himself the unflattering cognomen Vespillo, "The Undertaker." As happened with such names, the bearer passed it down to his branch of the family: two generations later a Quintus Lucretius Vespillo turns up among the victims of the dictator Sulla. The most distinguished of the Vespillo clan, however, was the latter's son (also Quintus Lucretius Vespillo), who fought against Caesar in the civil wars, narrowly escaped death in the proscriptions of 43 BC, and then survived to become consul under Augustus in 19 BC.

---

*The *aediles* were magistrates tasked with, among other things, keeping the city streets clean.

John Bodel, "Dealing with the Dead: Undertakers, Executioners and Potter's Fields in Ancient Rome," in V. Hope and E. Marshall, eds., *Death and Disease in the Ancient City* (London: Routledge, 2000) 128–151, esp. 138. *PIR*² L 412.

PARASITUS: PARASITE, TOADY, SPONGER

Parasitus: *he who says amusing things in order to fill his belly.*

(From a late antique glossary, *CGL* 4.266.50)

Q.: What are parasiti?

A.: Men who are fed like fish.

(From the anonymous *Dialogue of Hadrian and Epictetus* 73)

[Noble] houses are frequented by certain idle gossips, who express approval of every word uttered by the great man with various inventive flatteries, imitating the toadying jokes of parasiti in comedies. For just as those characters massage the egos of braggart soldiers by attributing to them the sacking of cities and battles against thousands of enemies, as though they rivaled the heroes of old, just so, these men too extol the nobles beyond merely mortal station, as they express wonder at the lofty columns in a façade or the glistening sheets of colored stone on the walls.

(Ammianus Marcellinus, *The Later Roman Empire* 28.4.12)

As for those virgins and widows who, idle and meddlesome, make the rounds of the houses of noble matrons, and who surpass in shamelessness even the parasiti of comedy, you should shoo them away like flies.

(Jerome to Eustochium, a noble lady of Rome, who in 384 took a vow of perpetual virginity. *Letters* 22.29.)

parasitus To call parasitism a job is a stretch, but it was a living, if sometimes a humiliating one. In origin the word is Greek, meaning literally "he who dines beside," and it comes into Latin through the theater. The parasite was a stock figure of Greek and then Roman comedy, like the cunning slave, the pimp, the prostitute, or the braggart soldier. The latter was often portrayed in the company of a ridiculously flattering parasite, looking for a dinner. The tone of the word is thus always derogatory, and reminiscent of fiction, like "Shylock" used to describe a moneylender. But *parasitus* outlasted its theatrical origins, which suggests that it applied quite well to a class of real people, or at least was felt to be a useful tool to criticize certain aspects of the Roman patron-client system. Like the English *groupie*, it is not something one calls oneself without a real loss of dignity. The biological use of the word for an animal or plant that lives on another organism is fairly late (eighteenth century) and derives from the enduring social phenomenon described here.

To glimpse the reality of Roman parasitism behind the comic exaggerations and moral denunciations of it is difficult. The word suggests a one-way street, the sponger profiteering off of the vanity and generosity of the host. But as a humorous ancient manual of the trade points out, the relationship is actually symbiotic: "The rich man, even if he has the wealth of Gyges, is poor if he eats alone . . . if he takes the air without a parasite in his company he is considered a pauper." Hosts gained in status. To have parasites was an aspect of *luxuria*, "living large." St. Ambrose, criticizing people who live high on credit, imagines the following scene of a man who has just returned flush from the moneylenders: "Suddenly parasites surround the man whom they used to despise. Now they greet him, escort him, urge him to be happy, and spur him on to expenditure, saying, 'Come, let us enjoy the good things of the world, and let us use up creation, as we did in our youth, quickly.'"

Besides having wit and a taste for the finer things in life, an important part of the job description was the ability to take abuse. For the host could turn nasty and resentful at any moment, or could act cruelly for his own jaded amusement. In Act Three of Shakespeare's *Timon of Athens*, the king serves his courtiers a dinner of water (as Roman emperors on occasion served their parasites wooden fruit) and then curses them: "You knot of Mouth-Friends . . . Most smiling, smooth, detested Parasites. Courteous destroyers, affable wolves!" Timon speaks here for all the nobles who feel betrayed by so-called friends who turn out to be freeloaders interested in nothing but good food and whatever gifts they can get. The entertainment aristocracy of today fosters the same "groupie" phenomenon: who is a real friend, and who merely a parasite? The parasite's-eye view can be glimpsed from a homily on the subject given by a fifth-century bishop. He emphasizes the humiliation and violence suffered by parasites and the cruel vulgarity and debasement of friendship on the part of the hosts. "Behold, man becomes a spectacle for man. In order to raise a laugh one must produce some lewd remark or a distorted expression. One man has his beard yanked as he chews, another his chair pulled out from under as he drinks, one dines on broken crockery, another drinks from a broken glass." The parasite "sells humiliation for wine," though for a laugh the host often gives him non-potable wine and inedible food, so that "it is hard to know whether it is better to starve or go thirsty."

TLL 10.316–318. *RE* 18, pt. 4.1397–1405. Cynthia Damon, "Greek Parasites and Roman Patronage," *Harvard Studies in Classical Philology* 97 (1995) 181–195. Lucian, *The Parasite* 58, trans. Harmon. Ambrose, *On Tobias* 5.17. W. Shakespeare, *Timon of Athens* III.vi.49–55. Valerian, bishop of Cemenelum, *Homilies* 10, *PL* 52.722–725.

THE SOCIAL CONTRACT

cliens

amicitia

consilium

collegium

auctoritas

CLIENS: A DEPENDANT ON A WEALTHY PATRON

One testifies on behalf of a cliens against a relative, but no one testifies against a cliens.
> (Cato the Elder, quoted by Aulus Gellius, *Attic Nights* 5.13)

One cannot abandon one's clientes without incurring the greatest disgrace.
> (Julius Caesar, quoted by Aulus Gellius, *Attic Nights* 5.13)

Little by little our friendship grew, to the point where he did not mind, and I was not ashamed, that he obediently did for me such things as clientes and loyal, industrious freedmen do; there was in this neither arrogance on my part nor flattery on his. Rather our mutual affection and true love freed both of us from all reluctance in calculating favors.
> (Fronto, speaking of a more junior senator, Gaius Clarus, *Letters* 2.150–152 ed. Haines)

If a man has let the apartments rent-free to his freedman or his own or his wife's clientes, Trebatius says he is liable in their name [if someone on the street is hurt by debris thrown out of a window].
> (Ulpian, in Justinian's *Digest of Roman Law* 9.3.5.1)

He lost my pajamas, which a cliens of mine gave me on my birthday.
> (Petronius, *Satyricon* 30.11)

Often they left their kingdoms and, wearing togas without any mark of their royal status, they paid Augustus daily attendance in the manner of clientes—not only at Rome but also when he was visiting the provinces.
> (Suetonius, referring to the "client kings" on the frontiers of the empire, *Augustus* 60)

cliens In English, *client* is usually just a fancy word for customer. The Roman *cliens*, by contrast, was part of a more lasting, more personal, and more unequal relationship. *Clientes* attached themselves to a more powerful person, the *patronus* or *patrona*, in what was in theory a mutually beneficial bond. The typical duties of the client were public attendance (for example, escorting the patron to the forum in the early morning) and the willingness to perform various small services (*obsequia, officia*) whenever asked. In return, the patron provided protection, especially in the courts (*patronus* can mean "lawyer"), and other courtesies such as dinner invitations, seats at the shows, regular cash gifts, or even, as in the legal text quoted here, a rent-free apartment. More democratic societies find this sort of semipermanent dependency uncomfortable. We have mentors, but only temporarily; we work for bosses, but we don't form their daily retinue in public so as to augment their prestige. "Clientage" to us is feudal and corrupt. To the Romans it was fundamental to a well-ordered society, second in importance only to the parent-child relationship, and almost as sacred. Vergil reserved a special place in the underworld for the punishment of patrons who defrauded their clients. One of the first recorded Roman laws in fact protects the vulnerable *cliens* against a patron's abuses. And the young Julius Caesar gained an excellent reputation by his zeal on behalf of his clients' interests. If you were rich, people paid attention to how good a patron you were.

Being a client, on the other hand, was also an honorable estate, because it was nominally based on reciprocity rather than merely the receiving of a handout, and because, when done right, it freed one from actually having to work for a living at some other trade. Yet it exposed one regularly to small humiliations about which Roman satirists loved to complain: the great man is busy and you must wait; at dinner he serves you inferior wine or meat; he is stingy with his gifts; he expects you to be at his door at dawn wearing a clean toga; he prefers other, less worthy clients. Patrons naturally complained about the effort involved, the ingratitude of clients, and they were known to slip out a back door to avoid a particularly annoying client waiting in the atrium.

But despite its awkwardness, the patron-client relationship was part of the natural order for the Romans and easily extended, for example, to the realm of foreign relations. Augustus treated the petty kings on the borders of the empire just as any Roman aristocrat treated his dependents. The patron-client relationship was as basic to the Roman mindset as the corporate-consumer relationship is to our consumer society. Government now is encouraged to see citizens as consumers, but the Roman view was that, in a way, the citizens were *clientes* of the biggest *patronus* of them all, the emperor.

TLL 3.1343–1346. R.P. Saller, *Personal Patronage Under the Early Empire* (Cambridge: Cambridge University Press, 1982). A. Wallace-Hadrill, ed., *Patronage in Roman Society* (London: Routledge, 1989). Vergil, *Aeneid* 6.609. Suetonius, *Julius Caesar* 70.1.

AMICITIA: FRIENDSHIP

They say that amicitia *is one soul and two bodies.*
(Dicunt amicitiam animam unam esse et duo corpora.)
(Proverb quoted by Porphyrio, Commentary
on Horace, *Odes* 2.17.5)

It is true what they say, that you have to share
many quarts of salt together to know what
amicitia *really means.*
(Proverb quoted by Cicero, *On Friendship* 67)

Vulgar people judge amicitiae
by their usefulness.
(Ovid, *Letters from Pontus* 2.3.8)

He was deceived by his hopes and by many of his friends [amici],
though he deserved good treatment from them.
(Grave monument of L. Licinius Nepos, who had hoped
to succeed in business but did not; *ILS* 7519)

The poor man cultivates amicitiae *that
yield no return. Who bestows wealth on
an old and trusted companion, or is
accompanied on his walks by an eques of
his own making?*
(Martial, *Epigrams* 5.19.8-10)

How closely flattery resembles amicitia!
(Seneca, *Letters* 45.7)

I defiled the pure stream of amicitia *with the filth of lust,
I darkened its radiance from a smoking hell of desire.*
(Augustine, *Confessions* 3.1)

amicitia To confess on one's tombstone as did Licinius Nepos, "my friends let me down," seems to us an odd public airing of a private grudge, not the kind of thing we would want posterity to remember. Yet commentary on the duties of friendship—praise of good and dutiful friends, reminders for those falling short, public defense of one's own behavior as a friend, bitter reproaches of perceived backstabbers—appears throughout Roman literature. It is found in poetry, speeches, published letters, autobiographies, histories, and even in that most permanent of genres, the grave *titulus*. The Romans clearly placed a high value on friendship and its reciprocal duties. Many proverbs reflect this, and I quote two. Part of the reason for this preoccupation is the wide field covered by the notion of *amicitia*. It included several kinds of relationships, including personal friendships, but also temporary political alliances, the bond of patron and client, and alliances between states and rulers. An *amicus* might be a friend, a lover, a political supporter or associate, a king's courtier or counselor, or a philosopher's disciple. In politics, *amicitia*, rather than ideology or party platform, often determined alliances and the results of elections. This can be seen throughout the electioneering manual attributed to Quintus Cicero (brother of the orator). It says almost nothing about the issues but a great deal about the choosing and winning of "friends" and the swapping of favors.

Friendship of a sort was central to the client-patron system as well. The clients and hangers-on of rich men tended to be referred to charitably as *amici*, rather than the harsher but more accurate *clientes*. The cherished ideal of reciprocity meant that in exchange for years of loyalty, small services, and daily attendance, the poor but free *amicus* could fairly expect some return. In this way the poet and wit Martial earned a living, such as it was. But he often complains that patrons of his day were stingy, especially when it came to the ultimate prize: 400,000 sesterces of capital, which would guarantee financial independence and social status of an *eques*. In this kind of environment *amici* were of very different social standing, and true intimacy must have been rare. Well might the fabulously wealthy Seneca complain (like a modern celebrity) that it was hard to tell a flatterer from a friend.

TLL 1.1891–1898. P. A. Brunt, "*Amicitia* in the Late Roman Republic," in *The Fall of the Republic and Other Essays* (Oxford: Oxford University Press, 1988) 351–381. Roland Mayer, "Friendship in the Satirists," in S. H. Braund, ed., *Satire and Society in Ancient Rome* (Exeter, UK: University of Exeter, 1989) 5–22.

CONSILIUM: A GROUP OF ADVISORS; WISDOM, JUDGMENT

If you ask somebody, "What did you do today?" the answer
would be, "I attended a donning of the toga of manhood, I went
to an engagement ceremony or a wedding, one man summoned
me to witness a will, another to a legal consultation, still another
to a consilium."

(Pliny the Younger, *Letters* 1.9.2)

The Roman Senate is the consilium of the world.

(Cicero, *Philippics* 4.14)

I brought into my consilium two men whom our community
at that time considered most distinguished, Cornelius and
Frontinus. Surrounded by these men I sat down in my chamber.
Curianus spoke on his own behalf.

(Pliny the Younger, *Letters* 5.1.5–6)

Force devoid of wisdom falls headlong under its
own weight. (Vis consili expers mole ruit sua.)

(Horace, *Odes* 3.4.65)

Yours are the arms and the desire to fight; leave to me the
consilium and the guidance of your valor.

(The emperor Otho speaking to his soldiers in Tacitus,
Histories 1.84.10)

The angry man thinks even a crime is consilium.

(Publilius Syrus, *Sententiae* I 33 = 301 ed. Duff)

The valor of the soldiers hangs on the consilium of the general.
(Ducis in consilio posita est virtus militum.)

(Publilius Syrus, *Sententiae* D14 = 159 Duff.)

consilium Consilium is the wisdom that results from consultation, discussion, and debate. "No one is wise alone," says the Roman proverb (*Nemo solus satis sapit*). *Consilium* is the wisdom not of the philosopher but of the general—a good plan, a strategy, a way to get things done. Cicero attributes courage and practical wisdom (*virtus et consilium*) to great and clever commanders such as Hannibal, Scipio Africanus, Lucullus, and Pompey. As an abstract quality ("good sense," "intelligence," "judgment") *consilium* neatly combines leadership and consensus. It is the ability to think up plans that, in consultation, will win everybody's approval. This is the style of leadership that the Romans most admired.

For those not in positions of power, for example the young, *consilium* is the disposition to act sensibly and listen to reason. The reckless Gaius Cato insulted Pompey in an assembly by calling him a civilian dictator, an act that Cicero took as proof that he was "a young man without *consilium*." Propertius, the love poet, at the beginning of his first published work, says that he has given up on respectable women and decided "to live without *consilium*," that is, in the thrall of his mistress, Cynthia.

In a more concrete sense of the word, a *consilium* is a small, informal group of advisors called in to help make decisions and resolve disputes. Magistrates and emperors had their *consilia*, as did any *pater familias*, whose technically absolute authority over his family was always tempered by the expectation that he would not act arbitrarily but only after consulting others. Pliny the Younger's typical round of social obligations included being called into a friend's *consilium*. The importance of this custom is another example of the Roman pride in settling disputes fairly, without violence, in accordance with rules and based on consensus—a general cultural tendency whose main manifestation is the elaborate Roman law codes.

TLL 4.440-461. Cicero: *Letters to Quintus* 1.2.15. Propertius: *Elegies* 1.1.6.

COLLEGIUM: TRADESMEN'S GUILD OR BURIAL ASSOCIATION

To the departed spirit of Gaius Calventius Firminius. The keepers of the equipment, members of the fireman's collegium of Verona [set up this grave monument].

(*ILS* 6697)

In short, take the whole city into account, all the collegia, all the neighborhoods and districts; if you can win over the chief men from these to your friendship, you will easily have the rest of the crowd through them.

(Quintus Cicero, *Manual of Electioneering* 30)

[The poet Accius] never rose when Julius Caesar came into the collegium of poets. Not that he was unmindful of Caesar's majesty, but when it came to comparison in their common field of interest, he was sure he was somewhat better.

(Valerius Maximus, *Memorable Deeds and Sayings* 3.7.11)

If any slave member of this collegium dies, and his body is unfairly denied burial by his master or mistress and he has not made a will, his funeral will be taken care of. It is decided: whoever for whatever reason causes his own death, his right to burial [at the expense of the collegium] shall not be honored.

(From the regulations of a burial club at Lanuvium in Italy, AD 136; *ILS* 7212)

The collegium of trumpeters always draws the gaze of the crowd when in the midst of serious public and private business it plays a chord, wearing masks, with covered heads, and dressed in multi-colored clothing.

(Valerius Maximus, *Memorable Deeds and Sayings* 2.5.4)

Consider, my Lord, whether you think a collegium of firemen should be formed, up to a limit of a hundred and fifty men [in Nicomedia]. I will make sure that no one but a fireman is admitted, and that the privilege, once granted, will not be diverted to any other purpose; it will not be hard to keep an eye on so few men. [Trajan denied the request, afraid that the *collegium* would become politically disruptive.]

(Pliny the Younger to the emperor Trajan, *Letters* 10.33.3)

collegium Many observers have argued the benefits to a civil society of private clubs like the Lions, the Rotary, or amateur sporting leagues. The Romans were firm believers in this kind of thing, although their clubs were generally organized around a single profession or type of public office. There were *collegia* of magistrates, priests, and above all of tradesmen, who paid dues, met periodically for banquets, had bylaws, and in many cases provided insurance for the proper burial of members. Since *collegia* were not class restrictive, they were one of the few settings in which the free, freed, and slaves (with their masters' permission) might meet on a more or less equal footing. There were associations of trumpeters, ring makers, water carriers, spice dealers, ass drivers, firemen, imperial cooks, secretaries, war veterans, tanners, runners, druggists, potters, ushers at the arena, doctors, sailors, pavers, bakers, poets, tasters, rope dealers, and even one for the people who operated the foot clappers used in the theater (the *scabillarii*). During the turbulence of the late Republic, *collegia* were often misused as platforms for political gang warfare, and both Julius Caesar and Augustus dissolved some *collegia* that were thought to be illegitimate. Under the Principate, *collegia* were seen by the authorities as dangerous and disruptive, especially in the eastern provinces, and their establishment was strictly limited and controlled by the emperor. The *collegium* was one of the civil institutions that died out with the fall of the empire, only to be revived in a rather different form in the guild system of the Middle Ages.

TLL 3.1591–1599. *RE* 4.380–480. Dissolved some *collegia*: Suetonius, *Julius Caesar* 42, *Augustus* 32.

AUCTORITAS: AUTHORITY, CREDIBILITY, INFLUENCE, REPUTATION

When men of literary talent are punished, their auctoritas only grows.

(Tacitus, *Annals* 4.35)

Not only was he not following the truth in these matters, but he was also weighed down by the auctoritas of tradition.

(Augustine, discussing the religious scholarship of Varro, a contemporary of Cicero; *City of God* 7.17)

Finally, she drove him to it, rather by sarcasm than through pleas or parental auctoritas, since she constantly taunted him, calling him his brother's footman.

(Suetonius, on Emperor Vespasian's mother, who in his youth only persuaded him to go for a seat in the Senate by comparing him to his brother, who already had; *Vespasian* 2.2)

Then came P. Caesennius, vendor of the estate, a man whose body is rather weightier than his auctoritas.

(Cicero, discrediting an opposing witness, *Pro Caecina* 27)

One who deals in threats has no auctoritas among free men.

(Brutus and Cassius, the assassins of Caesar, in a letter to Marc Antony preserved in the correspondence of Cicero, *Letters to Friends* 11.3.3)

At that time Evander, an exile from the Peloponnese, ruled that region [Rome] more with auctoritas than with statutory power [imperium]—he was a man venerated because of his miraculous invention of the alphabet . . . all the more so because his mother Carmenta was believed to be a goddess.

(Livy, *Roman History* 1.7.8)

Now, auctoritas is also extremely important in the waging of war and the exercising of military command. Certainly, no one doubts that that same man [Pompey] is pre-eminent in that department as well. For who is not aware, what a huge difference it makes for waging war what the enemy thinks, and what our allies think, about our commanders.

(Cicero, *On the Manilian Law* 43)

auctoritas Auctoritas is the most precious of political commodities, credibility, and influence, not so much authority in the formal sense as the intangible quality that makes people take you seriously. It can be based on family ties (the *auctoritas* of a mother over her children, as in the case of Vespasian), but more usually it comes from some kind of achievement, military, political, or cultural, that makes one's words carry weight. To have earned *auctoritas* is to be trusted on matters of importance. Old age is no guarantee, but great learning, and even impressive clothing, can confer it. Indeed, appearances and circumstances matter. Juries, as Cicero frankly admits, attribute more *auctoritas* to a witness if he is rich.

It is spoken of as being "heavy" (*gravis*). Someone's *auctoritas* can weigh you down or crush you. Alternatively, if you "follow" (*sequor*) another's *auctoritas* in a senatorial debate, for example, you adopt his position and give support, without, however, surrendering autonomy. In a group of theoretical equals, acknowledging another's *auctoritas* allows one to comply without submitting. Other common metaphors involve shrinking or growing, as when Tacitus comments, in the passage above, that the banned historian Cremutius Cordus' *auctoritas* only increased after the emperor Tiberius forced him to commit suicide and suppressed his histories.

Etymologically, the word is related to the legal term *auctor*: one who guarantees that something is the case, one who takes responsibility. *Auctoritas* belongs properly to those with full legal rights, to the *pater familias*, who takes responsibility for his household. The Senate, which under the Republic acted in many ways as a kind of collective *pater familias* to the state, was the preeminent repository of *auctoritas*, and the phrase *auctoritas senatus* became shorthand to refer to its considerable but largely informal power. Cicero, the great defender of senatorial dominance, says that when he went into exile, the *libertas* and *auctoritas* of the Senate went with him. The word's strong Republican and senatorial flavor was put to propagandistic use brilliantly by Augustus, who emphasized his own *auctoritas* (and thus the consensual, earned, and legitimate quality of his extraordinary powers), even as he smashed the power of the Senate itself. It is not surprising that the word is almost never used by historians of the emperors. What they had was not *auctoritas*, freely acknowledged by a society of theoretical equals, but *imperium*, statutory authority held over subjects.

TLL 1.1213–1234. K. Galinsky, *Augustan Culture* (Princeton, NJ: Princeton University Press, 1996) 12–16. J. Hellegouarc'h, *Le vocabulaire latin des relations et des parties politiques* (Paris: Les Belles Lettres, 1972) 295–320. Cicero frankly admits: *Topics* 73. When he went into exile: Cicero, *Speech of Thanks in the Senate* (*post reditum in senatu*) 34.

GOVERNMENT AND POLITICS

candidatus

ambitio

fasces

decurio

dignitas

CANDIDATUS: A PERSON DRESSED IN WHITE; OFFICE-SEEKER

Virtue, honesty and integrity are the customary requirements in a candidatus, not a ready tongue, not skill, not knowledge.
(Cicero, *Pro Plancio* 62)

You called him a friend in the same way we call all candidati "good men" [i.e., without thinking].
(Seneca, *Letters* 3.1)

Occasionally he seemed more like a man seeking than holding a magistracy: he vilified the nobles, praised all the most worthless and lowborn candidati, and himself began to fly around the forum in the company of former tribunes, men like Duillius and Icilius, using them to court the plebs....
(Livy, on the insincere electioneering by the aristocrat Appius Claudius, 451 BC, *Roman History* 3.35.4–5)

And so the Roman plebs should not be deprived of those benefits which all our ancestors gave to them—the games, the gladiators, the banquets— nor is that opportunity for earning good will to be taken away from candidati, something which sig- nifies liberality more than bribery.
(Cicero, referring to the practice of candidates giving away free meals and seats at the spectacles, *Pro Murena* 77)

We are, so to speak, candidati for immortality.
(Lactantius, speaking of Christians, *Divine Institutes* 6.18.35)

At the last election, the Senate expressed the very noble resolution that "Candidati should not provide dinners, distribute presents, or place money with third parties." The first two of these practices were going on openly and rampantly; the third practice, though secretive, was common knowledge.
(Pliny the Younger, referring to the practice of candidates placing money with bribery agents, or *sequestres*; *Letters* 6.19.1–2, probably AD 107)

candidatus Aspirants for office, it should be obvious, are not called candidates because they are candid. As Roman observers mention, quite the opposite is true. *Candidati* promise lavishly, whether or not they think they can deliver. "People want not only promises, especially when asking something from a candidate, but they want the promises to be made in an expansive and complimentary way," says Quintus Cicero's manual of advice to an office seeker. Abject flattery (*blanditiae*) and entreaties (*preces*) were customary in Roman elections. The candidate "wears out with kisses the hands of men with whom, once he has been elected, he would scarcely deign to shake hands." A recognized candidate's license (*candidatorum licentia*) permitted one, for example, to adopt opportunistically a cognomen that suggested antique lineage.

Yet there is a connection, however distant, between honesty and electoral politics. Those running for office wore togas chalked white. The word for white is *candidus*, the whitened toga is the *toga candida*, and a *candidatus* is one "dressed in white." Certain priests, such as those of Isis, were also *candidati* in their apparel, and the *toga candida* was worn on various ceremonial occasions. The color suggested moral purity, as it does today in the bridal costume. *Candidus*, though it does not mean "candid" in Latin, does apply to people who are good-natured and kind, and to writing that is clear and lucid. Cicero claims that what was wanted in a Roman office seeker was not so much knowledge or skill as virtue, honesty, and integrity (*virtus, probitas, integritas*). This impression is bolstered by the habit of advocating for a candidate by saying simply, "He is a good man" (*vir bonus*), an expression so common in campaign graffiti at Pompeii that it can be abbreviated, as in a preserved example: "I ask you to elect Publius Carpinius *duovir*. VB."

Roman electoral and voting procedure was elaborate and unique. Rather than deciding matters by a simple majority, votes were always cast in assigned groups, so that a majority of individual votes decided the vote of each group, and a majority of groups decided the vote of the assembly as a whole. Scholars debate the actual importance of the element of electoral democracy in the (unwritten) constitution of the Roman Republic. It has been pointed out that members of the same families were elected to office, generation after generation. How democratic could this system really have been? On the other hand, elections in the Republican period were contested fiercely, to the point where bribery became a serious and recurring problem, and riots and other upheavals sometimes prevented elections from being held. Cicero's letters are full of electoral news, and senior senators remembered their candidate days as a time of intense striving and risk. If elections were unimportant, no one told the *candidati*.

The importance of elections lessened, however, under the Principate. Tiberius took most elections out of the popular assemblies and transferred them to the Senate and also began the practice of formally designating certain candidates as his favorites every year. The Senate routinely elected these *candidati Caesaris* ("Caesar's candidates") like a rubber stamp. A well-known humorist of the Augustan period, Gabba, once saw a man running nonchalantly for a ball and quipped, "You run like a Caesar's candidate," (*petis tamquam Caesaris candidatus*), a remark that reveals the dampening influence the presence of the emperor was already having on electoral politics. By the early third century, laws against electoral bribery were no longer in force in Rome, because, as a contemporary jurist remarks, "the election of all magistrates belongs to the discretion of the emperor."

In the later imperial period, the political use of *candidatus* for an office seeker receded along with political liberty, but it remained useful as a metaphor for those who eagerly seek something. In particular, the early Christian writers speak of Christians as "candidates for heaven" (*candidati regni caelestis*), "candidates for eternal life" (*candidati aeternitatis* or *immortalitatis*), or "candidates for God" (*candidati Dei*). In the fourth century the custom of dressing the newly baptized in a white tunic became general (this is still done by many Christians), and so they too are called *candidati*. In this case the word regains its old, nonpolitical symbolism, connoting purity of heart.

TLL 3. 237–239. *New Pauly* s.v. "*candidatus.*" Manual of advice to an office seeker: the *Commentariolum Petitionis*, attributed to Quintus Cicero, ch. 44. Wears out with kisses: Seneca, *Letters* 118.3. Candidate's license: Cicero, *Letters to Friends* 15.20. I ask you to elect Publius Carpinius: *CIL* 4.17. You run like a Caesar's candidate: Quintilian, *The Orator's Education* 6.3.62 with *PIR*[2] G 1. Contemporary jurist: Modestinus in Justinian's *Digest of Roman Law* 48.14.1.

AMBITIO: ELECTORAL CAMPAIGNING; CORRUPTION, GRAFT; AMBITION

Not once did I give away money—neither my own nor that of the allies—in the search for office [ambitio].
(Cato the Elder, "On His Own Expenses," p.37 ed. Jordan)

We are overwhelmed by the hunt for office and the business of the law courts. [Obruimur ambitione et foro.]
(Cicero, *On the Orator* 1.94)

Corruption [ambitio] is now hallowed by custom, it's unhindered by the laws.
(Plautus, *Trinummus* 1033)

But discord and greed and ambitio and the other evils that usually arise in prosperity increased tremendously after the destruction of Carthage.
(Sallust, *Histories* fragment 1.11)

We must beware of these sins: first arrogance, then disobedience, excessive talking ... anger ... fornication ... trickery ... ambitio.
(From an anonymous monastic manual probably composed in the sixth century AD near Rome, *Rules of the Teacher* 5.1)

Others he puffs up with ambitiones: those direct all the work and care of their lives toward filling magistracies just so they can put their names on the consular lists and the years. [The most common way to specify a year in Latin is to name the consuls who served in that year.]
(Lactantius, *Divine Institutes* 6.4.21)

But both of these must be rejected by the servants of God, we who renounce both luxury and ambitio.
(Tertullian, *To His Wife* 1.4)

The honor of this world passes away, ambition passes away. (Transit honor huius saeculi, transit ambitio.)
(Augustine, *Letters* 23.3)

ambitio In the Roman Republic aspiring candidates had to "go around" (*ambire*) and solicit support, both from ordinary citizens and from influential insiders. They did this by visiting (*occursatio*), calling people by name with the help of a name-remembering assistant or *nomenclator*, taking them by the arm (*prensare*), telling them what they wanted to hear (*blanditiae*), general toadying (*observantia*), and by spreading around the all-important gifts (*liberalitas, largitio*). The line between energetic glad-handing and plain bribery was crossed often, so that the word itself came early on to mean "electoral corruption, graft." Many laws (dismissed as ineffective by a character in Plautus) were passed in an effort to keep the *ambitio*—that is the money and special interests—out of politics. The upright Cato tried to fend off the charge, and historians such as Sallust (quoted above) and Livy rightly saw it as one of the "evils of prosperity" that contributed to the fall of the Republic. Still, in Cicero and other pagan writers, *ambitio* can have a neutral or positive sense—"the search for office." To Christians, keen to suppress worldly passions, *ambitio* is always bad, a personal failing associated with greed, luxury and vanity. This was a radical break with the pagan tradition of public life, in which serving in office, especially as one of the consuls who gave their names to the year, was the highest possible goal. In the sixth century, when the institutions that spawned it were long dead, the Roman politician's chief modus operandi endured as a vice to which even a monk could be susceptible.

TLL 1.1851–1854.

FASCES: BUNDLES OF RODS, USUALLY INCLUDING AN AXE, GIVEN TO SENIOR MAGISTRATES AND CARRIED BY ATTENDANTS CALLED *LICTORES*

Sisyphus lives. He is before your eyes, the man who thirsts
to be given the fasces and the savage axes by the people;
and beaten every time, he withdraws in misery.

(Lucretius, *On the Nature of the Universe* 3.995-996)

Cynthia doesn't follow after the fasces,
she doesn't care what office you've
held—she weighs only one criterion, the
size of her lover's wallet.

(Propertius, *Elegies* 2.16.11–12)

Then [the mob] snatched the fasces from the grove of Libitina
and brought them . . . to the gardens of Gnaeus Pompeius,
shouting out and calling him now consul, now dictator.

(Asconius, Commentary on Cicero, *Pro Milone* 29)

And when [Gaius Piso, the consul] had ordered the lictor to
arrest the men who kept making threatening gestures at him, his
fasces were smashed and rocks were also thrown in the direction
of the consul from the fringe of the crowd.

(Asconius, Commentary on Cicero, *Pro Cornelio* 51,
referring to events of 67 BC)

The unavoidable circumstances of war gave Gaius
Caesar the authority to command, but the Senate
gave him the fasces [thus legitimizing his position].

(Cicero, *Philippics* 11.20)

fasces The rods are of the kind used to flog, and the axe might chop off a person's head. So the *fasces,* though they were not apparently used in this way regularly, symbolized the power to punish. They inspired awe and fear (*terror*) says Livy; they were "the savage *fasces.*" It was said that the early kings had them and, when the kings were driven out and the Republic was founded, the consuls kept them, but with some important symbolic restrictions. Within the city of Rome the axes were removed; one of the early consuls instituted the custom of lowering them when he spoke in public, so as not to intimidate his audience; since there were two consuls—and two sets of *fasces* would have been too much—they alternated, one month at a time. Most importantly, the *fasces* passed to different men annually, so that this sign of royal omnipotence became a symbol of the orderly transfer of power under the Republic. The *fasces* in this anti-monarchical, "republican" guise appeared on the seal of the new French Republic (1792) and can be seen today in the U.S. House of Representatives behind the rostrum, axe tactfully removed. The binding of the rods suggests forceful but restrained authority.

Under the Principate, when Rome was again ruled by one man, the *fasces* became rather less important. But their symbolism also changed and widened, as they came to represent imperial power itself, rather than restrained consular power. A historian says that the emperor Diocletian "abandoned the imperial *fasces*" of his own free will and grew old on his estates. Another refers to the provincials as "those subject to the Roman *fasces.*"

"[Fascism] wants to remake not only the forms of human life, but the content: man, character, faith. To this end it requires discipline, and an authority that would impress the spirits of men and dominate them fully. Its sign is thus the *fascio littorio* [the lictor's *fasces*], symbol of unity, force and justice." So said Benito Mussolini in 1932, explaining the decision to adopt the *fasces* as the central symbol of his "fascist" regime. The *fasces* started appearing on Italian stamps and coins in the early 1920s and eventually appeared on everything from manhole covers to children's toys. Ostensibly what appealed was the bound rods as an image of social unity and discipline—which has nothing to do with their significance for the Romans. But in the end Mussolini returned to the *fasces* of the early regal period, a sign of fear, to impress the spirits of men and dominate them fully.

TLL 6.302–308. Livy: *Roman History* 2.1.8. A historian: Rufinus's Latin translation of Eusebius, *Church History* 2.5.3. Mussolini: *Scritti e discorsi* viii.73, quoted in S. Francesca-Zamponi, *Fascist Spectacle* (Berkeley: University of California Press, 1997) 96.

DECURIO: A MEMBER OF A TOWN COUNCIL OR MUNICIPAL SENATE OUTSIDE ROME, TYPICALLY COMPOSED OF TEN DIVISIONS OF TEN MEN EACH

Do you know the man called Barbarus, a decurio in our city, the one whom the people call The Scorpion because of the harshness of his temper?

> (Apuleius, *Metamorphoses* 9.17)

It is permitted to vote subsidies for decuriones whose fortunes have fallen, especially if they exhausted their patrimony by generosity to their homeland.

> (Hermogenian, in Justinian's *Digest of Roman Law* 50.2.8)

Decuriones are not to be compelled to provide grain at a price cheaper than the going rate in their homeland.

> (Paulus, in Justinian's *Digest of Roman Law* 50.8.7)

Has he not paid numerous quarterly fees regularly for the privilege of being a decurio? Has he not enjoyed for forty-five years all the rewards and privileges of decuriones, at public banquets, in the Senate house, in the games?

> (Fronto, on Volumnius Serenus, a *decurio* from Concordia in northern Italy in the mid-second century AD; *Letters* 2.179 ed. Haines)

Any seat given, assigned, or reserved for the decuriones at the games . . . let no one but them . . . sit in that seat, nor let anyone lead another to be seated there nor, with malice aforethought, order anyone else to be seated there.

> (A municipal law from Urso in Spain, first century BC, *ILS* 6087.125)

decurio *Decuriones* were responsible for running cities and towns—an important role, given the extremely limited extent of the imperial bureaucracy. They took care of local needs in government, law enforcement, and public works, contributing some of their own money rather than simply spending tax money as modern town councilors do. In return they got an important boost in personal prestige: dinners at public expense, special seats at the spectacles, and the right to speak in public deliberations. Men of certain disreputable professions were at times excluded by law from being *decuriones*, but bastards and Jews were not. An imperial decree specifically included the latter, and stipulated that their duties should not conflict with religious obligations. Required payments ensured that *decuriones* were in a fairly high tax bracket, and at least some ruined themselves by building too lavishly or subsidizing cheap grain. What modern cities achieve bureaucratically and anonymously by taxing the whole population, Roman cities accomplished through socially expected munificence by the rich, who in turn received the intangible but all-important benefit of honor and prestige (*dignitas*).

TLL 5.224–226. A.H.M. Jones, *The Later Roman Empire* (Oxford: Blackwell, 1964) 737-757. Imperial decree: Ulpian, in Justinian's *Digest of Roman Law* 50.2.3.3.

DIGNITAS: RANK, STATUS, DIGNITY, WORTH; PUBLIC OFFICE, OFFICIAL CAREER

My dignitas was begun thanks to the emperor
Vespasian, increased by Titus, and carried forward
further by Domitian.

(Tacitus, *Histories* 1.1)

Dignitas in an unworthy man serves only as a disgrace.

(Publilius Syrus, *Sententiae* L 1)

To the departed shade of Marcus Aurelius Propinquus, senator
and father. Through the labor of military service and the merit
of his energy [industria] he increased the family fortune and
attained an outstanding glory of dignitas. His most devoted
children made [this monument].

(Epitaph from Nepi in Italy, *CIL* 11.7540)

Do you really expect me to take up arms and oppose Caesar, my
own general under whom I commanded a company, and his army
for whose dignitas and victory I have fought for more than
thirty-six years? I will not.

(A centurion of the 14th legion, to an opposing commander by whom he
had been taken prisoner of war, as imagined by an anonymous but
pro-Caesarian historian, *The African War* 45)

[Govern] in such as way that you maintain distinctions of rank
and dignitates. If they become confused, jumbled and mixed,
nothing is more unequal than that equality.

(Pliny the Younger, giving advice to a friend serving
as a provincial governor, *Letters* 9.5.3)

dignitas *Dignitas* refers primarily to the social prestige of office holders and their families, and it has a very positive ring, since such distinctions were, through an ideological trick central to the word, seen as based on worth. *Dignus* means "worthy," and *dignitas* is the personal worth that earns high office, or the high office itself. One's *dignitas*, in the senses of both career and prestige or honor, had to be maintained and reasserted by winning new offices and distinctions through election or preferment, by the behavior of the individual, by exercising leadership in the Senate, and through recognition by the voters. The word had moral content and implied that the man was worthy of such leadership, advancement, and promotion. There was thus a kind of productively vague slippage between political prestige, management of the state, and moral worth. It is often impossible to separate the various shades of meaning: the office itself, the rank in society it entails, and the quality of the office holder's life.

A Roman animal fable about the loss of *dignitas* casts in the leading role an old lion who has lost his roar and bite. This is fitting, because, unlike dignity, which in theory belongs to everyone to some degree just by being human, *dignitas* belongs to the lions of the social world. As he is drawing his final breaths, a boar comes up and gores him, avenging an old hurt; then a bull attacks with his horns; finally an ass, seeing that the lion is putting up no resistance, kicks him in the head. "I resented being insulted by the brave," says the dying lion to the ass, "but having to endure you, you shame of nature, I feel I am dying twice." The moral is that loss of *dignitas* means being exposed, helpless, to the insults of one's inferiors. Cicero experienced something like this when, after Julius Caesar invaded Italy in 49 BC, he sat in virtual exile and waited for Caesar's men, whom he despised, to take control of the capital. The ex-consul wrote to his friend Atticus, "I have given up thinking about the *dignitas* I have lost, the honors, the position in life. I think about what I have accomplished, what I have provided to others, in what glory I lived, and finally, in these terrible circumstances, what a difference there is between me and those men thanks to whom I have lost everything."

It was to prevent such a humiliating loss of *dignitas* that Caesar himself had crossed the Rubicon with the army he had commanded in his Gallic provinces, rather than laying down the command and returning to civilian life. His enemies in the Senate were insisting that he put aside his military command before returning to Rome and running again for office, an interval that would have given them an opportunity to end his career through prosecutions and the like. Just after Caesar invaded Italy, making war inevitable, there was a testy exchange of messages between Caesar and the leader of the anti-Caesarian forces, Pompey, on the subject of *dignitas*. Pompey fulsomely stated that he himself had always held the public interest to be more important than private quarrels and urged Caesar to give up his anger at his enemies "for the sake of his *dignitas*" and in the name of the Republic. Caesar replied that he had always held his *dignitas* to be more important than life itself, and that he was angry now because his enemies in the Senate had deprived him of the honors voted to him by the Roman people, especially the right to run for the consulate in absentia. In other words, it was precisely for the sake of his *dignitas* that he was intending to fight and, potentially, die.

How, many people have wondered, could Caesar get away with advancing such an intensely personal reason for resorting to civil war? The indulgence given here to claims of personal honor seems to verge on the insane. On the other hand, perhaps it is not human behavior that changes, but merely the degree of honesty with which we describe it. Caesar started a war to save his political career. How many modern leaders have done the same while dressing up the cause in other terms? What is peculiarly Roman is the candor with which Caesar admits it and the readiness of his supporters to march behind the flag of Caesar's honor, his accumulated *virtus*, as opposed to any concrete program he may or may not have had.

One of the few things that "dignity" and *dignitas* have in common is that both can form the basis of a concept of justice, though those concepts are radically different. The United Nations Universal Declaration of Human Rights of 1948 begins its preamble by stating that "the recognition of the inherent dignity and of the equal and inalienable rights of all members of the human family is the foundation of freedom, justice and peace in the world." Such a sweeping egalitarian idea of dignity, applicable by right to all persons, was never contemplated in the ancient world. Indeed the importance of *dignitas* militates *against* exactly this kind of thinking. Cicero defines justice as a habit of mind that gives to each his *dignitas* while preserving the common good. That "while" is crucial: giving each his *dignitas* means acknowledging the privileges of higher status individuals to be treated as they deserve. But the claims of *dignitas* must not be so excessive that they damage the overall well-being of the community, as in the case of Caesar's outsized *dignitas*. Status distinctions are the very basis of justice, not obstacles to it. But (and here Cicero is progressive) they must be balanced against the common interest. He makes matters clearer in a discussion of the drawbacks of the various types of government: "In a monarchy the rest of the people are too cut off from common rights and executive authority; and in an oligarchy the multitude can scarcely be free, given its lack of power in all deliberative authority; and when everything is done through the people [i.e., democracy], even if it is a just and moderate people, still that very equality is unfair, since it recognizes no status distinctions [*gradus dignitatis*]." The shift in meaning from the *dignitas* of the privileged, to the dignity of every human being, is a radical one that marks the distance between that social world and ours, even if the dignity of the UN Declaration is still a dream in many parts of the world, and the old claims of *dignitas* are still much honored.

TLL 5.1.1133-1140. Peter Garnsey, *Social Status and Legal Privilege in the Roman Empire* (Oxford: Oxford University Press, 1970), esp. 224–225. Susan Treggiari, "Ancestral Virtues and Vices: Cicero on Nature, Nurture and Presentation," in D. Braund and C. Gill, eds., *Myth, History and Culture in Republican Rome. Studies in Honour of T. P. Wiseman* (Exeter, UK: University of Exeter Press, 2003) 139–164. Roman animal fable: Phaedrus, *Fables* 1.21. Cicero's loss of *dignitas: Letters to Atticus* 10.4.1. Caesar and Pompey on *dignitas*: Caesar, *The Civil War* 1.8–9. Cicero's definition of justice: *De inventione* 2.160. Drawbacks of types of government: *The Republic* 1.43.

ARMY AND EMPIRE

barbarus

castra

caliga

triumphus

BARBARUS: FOREIGN; UNCIVILIZED, SAVAGE

Are we barbari, because we hang innocent
men on the gallows, but you are not barbari
because you throw criminals to the beasts?
(Varro, *Menippean Satires* 24 ed. Astbury)

[The Greeks] have sworn a sacred oath amongst themselves to kill all
barbari with their "medicine"; and what is more they do it for a fee.
(Cato the Elder, quoted by Pliny, *Natural History* 29.14)

Of course you will not overlook my speeches before the Senate and
my addresses given to the army. I will also send you my discussions
held with the barbari. These will be of much use to you.
(The emperor Lucius Verus to his teacher Fronto,
in Fronto's *Letters* 2.196 ed. Haines.)

A "cohort" of soldiers comes from their
mutual exhortation [cohortatione]. True,
we commonly hear the word pronounced
chortes, but this is a barbare dici.
(Velius Longus, *On Orthography* 74)

But how insulting in his edicts,
how barbarus, how crude!
(Cicero, on Marc Antony,
Philippics 3.15)

barbarus Latin originally had no single word to refer simultaneously to all non-Romans. Foreign peoples were called *nationes* (or *gentes*) *externae*, which is a neutral, geographic term. Politically they had a series of graded relationships with foreign peoples. Some might be styled "friends" (*amici*) of the Roman people, others allies (*socii, foederati*) of some specific type, still others were treated as open enemies. The Romans' sometimes elaborate system of alliances and qualified forms of citizenship was the cornerstone of their foreign policy and imperialism. Even in the late empire the Roman relationship with the various tribes and states on its borders was extremely varied, a fact that belies the common image of beleaguered Roman troops desperately struggling to keep the barbarians off the gates. Quite often the barbarians were invited in and given land and a spot in the Roman army, if only to help fight against some nastier group of *barbari* elsewhere.

Yet despite their typically pragmatic approach to foreign relations, the Romans early on adopted the Greek term *barbaros*, onomatopoeia for those uncivilized beings who spoke no Greek and produced only gibberish. A mistake in proper Greek (or Latin) is called a "barbarism." Since the Romans originally fell into this category themselves, they were quite aware of the extremity of the ethnocentrism inherent in the term. But once they had, by dint of sheer military and cultural dominance, earned the right to call other people *barbari*, they did so frequently and with gusto, whether referring to the nomads of Scythia or to temporary political opponents, to Attila and his Huns or to Roman pagans or (from the other side) the Christians. The same can be said of the various states that succeeded the Romans, such as the erstwhile barbarian tribes who made up the Carolingian realm. When the Franks, Suebi, and Thuringi took over, these ex-barbarians began referring to all those outside their empire as *barbari*, just as the Romans had.

But what makes a barbarian a barbarian, besides language? When it doesn't mean simply "foreign," *barbarus* can be applied to various traits, qualities, and customs: wildness, frenzy, cruelty, inhumanity, insolence, arrogance, fearsomeness, lawlessness, greed, lust, cunning, perjury, ostentation, thievery, double-crossing, effeminacy, hot temper, stupidity, foolhardy courage, cannibalism, human sacrifice, the wearing of pants, body painting, hair-dyeing, brightly colored clothing, a habit of screaming loudly when going into battle, and a lack of moderation, prudence, or education. All these and more are imputed to *barbari* at various times and places. A few Roman and Greek writers admire, at least in the abstract, the simplicity of barbarian life, so uncluttered by luxury and the moral corruption it brings.

It would be easy to extract from this list a flattering mirror image, showing how Greco-Roman civilization saw itself as humane, lawful, moderate, and honest, and then to point out the various ways in which Greco-Roman civilization fell short, the ways in which the Romans themselves were the barbarians. This is quite true. What is also interesting, however, is the Romans' own awareness of the contingency and shiftiness of the term, their willingness both to throw it around and to question its applicability. Already in the fourth century BC, Plato had said, "Whatever we do not know about is a barbaric thing." The strange statement of a late-antique veterinary manual that the differences between Romans and barbarians extend even to their animals ("barbarian animals are different" [*barbaricorum animalium alia natura est*]) is exceptional. More often there seems to be at least a tacit recognition that the designation *barbarus* is a relative term, a cultural judgment, nothing immutable or ethnic per se. A graffito from Pompeii, probably written by a less-than-successful client in search of a dinner invitation, says, "To me that man is a *barbarus* at whose house I do not dine."

But this comparative open-mindedness should not obscure the fact that the power and persistence of the notion of the *barbarus*—which is in a sense at odds with the nuanced relationships the Romans actually had with foreign peoples—is a sign of severely limited vision and curiosity. It consigns a large portion of the human race to a spot beneath the notice of educated men and women. The ethnographic writings even of those who had visited barbarian lands, are notably lacking in substance and often rely on fables transmitted by ill-informed Greek writers rather than first-hand information. As a result of this pervasive lack of interest, scholars even today have little information about those peoples at the fringes of the empire whom they still usually end up calling, although without the pejorative ring, "the barbarians."

TLL 2.1735-1744. W. Speyer and I. Opelt, "Barbar: Nachträge zum Reallexicon für Antike und Christentum" *Jahrbuch für Antike und Christentum* 10 (1967) 251–290. Patrick J. Geary, "Barbarians and Ethnicity," in G. W. Bowersock et al., eds., *Late Antiquity: A Guide to the Postclassical World* (Cambridge: Harvard University Press, 1999) 107–129. Whatever we do not know: Plato, *Cratylus* 421C. Barbarian animals are different: Vegetius, *Mulomedicina* 2 pref. 2. Graffito: *CIL* 4.188 = *CLE* 933.

CASTRA: A MILITARY CAMP

Uneven places, which our ancestors used to call "stepmothers" should be avoided at all costs: no mountain should overlook the castra, so the enemy cannot climb it and look down at what is going on in the camp.

(ps.-Hyginus, *On the Fortification of the Camp* 57)

Every lover is a soldier, and Cupid has his own castra.

(Ovid, *Amores* 1.9.1)

I'm heading for the castra: goodbye Venus and goodbye girls!

(Tibullus, *Elegies* 2.6.9)

[The emperor Hadrian] himself lived a military life among the troops, even eating the food of the camp [cibis castrensibus] openly and with evident pleasure—that is, lard, cheese and posca. [*Posca* was a mixture of vinegar and water.]

(*SHA, Hadrian* 10.2)

[Scipio Africanus] restored the army to very strict military discipline. He removed all the instruments of luxury and self-indulgence, and ejected two thousand prostitutes from the castra.

(Livy, *Roman History*, epitome of Book 57)

And if anyone scales the exterior fortifications or enters the castra over the wall, he is punished by death.

(Modestinus, in Justinian's *Digest of Roman Law* 49.16.3.17)

[Fabius Maxius] possessed an equal talent for the camp and for the toga [castris togaeque].

(Silius Italicus, *Punica* 6.617)

castra In the Republican period Roman military marching camps were usually temporary, fortified quickly, and then dismantled as the army moved on. Under the Principate more permanent bases were sometimes built, the so-called *castra stativa*, especially when the enemy was near. Over time the *castra stativa* could become the nucleus of a city, and several European cities that started out this way retain the distinctive grid street plan originally laid down by Roman army surveyors.

The many metaphorical uses of the word in Latin show the central place of the military camp in the Roman imagination and the militarized quality of Roman culture in general. The *castra* symbolized military life, as the toga symbolized civilian life. But even outside the military sphere, to leave a place was to "move camp" (*castra movere*). To adhere to someone's side in any conflict was to "follow his camp" (*castra sequi*). The Christian writer Tertullian sees the battle of good and evil as that between the *castra* of light and the *castra* of darkness, and Christians saw the church itself as their *castra*. Heaven was the "camp of the saints" (*castra sanctorum* or *castra caelestia*). To beat someone at his own game was to "slay him in his own camp" (*in suis illum castris cecidit*). To Roman writers on nature, the bee's hive was his *castra*.

In later Latin the word came to refer to any fortified place, and as such it has had an enormous impact on the maps of Europe and the new world. The diminutive form *castellum* produced nineteen separate roots in later spoken or "vulgar" Latin, which in turn yielded the Spanish *castillo*, Italian *castello*, French *chateau*, English *castle*, and many, many others. By one scholar's count, late Latin *castellum* provided the root for 143 distinct form classes in actual use as European place names (Castilla, Castelo, Castillon, etc.). In England, too, it yielded the suffixes -*caster* (as in Lancaster) and -*chester* (as in Winchester). Castro is a common Spanish surname (especially in Aragón, Castile, and Catalonia) meaning "one who lives at, or near, one of the many towns called Castro." Spanish, French, and English settlers brought these names to the Americas, and thus by linguistic diffusion the Roman *castra* invaded the New World long after conquering the Old.

TLL 3.548-564. H. Diamant, *The Toponomastic Reflexes of Castellum and Castrum* (Heidelberg, Germany: Winter, 1972). Tertullian: On *Idolatry* 19.

CALIGA: THE COMMON SOLDIER'S BOOT

He served seventeen years in caliga.
(Epitaph of a soldier, *ILS* 2149)

Gaius Marius went from the caliga *to seven consulates,*
having conquered the Numidians in Africa, and the
Cimbri and Teutoni in Gaul.
  (Lucius Ampelius, on the phenomenal upward mobility of the
  famous general of the late Republic; *Liber Memorialis* 18.15)

As for military distinctions [Augustus] granted medals and
torques, valuable for their gold or silver, somewhat more freely
than he did the garlands intended for those who first scaled an
enemy wall or crossed a camp-fortification, which carry more
honor; these he gave out very sparingly, without favor, and
*often even to common soldiers [*caligati*].*
(Suetonius, *Augustus* 25.3)

Then there was her little son, born in the camp and brought up
in the company of the legions, whom they called "Caligula,"
using the soldier's word, because he usually wore that kind of
shoe to win the affection of the rank and file.
(Tacitus, speaking of the son of Germanicus and Agrippina,
the future emperor; *Annals* 1.41.2)

caliga The *caliga* was a thick sandal of various designs with iron nails securing its leather straps or upper. Not a boot in the modern sense, it needed some kind of shin protection or greave (*ocrea*). Though farmers and peasants also wore the *caliga*, it was above all associated with the common soldier, who was often called a *caligatus*, "boot wearer." Similarly, in the U.S. Marine Corps new inductees used to be called "boots," hence the term "boot camp," which arose in the 1940s. *Caligatus*, by contrast, went for all Roman foot soldiers, including centurions, not just new recruits. And just as we say "boots on the ground" to mean troop strength, Latin too personifies the boot, as when a satirist urges a friend not to be so rash as to take a soldier to court for beating him up, and to risk alienating his comrades: you'd have to be crazy, he says, "to offend so many boots, so many thousands of hob-nails."

Soldiers' slang has always been rich in nicknames. A centurion on the German frontier, one Lucilius, got the moniker "Another-please" (*cedo alteram*), because that is what he would say in a loud voice after breaking a stick over the back of a soldier being punished for some offense. (He was killed by his men in a mutiny.) The future emperor Tiberius, whose full name was Tiberius Claudius Nero, was re-christened by the soldiers "Biberius Caldius Mero" ("Drinks Hot Strongwine"), after his early penchant for heavy drinking. But the soldier's nickname that stuck the longest was *Caligula*, "Little Boots." It was a term of endearment given by the soldiers in the legions stationed on the German frontier to the little son of their beloved commander, Germanicus. The name suggests two things: that as a boy he was dressed in military, rather than civilian, fashion; and that he wore the costume of the common soldier (*caligatus*), not of an officer like his father, who would have served in civilian shoes (*calcei*). It was Little Boots' pathetic appearance, as he and his mother Agrippina were being rushed out of camp, that shamed the soldiers into stopping a mutiny after the death of Augustus in AD 14.

The word *caliga* itself is "low" in tone, and is used not at all, or only with distaste, by educated writers. "I did not care for his *caligae* and chalked-white leggings," says Cicero of somebody he doesn't like. The humble tone of the word may account for the fact that Caligula once became angry at a centurion who addressed him by his cognomen (as opposed to the more dignified "Caesar"), though this is what soldiers had always called him. Seneca gives this as an example of his hypersensitivity to insult.

TLL 3.154.55. RE 3.1355. J. F. Gilliam, "Milites Caligati," *Transactions of the American Philological Association* 77 (1946) 183–191. Satirist: Juvenal, *Satires* 16.24–25. Another-please: Tacitus, *Annals* 1.23.3. Biberius Caldius Mero: Suetonius, *Tiberius* 42.1. Cicero: *Letters to Atticus* 2.3.1. Seneca: *On Firmness* 18.4.

TRIUMPHUS: VICTORY PROCESSION

It is called triumphare because the soldiers returning with the general shout "io triumphe!" Possibly this derives from thriambos, a Greek title of Bacchus.

(Varro, *On the Latin Language* 6.68.8)

On the day of his Gallic triumphus Caesar's chariot broke an axle while passing the Velabrum area, and he was almost thrown out. He ascended the Capitoline hill [on foot] to the light of torches which were carried in the trunks of forty elephants on either side. In his Pontic triumphus, instead of the usual tableaux showing scenes of the campaign, there was an inscription of three words only: VENI VIDI VICI ["I came, I saw, I conquered"] thus showing the speed of the whole operation.

(Suetonius, *Julius Caesar* 37.2)

The victor is here! Behold the great ornament of a great triumphus, victor afar on land and sea, carrying the grim representations of the fight with the barbarians.

(From a verse encomium on Valerius Messalla Corvinus, who triumphed over Aquitania in 27 BC; ps.-Vergil, *Catalepton* 9.3–5)

Lucius Paulus, while reciting in the traditional fashion a record of his deeds in a public meeting outside the city before the day of his triumphus, prayed to the immortal gods that, if any of them felt envy [invidere] towards his works and his good fortune, that they rage against himself, rather than against the state. [Two of Paulus's sons died within days of his triumph.]

(Velleius Paterculus, *Roman History* 1.10.4)

triumphus The name of this most distinctive Roman celebration does not sound like Latin at all. Every other Latin word with *-mph-* in it is of Greek origin—e.g., *amphitheatrum, symphonia, nympha, emphasis, amphora*. But there is no Greek word *triumphus*, and no analogous Greek ceremony. The best that Roman scholars such as Varro (quoted above) could do was suggest an origin in *thriambos*, a Greek title of the god Dionysus. Not very close, granted, and no *-mph-*. But the similarity lies in the use of the word *triumphus* as a kind of ritual, celebratory address or shout ("Hey! Triumphus!"), the same way that Dionysus's cult titles were often used. The best modern guess has it that *trium-phus* is of distant Greek origin but passed into Latin via the Etruscans, who did apparently have a triumph-like ceremony, and from whom the Romans adopted much of their public regalia and ceremonial in the early Republican period.

So *triumphus* seems to be originally a kind of shout or chant that then gave its name to the celebration of military victory. The triumph procession, as it developed over the course of the Republic, was part thanksgiving service, part military parade, political propaganda, and public spectacle. References in the poets and elsewhere about the fun to be had suggest that the triumph was not, however, a North Korean-style orchestrated political rally but a genuine holiday for everybody. For the returning victor it was a glorious but inherently transitory event, a day of unique magnificence, the highest single honor to which a Roman man could aspire. Artists tried to catch some of the magic of the day and preserve it, and this urge is probably the single most fertile source of distinctively Roman visual art, architecture, and poetry. Coins, medallions, cameos, gems, statues, and sculpture were all used for commemoration, and there were special forms of architecture created to serve the same purpose—the triumphal arch and a type of column with spiral bands of relief showing scenes from the war. A few of these columns survive in the piazzas of modern Rome. The distinctive flavor of Roman "official" art, with its blending of historical representation and myth, its mixing of fact and symbol, has a lot to do with the battle representations carried on the floats and the artistic effort to freeze the moment of triumph.

Listing and describing triumphs is also the essence of Roman historical writing. Written commemorations of the triumph begin with the primitive year-by-year lists of events kept by priests in early times and preserved in the bare-bones records of inscriptions. Triumphs became part of Roman historiography as it evolved in the third century BC and reached maturity in the sometimes elaborate descriptions of Livy, Plutarch, and others, who furnish accounts of senatorial debates and controversies about the granting of the privilege, lists of spoils displayed, peoples conquered, and noble captives driven before the chariot. Such an honor redounded not only to the general and his family but had a wider, communal importance that had to be preserved and recorded. The lavish display of wealth and power conveyed a message beyond the glorification of the individual general's deeds and provided, as a Jewish observer put it, speaking of the triumph in which the treasures of the temple in Jerusalem were displayed, "a testimony of the might of the Roman empire."

The accounts follow a stereotyped structure, beginning with the report by the general of his accomplishments (*res gestae*) and the formal request for the triumph, lodged from outside the city. The request was "that honor be shown to the immortal gods and that it be permitted to me to ride into the city triumphing [*triumphans*]." This suggests that the basic purpose was a sacrifice to give thanks to the gods, especially Jupiter, for the victory. Jupiter was the guarantor of the success and stability of the Roman empire, and the general acted, in effect, as his deputy. The goal of the procession was Jupiter's temple, where sacrifice was made and spoils deposited.

After the request came the debate in the Senate, which had to decide whether to grant the privilege (*triumphum decernere*) formally or to deny the request or grant a lesser honor, the *ovatio*. The senatorial decree traditionally used the language, "Whereas by reason of his valor [*virtus*] . . ." or "good fortune [*felicitas*]." The victor embodied *virtus* and stood at the pinnacle of human *felicitas*. But this position on the summit was precarious. It meant that he was vulnerable to the jealousy (*invidia*) of fortune or of the gods. This was an honor so great it needed to be counteracted to prevent attacks of *invidia* of the type that killed Lucius Paulus's sons. What was in effect a temporary deification (since he appeared with the dress and insignia of Jupiter) was counteracted in several ways: by a slave placed in the chariot and charged with holding over his head a golden Etruscan jewel-encrusted crown and occasionally whispering, "Look behind you, remember you are a mortal man" (*Respice post te, hominem te memento*); by comical and insulting songs and chants delivered by the soldiers, intended to deflate him a bit; and by a phallus strapped under the chariot, a *fascinum* to avert the forces of *invidia*. Victory was proof of the superhuman character of the victorious general, but the Romans understood the danger that such great honor would inebriate the already powerful man and endanger both him and the community.

The mention of the celebration is usually handled by the historians with the verb *triumphavit*, or by the more precise formulation "he rode into the city triumphing" (*triumphans urbem est invectus*). The people over whom the triumph was being celebrated were seen as the source of the triumph and so were preceded by the preposition *ex* or *de*, thus "Metellus and Pompeius triumphed from Spain" (*ex Hispanis*), or "there was a triumph from the Scordisci" (*ex Scordiscis*). Descriptions of the parade refer to the leading of the captives and sacrificial victims before the triumphal chariot (*ducere ante currum*). The booty and spoils borne on floats for display are often said to be "carried across" (*transvehere, transferre*), perhaps because the ritual crossing of the sacred boundary of Rome, the *pomerium*, was the formal start of every triumph. Finally the donative is mentioned, a cash bonus from the spoils to the soldiers, and sometimes to the people of Rome as well. In addition to the usual cash and food, Julius Caesar once remitted a year's rent to those in Rome who paid up to two thousand sesterces and in Italy up to five hundred. One can imagine the crowd cheering extra loud on that occasion.

For a summary of recent scholarship, Carlin Barton, *Roman Honor: The Fire in the Bones* (Berkeley: University of California Press, 2001) 54–56. See D. R. Dudley, *Urbs Roma* (Aberdeen: Aberdeen University Press, 1967) 58–66. Jane E. Phillips, "Form and Language in Livy's Triumph Notices,' *Classical Philology* 69 (1974) 256–273. A Jewish observer: Josephus, *The Jewish War* 7.133. That honor be shown to the immortal gods: Livy, *Roman History* 38.44.10. Look behind you: Tertullian, *Apology* 33.4.

TECHNOLOGY

antiquus

caementum

architectus

fornix

metallum

ANTIQUUS: ANCIENT; PREFERABLE, IMPORTANT, PRAISEWORTHY, GOOD

Generally people say that what is preferable is "more ancient" [antiquior].
(Fronto, *To Marcus Aurelius on Speeches* 2.114 ed. Haines)

Death is to be considered preferable [antiquiorem] to disgrace.
(From an anonymous treatise on rhetoric,
Rhetorica ad Herennium 3.3.5)

When properly placed, they often make a speech seem grander and more impressive [antiquior].
(Cicero, on the use of poetic words in public speeches,
On the Orator 3.153)

To Roman parents military discipline has been more important [antiquior] than love of their children.
(The jurist Paulus, explaining why, according to Roman law,
a son who is a deserter cannot be returned after the war
into the legal guardianship of his father; Justinian's
Digest of Roman Law 49.15.19.7)

Rome rests upon the old-fashioned strength of character of her men.
(Moribus antiquis stat res Romana virisque.)
(Ennius, *Annals* fr. 156 ed. Skutsch)

antiquus Nothing exemplifies the famous retro-ism of the Romans more clearly than the fact that words denoting novelty (*novus, recens*) often carry a note of disapproval, while words denoting age are generally approving. Quite often the comparative *antiquior* is simply equivalent to *melior* ("better") or *potior* ("preferable," "more important"). One of the puzzles of Roman culture is how a people whose very language enshrines this backward-looking stance managed to be so successful at adapting to new circumstances and so innovative when it came to architecture, politics, literature, and warfare. Constitutional change was ceaseless, and often those who most loudly invoked the past were planning the most radical changes. For us the words *new, modern* and *modernity* have some of the glamour, and offer a similar promise of happiness, order, and effectiveness, that words like *antiquus* and *priscus* ("ancient, archaic") did to the Romans.

In technology as in other areas of life, innovation per se was not prized by the Romans. Yet neither is it in our society, in every case. The fishhook and hammer remain essentially as they were in the Neolithic age, and many of the Roman tools used in agriculture and crafts are remarkably similar to their modern counterparts. Innovation is not a uniform process of technical improvement across all spheres. Development in educational software plods along, while computer-based games and gambling progress at an astounding rate. What makes certain technologies attractive or unattractive in certain places at certain times is culturally determined and often mysterious. Some technologies, known to the ancient Egyptians and Greeks but not much used, were exploited by the Romans with a will: the aqueduct and the arch, for example. When properly motivated, as they were in the case of mining and metallurgy, bridge making, war machinery, and monumental building with concrete, the Romans were capable of sustained innovation and astounding technical and organizational feats. Yet the potential of the water-powered mill was slow to be exploited, the crank and wind power were neglected, and medical advances were modest.

Is technological success to be measured in terms only of high technology and inventions or also in modest advances that affected a large number of people? Do we consider the needs of the elite, of the army, or of the population at large? It will not do to stereotype the Romans (or any other premodern people) as backward, or backward-looking, without examining the perceived needs and responses—what people thought about technology—as much as what technologies emerged. *Antiquus, mos maiorum*, and other words that are usually used to evoke Roman conservatism are in some ways a hindrance rather than a help in understanding what was really going on. The preferred Roman ways of talking show how they liked to see themselves, as wary, pragmatic traditionalists. The language of modern advertising attempts to flatter us into believing that we can be bold revolutionaries every day, just by using a new product. The truth is that all cultures, in their peculiar attachment to some technologies and disdain for others, are equally quirky, and that the interesting question historically is often not, "What was invented?" but "Who benefitted?" (*Cui bono?*).

TLL 2.177–183. Kevin Greene, "Industry and Technology" in A. K. Bowman et al., eds., *The Cambridge Ancient History*, 2nd ed., vol. XI: *The High Empire, AD 70–192* (Cambridge: Cambridge University Press, 2000) 741–768.

CAEMENTUM: SMALL ROCK, RUBBLE; CONCRETE

> But people nowadays, in a hurry, pay attention only to the faces
> [of walls], putting stones on end, and fill up the middle separately
> using broken caementa with mortar.
>
> (Vitruvius, On Architecture 2.8.7)

> The fish perceive the lessening of the sea when piers have been
> built out into the deep: again and again the contractor with his
> gang of slaves throws caementa down there, and the owner,
> disdainful of dry land [looks on]. But Fear and Dread climb as
> high as he does.
>
> (Horace, commenting on the fashion among the wealthy of
> building high concrete terraces out into the sea to support
> their beachfront pleasure villas; Odes 3.1.33–38)

> Why, you might as well believe that the temples of today are weaker
> because they shine with marble and gleam with gold instead of being
> constructed from crude caementum and ugly roof tiles.
>
> (Tacitus, arguing against critics of more elegant, modern
> oratorical style, Dialogue on Oratory 20)

caementum Walls made of rubble that has been stiffened with a mortar of slaked lime, water, and sand are undoubtedly one of the technological signatures of Roman civilization. The development (over the course of the late Republic and early Principate) of concrete mixes of varying composition and appropriate strengths ranks among the most outstanding contributions of the Romans to structure. The Roman use of concrete to vault and dome large spaces was truly revolutionary, in that it gave architects new freedom to create rooms of almost any conceivable size and volume. It was far more flexible and easy to build with than the method preferred by the Greeks—post and lintel construction using cut stone. More than any other innovation, the mastery of concrete technique made possible the spectacular building binges of the emperors and gave to an unprecedented number of people the benefits of aqueducts, baths, and huge temples, not to mention harbor moles that allowed African grain ships to park safely within a few miles of the city of Rome.

Roman authors were aware of the distinctiveness of this Roman building method. Discussing the peculiarities of the German tribes, Tacitus says (writing in AD 98), "Everybody [among the Germans] surrounds his house with open space, whether to protect against accidental fires, or through ignorance of building technique. They do not even use *caementa* or roof tiles, but employ timber for everything, unshaped and without beauty or attractiveness." He unkindly attributes the Germans' un-Roman building methods not to a tendency to use locally abundant materials but to ignorance. A couple of centuries later, however, things had changed in Germany. When the emperor Julian visited the area with his legions on a punitive expedition across the Main River (AD 357), he found that the locals had learned. "None was spared. Prisoners were taken from the houses, which were carefully built in Roman fashion, and all were set on fire and burnt to the ground." Ah, Romanization. To this day many German terms having to do with building are of Latin origin: *Kalk*, "lime" from the Latin *calx*; *Mörtel*, "mortar" from *mortarium*; *Ziegel*, "brick" from the Latin *tegula*; and also *Zement* from *caementum*.

Characteristically, the technological change and innovation involved with the rise of concrete construction had next to no impact on the Latin language. It is constantly stated in reference books that the Latin term for concrete is *opus caementicium*, but this is only a half-truth. *Opus caementicium* is a rare technical usage, found in Pliny and a few inscriptions; much more common is the vague (and plural) *caementa*. The word *caementa* existed well before the concrete boom of the late Republic and refers simply to small bits of broken stone (not building stone cut to order, which would be *saxa* or *saxa quadrata*). The word derives from *caedere*, to crush. Writers who know what they are talking about refer to concrete walls or foundations as made "from small rubble and lime cut with sand" (*caementis minutis et calce harenato*), an admirably accurate description, or just "from rubble and lime" (*ex caemento et calce*), with variations. To distinguish between *caementa* as rubble, a transportable raw material, and *caementa* as a finished work, the word *structura* is sometimes used. A bath or theater can be made with *structile caementum*, "building rubble," or *ex structura caementorum*, "out of a structure of rubble." The layman probably said *caementa* in a vague way to refer to any stone wall or any concrete structure, without thought of the exact methods used to make it stand up. The *caementa urbis* were the concrete walls that made up the bulk of the city by the imperial period. But the temple of Solomon (surely built without concrete) is called "that *caementum*" by the fourth century AD poet Prudentius.

Every new technology brings its own eagerly embraced vocabulary. So it seems odd that no new term besides "rubble" was felt to be needed for this highly visible innovation. In part the reason could be that most people saw concrete not as a sign of an architectural revolution but as a cheap, vulgar, and unsightly building material, and had feelings about it, if they had any at all, akin to the feelings many have today about sheet rock. It was to be covered up at all costs, and architects became expert at using various facing materials—stucco, stones, bricks, and fine marble veneers—to give a more pleasing effect. The glory went to the veneers, and when Augustus boasted he had found Rome a city of brick and left it a city of marble, he was speaking of the use of marble veneers over concrete cores, especially on temples. Latin possesses a huge vocabulary to refer to different types of marbles but wasted no words on what, in hindsight, we see as the wonder material of the Roman world.

TLL 3.95–96. C. Densmore Curtis, "The Difference between Sand and Pozzolana," *Journal of Roman Studies* 3 (1913) 197–203. Tacitus: *Germania* 16. Julian in Germany: Ammianus Marcellinus, *The Later Roman Empire* 17.1.7, trans. Hamilton. The most outstanding contribution of the Romans to structure: K. D. White, *Greek and Roman Technology* (Ithaca, NY: Cornell University Press, 1984) 204–205. *Caementa urbis*: Jerome, *Commentary on Hosea* 1.4.113. Prudentius: *Apotheosis* 514.

ARCHITECTUS: CHIEF BUILDER, ARCHITECT

When a completed building makes a magnificent impression, the expenditure undertaken by the patron will be praised; when the craftsmanship is fine, the supervision of the foreman will gain approval; but when it wins esteem through its grace and harmonious proportions [proportionibus et symmetriis], then the glory will go to the architectus. These things are arranged correctly when he permits himself to take advice both from craftsmen [fabri] and from private citizens.

(Vitruvius, On Architecture 6.8.9–10)

Only let this be our fixed intention . . . if anyone wants to employ us as architecti to help in rebuilding the state, or even as workmen [fabri], not to hang back but rather to come running willingly.

(Cicero to Varro in 46 BC, after the loss of their side and the victory of Julius Caesar in the civil war of 49–46; Letters to Friends 9.2.5)

[Plato] names three sorts of gods, of which the first is that single unique and highest god, beyond the visible world, incorporeal, whom we have shown above to be the father and architectus of this divine orb.

(Apuleius, On Plato and his Doctrine 1.11)

When building a villa at Baiae, Lucullus became so obsessed [with keeping his fish cool] that he gave the architectus a blank check, provided that he lead a tunnel from his fish ponds into the sea opposite a jetty, so that twice a day the tide could go in and come out again and cool down the fish ponds.

(Varro, referring to the statesman and general of the first century BC, who was famous for the luxury of his villas; On Agriculture 3.17.9)

architectus An *architectus* is distinguished from a workman or craftsman *(faber)* by being in charge. *Tekton* is the Greek equivalent of *faber*, and *archi-* is a prefix meaning "master" or "chief," as in *arch-enemy* or *arch-druid*. An *archipirata* is a pirate king, an *archigallus* the head of a band of self-castrating priests called *galli*, and an *archidiaconus* is an archdeacon. Such compounds are relatively rare in classical Greek and Latin but pop up like liver spots in late antiquity and the Middle Ages with the growth of the imperial and church bureaucracies, yielding dozens of ridiculous words along the lines of *archiphonista*, a choir director, and *archiclavis*, a chief key keeper. In contrast to the *faber*, the *architectus* was not a specialist but expected to be broadly educated and to possess many skills. *Faber* is usually paired with a defining adjective denoting the specialty, such as *faber tignarius* (carpenter), *faber argentarius* (silversmith), or *faber pectinarius* (comb maker). *Architectus* typically stands alone and denotes one competent to design and direct the building of any kind of structure.

Vitruvius, a practicing architect who worked for Augustus and wrote a treatise on the subject, places great emphasis on the intensive education necessary in both practical matters (*fabrica*) and theory and book learning (*ratiocinatio, litterae*). Not only must the aspiring architect know the properties of raw materials and the various skills involved with building, but he must also know a fair amount of history, geometry, mathematics, philosophy, music, medicine, and law. Of all these intellectual accomplishments, perhaps the most important to Roman architects (or to Greek architects working for Roman patrons, since many were Greek immigrants) was geometry. As a rule Roman architects preferred to use squares, segments of circles, and rectangles of certain simple ratios as units of design. Not that such units were applied mechanically. What Roman architecture seems to be aiming at is rhythmic proportion (*symmetria*) that creates an orderly and dignified, yet dynamic impression. Think of the spherical dome of the Pantheon, or the façade of the Colosseum, whose geometrically designed yet subtly changing proportions people still find pleasing.

Symmetria is not symmetry but the principle of mathematical harmony and commensurability of parts, as in a well-shaped man. The idea is that this aspect of beauty is *not* in the eye of the beholder. Rather, nature dictates that certain kinds of simple numerical ratios yield a satisfying aesthetic experience. In the ideal human form, the face takes up one-tenth of the total height, and man is bisected at the genitals. Arm span is equal to height, which means that if you extend your arms you can be inscribed in a square. Leonardo has a slightly different system of ideal human proportions from the one developed earlier by Vitruvius, but he embraces the same concept: *symmetria* is the mathematical harmony that comes of commensurable numbers and shapes used in design.

Vitruvius tells a little story about the origin of architecture. Primitive man learned to build huts in imitation of the nests of swallows, he says. Gradually he got better at it, in rivalry and competition, at first using sticks and straw; then, those who had aptitude and industry specialized and called themselves *fabri*. The work of these early craftsmen proceeded from the building of houses, step by step, to "the other arts and disciplines, and we progressed from a wild and rustic life to peaceful civilization." So *fabri* deserve honor for bringing us out of barbarism. But the crucial innovation was the synthesizing and aestheticizing intellect of the *architectus*: "through greater cogitations arising from a variety of arts, they began to build not just huts, but houses with foundations, and brick or stone walls, and roofs of wood and tile. Finally, by observations in their studies, they progressed out of wandering and uncertain judgments to fixed and rational methods of proportion [*certas symmetriarum rationes*]." The quest for empirically fixed aesthetic principles was part of the Greek heritage of architecture. It informed in a flexible way the most successful Roman buildings and has remained a part of the profession, as passed on through Vitruvius's influential treatise, up to the present day.

The high prestige of architecture among the professions meant that *architectus* was available as a metaphor for the creator of the universe, whereas *faber* would be rather insulting to a supreme being. Still, the fact that architects were frequent companions of Roman aristocrats with a taste for ostentatious building (like Lucullus and his fish ponds) led to disparaging remarks from moralists, such as Seneca, who disapproved of the wasteful expense: "Believe me, blessed was that age before architects and before builders [*tectores*]."

TLL 2.465-466. Mark Wilson Jones, *Principles of Roman Architecture* (New Haven: Yale University Press, 2000). Fixed and rational methods: Vitruvius, *On Architecture* 2.1.7. Seneca: *Letters* 90.9.

FORNIX: ARCH, VAULT; BROTHEL

It hangs on high, supported with delicate skill on arched fornices.

> (Prudentius, referring to temple architecture, *Apotheosis* 523)

Before he left the city he built a fornix on the Capitoline hill, facing the street by which one climbs the Capitoline, with seven gilded statues and two horses [on top] and two basins of marble before the arch.

> (Livy, on the general Scipio Africanus, referring to events of 190 BC, *Roman History* 37.3.7)

May he spend a cold, miserable winter in a shuttered fornix, an endless December of rainy storms.

> (Martial, cursing one of his enemies, *Epigrams* 10.5.7)

Marcus Cato the Censor, when he saw a socially prominent man coming out of a fornix, praised him for mastering his sexual urges without committing any misdeed.

> (Porphyrio, Commentary on Horace, *Satires* 1.2.31)

fornix Arches were known in ancient Egypt and Greece but considered unsuitable for monumental architecture and rarely used. To the Romans, the arch was a marvel. "If someone were to remove from the arch the crucial stone upon which everything leans, all the rest would come crashing down at once," said an admiring poet. Learned men ascribed the idea to the phenomenal Greek philosopher Democritus. It allowed pure water to travel for miles in suspension, buildings and bridges to hover over empty space, stable yet splendidly precarious. During the earthquakes to which Naples is prone, it was seen that buildings which "hang" (*pendent*) over arched vaults are much stronger than solid construction. The victorious Roman general used the proceeds of conquest to set up a perverse tribute to himself and his works: a *fornix* that supported nothing but an attic, the abstracted form, useless and decorated with testaments to his glory. The triumphal *fornix* and the aqueduct *fornix* are two of the most recognizable symbols of Roman power—the one a revolutionary public convenience, the other a monument to military ego.

Around the time of Augustus, however, the term *fornix* stopped being used for the triumphal arch. It was replaced by the ancestor of our term, *arcus*, for reasons that have to do with an important change in Roman architecture and society. In the late Republic, as the population of Rome boomed, architects had to build up, not out. Tall buildings with vaulted ground-floor rooms, which were also called *fornices*, became ubiquitous. Proverbially dank and sooty, such cellars gave homes to humble craftsmen, beggars, drunks, and above all to prostitutes. By Julius Caesar's day, *fornix* meant brothel. Along with the cookshops (*popinae*), the *fornices* became one of the chief attractions of city life, to men at least. Soon, using the same word for a whorehouse and a triumphal arch just did not seem right. In the Christian era, the Latin Bible used *fornix* as the usual term for brothel, and its architectural origin was abandoned and forgotten altogether. The church fathers, blasting pagan vice, relished the word and gave us derivatives like *fornicari*, "to go whoring," or to become a spiritual "fornicator" by worshipping idols. "The soul fornicates when it is turned away from You," said St. Augustine, who knew something about fornicating from his younger days.

TLL 6.1125–1127. *RE* 7.8–12. Admiring poet: Ausonius, *Eclogues* 24.15–17 ed. Green. Learned men: Seneca, *Letters* 90.32. Earthquakes: Pliny the Elder, *Natural History* 2.197. Attractions of city life: Horace, *Letters* 1.14.21. St. Augustine: *Confessions* 2.6.14; on his youthful carnality, see Book 2 as a whole.

METALLUM: MINE; METAL

Gold is more useful before it is excavated from the metalla because after being dug up it provides reasons for greed and crime.

(Porphyrio, Commentary on Horace, *Odes* 3.3.49–50)

Now we shall discuss metalla and the actual resources which are used to pay for things. These are carefully sought within the earth in a multitude of ways, in as much as in some places the goal of excavation is wealth, people seeking gold, silver, electrum, bronze; in other places the purpose is luxury of gems and pigments; elsewhere rashness demands iron, which in the midst of war and slaughter is even more pleasing than gold.

(Pliny the Elder, *Natural History* 33.1)

But after the bronze generation was given to earth, no longer did the buried seeds of virtue resist vice; and when the metallum of the sword was invented the mind rejoiced, and the ox, accustomed only to the plow, now polluted the dinner table.

(Germanicus, *Aratea* 133–136)

We live in the ninth age, an era even worse than the times of iron, for whose criminality nature herself has yet to find a name or assign a metallum.

(Juvenal, *Satires* 13.28–30)

It is with your people [viz. non-Christian criminals] that the prisons swarm, with your people's sighs the metalla resound, on your people do the beasts [in the arena] feed, and from your people come the flocks of criminals kept by those who put on gladiatorial games. There is no Christian there, unless he is there solely because he is a Christian.

(Tertullian, *Apology* 44)

metallum Mining seems always to have attracted its own colorful vocabulary. In English we have such terms as *winze* (the vertical passage between levels in an underground mine), *stope* (a large underground room or area where ore has been mined out), *sourdough* (an experienced miner), and *grubstake* (to supply a prospector with food and gear in return for a share of his findings). Some mining terms have made it into common use. "Peter out," though its ultimate origin is unclear, is first attested in mining slang of the eighteenth century, referring to the dissipation of a mineral deposit. No Roman sourdough required a grubstake, since in most cases the workers were slaves or prisoners, the supervisors imperial employees or contractors. A lead sow (another fine mining term, for a large bar of raw metal from the smelting furnace), stamped with the name of the emperor and the mine, attests to imperial supervision: "[Property of] Imperator Caesar Hadrianus Augustus. From the mines at Lutudarum."

Latin mining vocabulary was exotic by classical standards. It was one of the few spheres in which Latin was relatively open to borrowings from languages other than Greek. In Spain, the site of the most important Roman gold and silver mines, the Romans encountered and took over mining operations already hundreds of years old, and in the process of using, presumably, native expertise, they admitted Iberian terms. Gold nuggets, for example, went by the strange (to Latin ears) names *palaga* or *palacurna*, and gold dust was *balux*. When prospectors went looking for deposits, they searched for *segutilum*, a surface earth that indicated the presence of gold below, or better yet *talutium*, surface gold that indicated more below. Neither word has any known Latin root or relatives. The digging of shafts through hard rock, when necessary, was done with crushing machines fitted with 150-pound iron heads and called by the unusual but Latin-ish term *fractariae* ("smashers"). A certain kind of earth made of a clay and gravel mix was supposedly even harder to dig through than rock and was called *gangardia*. Washing the raw ore was a crucial part of the process, and here Roman water-moving technology conferred a decisive advantage over earlier attempts to exploit the Spanish mines. Systems of special channels (*corrugi*) and cisterns allowed them to create high-pressure deluges. Another Iberian loan-word designated the mud and clay liable to pollute the watercourses: *urium*. The slag that still provides visible evidence of the activity of Roman miners was called *scoria* or *scaurea*, a word ultimately based on an old Indo-European root meaning "dung."

None of these barbarous terms was destined to issue from the stylus of a Cicero or a Vergil. The purist literary tradition discriminated against such words rigorously, and most of them occur in surviving written Latin only once, in a description of gold mining techniques in Pliny's *Natural History*. They give a glimpse, however, of the kind of linguistic mixing that must have gone on wherever Roman and pre-Roman cultures interacted in a work environment. Greek loan words like *metallum*, by contrast, had an excellent pedigree and were welcomed by educated writers. The Greek verb *metallan* means to inquire or search after, and *metalleia* is the search for metals and the like—in other words, mining. The Latin *metallum* is closer to its Greek ancestor than to our "metal." It refers primarily to a mine or quarry; then to anything dug out of the earth. This is why Pliny's long discussion of *metalla* in his *Natural History* includes items like marble, gemstones, and pigmented earths used in painting, as well as gold, silver, and copper.

The idea that the history of human kind could be divided into ages corresponding to metals of decreasing value and increasing lethality goes back to early Greek thought.

It is also attributed by some Roman authors to the esteemed but mysterious prophecies of the Sibyl. In the "golden" age, said the myth, all was primitive virtue, harmony, and peace. The golden age also had no technology: no sailing, no agriculture. The silver age inaugurated moral degeneration along with technological progress. "I shall hand over your generations," says the virgin goddess Justice in one Roman version, "to indomitable technology [*artes*] and bloody crime." In this age the seasons began, along with the necessity for agriculture and housing. The Bronze Age dimly recalls a real milestone in human development, the invention of bronze tools and weapons (ca. 2000 BC in Italy). In the myth it is another stage in the retreat of justice, with people more ready to resort to force, though not yet wholly wicked. The age of iron also preserves a memory of a real advance in metallurgy (ca. 1000 BC); it brings animal sacrifice, meat eating, and all kinds of wickedness: war, murder, sailing, private property, and moreover, mining. "They entered the guts of the earth," says Ovid, and brought up "the incitements to evil."

Pliny calls gold a "plague on the human race" and silver "the second insanity." The inclusion of private property and sailing in the catalogue of ills is not so much proto-communism or hydrophobia as a sign of the real target of the metal myth: greed. Mining and shipping, like war, are examples of the dangerous lengths to which man is pushed by the cursed love of possessions (*amor habendi*). Pliny's discussion of the technological innovations associated with metals is punctuated frequently by expressions of disapproval, on account of the danger of mining, the violence done to the earth, and above all the *luxuria* of their use in society. While apparently a simple antitechnology parable, then, the myth of metals is actually a more complex moral and social critique. It was attractive to the likes of Pliny, in whose mind the wicked pursuit of luxury, the violent disruption of nature in the quest for raw materials, the fashioning of weapons, and the frenzied lust for war are all of a piece and all center around the concept of *metallum*.

Early Christian authors knew *metallum* primarily as a punishment. Being sent to the mines (*ad metallum*), though a sure death sentence in the end, is treated in the late law codes and other sources as a comparatively mild punishment. It is, perhaps, when compared to being thrown to the beasts (*ad bestias*) or burned alive (*cremptio*), which are some of the other punishments inflicted on heinous and low-status criminals like brigands and pirates, and, in some episodes of persecution in the second, third, and early fourth centuries, on Christians as well.

TLL 8.870–875. K. D. White, *Greek and Roman Technology* (Ithaca, NY: Cornell University Press, 1984) 113–126. On the text of Pliny the Elder, *Natural History* 33.1 see *Classical Quarterly* 38 (1988) 206. English mining terms: The Western Museum of Mining and Industry, Colorado Springs, www.wmmi.org. Lead sow: *Roman Inscriptions in Britain* 2404.39. Gold mining techniques in Pliny's *Natural History*: 33.66–77. Technology and crime: Germanicus, *Aratea* 129–130. Incitements to evil: Ovid, *Metamorphoses* 1.138–140. Plague on the human race: Pliny the Elder, *Natural History* 33.2, 33.95.

DEBAUCHERY

luxuria
taberna
cena
amor
corona
crocus or crocum
acroama

LUXURIA: EXTRAVAGANCE, SELF-INDULGENCE

I declare that [vomiting] ought not to be induced for the sake of luxuria; but I believe that it is occasionally appropriate for reasons of health.

(Celsus, *On Medicine* 1.3.21)

Conception is made more difficult in the case of the male when he is weakened by his own luxuria in frequent sexual activity.

(Soranus, *Gynecology* p. 75.17 ed. Rose)

[Sempronia] was learned in Greek and Latin literature, could play the cithara and dance better than is necessary for a respectable woman, and many other things which are the equipment of luxuria.

(Sallust, referring to an aristocratic lady of the first century BC, *The War with Catiline* 25.2)

Then, from the western part of the world came their enemy, Luxuria, who had long since lost her reputation and ceased to care that she had lost it, her hair thickly smeared (with perfumed oil), eyes wandering, voice feeble, wasted by self-indulgence (deliciis); her only reason for living was pleasure, to soften her enervated mind, to wantonly drink in alluring delights and to undo her enfeebled understanding. She was still woozy and belching after an all-night banquet, reclining by chance at the table when at dawn she heard the blaring war trumpets ....

(Prudentius, describing the allegorical representation of Luxury as she prepares to do battle with the personified virtues, *Psychomachia* 310–318)

Luxuria is a revolt against nature. (A natura luxuria descivit.)

(Seneca, *Letters* 90.19)

luxuria In plants, *luxuria* is overgrowth, abundance that needs to be pruned away. "A grapevine of rank growth [*luxuriosa*], unless it is checked in its fruit, casts its blossoms badly and runs to wood and foliage," becoming unproductive, says a farming manual. By extension, this agricultural imperative applies to human beings, whose behavior is "luxurious" if it is unruly, willful, licentious, and heedless of moral restraints. When behavior insolently exceeds normal limits and enters the realm of *luxuria*, it expresses this immoderate flowering in three main realms: the consuming of delicious, very expensive food; the building of houses of exquisite materials such as colored marbles and precious metals; and having lots of sex (non-marital, of course).

    Luxuria thus takes in a much wider field than the English "luxury." While it includes elegant dining, homes, and transportation, these are not *luxuria* itself but the *instrumenta* or *apparatus luxuriae*, the "equipment" or "tools" of luxury. The immoral but talented Sempronia had in her toolkit of *luxuria* the ability to dance, play music, and discuss Greek poetry, according to the remark of Sallust quoted above. True *luxuria* is a state of mind and an attitude that combines material extravagance with moral self-indulgence and sensuality. It is always excessive. *Luxuria* has none of the positive associations of luxury, which can be a reward for hard work; luxury cars and luxury homes are the very goals of the American dream. *Luxuria* is decadent, debauched and depraved, unnatural and perverse—in short, all of the things that popular opinion associates most closely with ancient Rome.

Tales of Caligula and Nero have, since the early seventeenth century, made imperial Rome into the benchmark of gluttony and extravagance, a pristine model of decadence against which modern empires judge their own morals. Often-repeated stories culled from the more salacious historians—about baths in asses' milk, gold and silver mules' shoes, drinks into which costly pearls were dissolved, and meals of peacock brains and flamingo tongue—have conveyed the idea that the entirety of the Roman empire wallowed in a luxury that was fabulous, unparalleled, immoral, and senseless. But Caligula and Nero were special cases, of course, singled out exactly for their abnormality. These emperors had a mania to inspire the world with the idea of their omnipotence and to demonstrate the immeasurable gulf between the emperor and the common man. The next dynasty to establish itself after the death of Nero, the Flavians, declared their rejection of Neronian *luxuria*, and made it into a political slogan that earned them hearty approval. Their signature gesture was to replace Nero's massive pleasure villa in the center of Rome, the Golden House, with an amphitheater for public entertainment. At first called the "Flavian Amphitheater," it was later dubbed the "Colosseum," after a colossal statue nearby, a golden image of Nero, whose head was discretely replaced by that of the sun god. The success of this move vindicates the often-quoted dictum of Cicero: "The Roman people hates private luxury, but it loves public magnificence."

To keep Roman luxury in perspective, it is essential to keep in mind the exact nature of the behavior that earns the hated name of *luxuria*. Elaborate wall decoration of the Pompeian type is a prime target. Cooling one's drinks with snow, dining in an art gallery, using feather-stuffed cushions, gilding a ceiling coffer, wearing pearl jewelry and sheer clothing—all these were blasted as immoral, unnatural extravagance, the handmaidens of military weakness in men and of wanton promiscuity in women. Prudentius's description of *Luxuria* quoted above speaks with horror of the wearing of perfume, the drinking of wine, and the holding of long feasts. His description of the mental and physical effects of *luxuria* conjures men wasted and enfeebled by self-indulgence, mentally addled by their addiction to the pleasures of fine dining and flower-strewn bedrooms. Prudentius sees the ill effects of *luxuria* in the wandering eyes, weak voices, and supine posture of these dining dope fiends. Since luxury is so attractive, however, he imagines the troops of virtue being temporarily swayed, as "her alluring breath blows a subtle poison that weakens their limbs." This kind of shrill rhetoric is very common in Latin literature, Christian and pagan. So, in a way, if the Romans have a reputation for extraordinary decadence, they have no one to blame but their own puritanical moralists.

TLL 7.1919–1925. Andrew Wallace-Hadrill, *Houses and Society in Pompeii and Herculaneum* (Princeton, NJ: Princeton University Press, 1994) 143–174. L. Friedländer, *Roman Life and Manners Under the Early Empire*, trans. J. H. Freese and L. A. Magnus, vol. 2 (repr. New York: Barnes and Noble, 1965, orig. 1908) 131–230. A farming manual: Columella, *On Agriculture* 4.21.2. Dictum of Cicero: *Pro Murena* 76. Her alluring breath: Prudentius, *Psychomachia* 328-329.

TABERNA: RETAIL SHOP, BAR, INN, TAVERN

Obviously there is no such thing as a virgin working in a taberna, an adulterer-monk, or an innkeeper-priest.
(Jerome, *Against Helvidius on the Perpetual Virginity of Mary* 21)

As for the crowd of the poor and the dregs of society, some spend all night in bars [tabernis vinariis], others congregate under the shadow of theater awnings . . . and others fight fiercely at dice, all the while making a disgusting noise as the breath is sucked back in through their noses with a rough snort.
(Ammianus Marcellinus, *The Later Roman Empire* 14.6.25)

Men lounge in the doorways of the tabernae who lack tunics and even money for the following day. Yet they pass judgment on emperors and magistrates, and in fact to themselves they seem to be kings and generals. Drunkenness makes them rich, when in fact they are penniless; they give away gold and pass out cash to the people.
(Ambrose, *On Elias and Fasting* 42)

[Lucius Verus] was such a great rival of the vices of Caligula, Nero, and Vitellius that he wandered around at night through the tabernae and brothels, his head covered with a common traveler's cloak, drinking with con men, getting into fist fights, concealing his identity, and they say he often returned with bruises on his face.
(SHA, *Lucius Verus* 4.6)

taberna At Pompeii, inns were clustered around the city gates and bistros were scattered throughout the city with an almost Parisian lavishness. No such archaeological evidence is available for Rome, but the poet Martial, writing in the first century AD, says that Rome was "a giant *taberna*"—at least until an imperial edict, of which he heartily approves, made the tavern keepers, proprietors of cookshops, barbers, butchers, etc. get their businesses to stop spilling onto the sidewalks so people could pass without tracking through the muck in the streets. As Martial's comment suggests, *taberna* was a blanket word covering establishments of all types of service industries. Only in the Middle Ages did the meaning specialize and become restricted to a house for the sale of drink, the meaning of the English *tavern*, Italian *taverna*, German *taverne*, and Spanish *taberna*. In ancient Rome of various periods we hear of a *taberna casearia* (cheese shop/factory), *libraria* (book shop/production facility), *coactiliaria* (where felt was made and sold) *carbonaria* (charcoal shop), *vinaria* (for wine), *unguentaria* (for unguents and perfumed oils), *coriaria* (leather shop), and many others.

Rome was a city of shops, its people a nation of shopkeepers, and this implies not just retail but thousands of small-scale manufacturing operations and artisan workshops, all of which might be called *tabernae*. An inn, on the other hand, was a *taberna diversoria* or *meritoria*. The lines between this kind of establishment and the cook shop/bar (*popina, caupona* or *taberna cauponaria*) and the brothel (*lupanaria* or *taberna famosa*) were quite indistinct. At any given inn or cook shop the girl serving your wine was likely to be available for other services. Hence the implausibility of finding a virgin in a *taberna*, according to Jerome.

In Latin all these various realms—retail shop, artisan workshop, hotel, and tavern—were grouped under the notion of *taberna*, unlike in Greek where separate words designated an inn (*pandokeion*), workshop (*ergasterion*), and retail shop/tavern (*kapeleion*). But the ambiguity of the Latin word reflects a certain perceived unity. The world of the *tabernae* comprised a distinct Roman subculture characterized by leisure (*otium*) and the indulgence of all sorts of appetites, for wine, food, sex, gambling, and material comforts. As such it is something of an antithesis to the more familiar Roman public sphere that demanded work (*negotium*), self-denial, and state service and took a dim view of inactivity, luxury, fine food, and merely self-interested commerce.

The *taberna* world was also the scene of social mixing of slaves, freedmen, and the lower-class free to an extent that is not clear. The scene usually painted of the bar/restaurant *tabernae* involves male patrons of humble or freed status, drinking heavily in the company of a *meretrix*, "harlot," a relatively sophisticated woman of the demi-monde who could be relied on for sassy, racy conversation, and possibly also would provide music for dancing. The language of the *taberna* was rough and obscene. *Tabernariae blanditiae* were bar pick-up lines, to be contrasted with the sophisticated wooing of love poetry (*versus amatorii*). A certain courtier of Nero who had grown up in and around *tabernae* was known for his dirty jokes. Horace says that his country-bound farm supervisor, a freedman, longed for "whore houses and greasy spoons (*fornix . . . et uncta popina*) . . . and a neighborhood *taberna* to provide you with wine, and a flute-playing *meretrix* at whose noisy music you can dance and do the stomp." Food, consumer goods, wine, women, and dancing in a milieu hospitable to all sorts—these were the pleasant, carnal associations of the *taberna*.

RE 2nd ser., 4.1863–1872. Martial: *Epigrams* 7.61. Courtier of Nero: Vatinius, according to Tacitus, *Annals* 15.34.2. Horace: *Letters* 1.12.21-26.

CENA: DINNER OR BANQUET, TRADITIONALLY HELD IN THE EARLY EVENING AFTER A VISIT TO THE BATHS

An egg is the beginning of the cena, served
as an hors d'oeuvre as soon as people walk
in from the baths.

(Porphyrio, Commentary on Horace,
Satires 1.3.6–7)

Why isn't the same cena given to me
as to you? You dine on oysters bred
in the Lucrine lake, while I chew and
suck on a mussel.

(Martial, *Epigrams* 3.60)

What? Did not the dictator Caesar also distribute jugs of
Falernian wine and casks of Chian wine among the diners
at the cena held in celebration of his triumph?

(Pliny the Elder, *Natural History* 14.97.2)

Resolved, that every August 11, the anniversary of the reign of
Hadrian Augustus, a proper banquet [cena recta] shall be given.

(From the bylaws of a guild of ivory and citron-wood workers in Rome,
second century AD, *ILS* 7214.17–18)

Being in on all of Nero's plans and secrets, on the day which
Nero had set for killing his mother Otho gave a cena of the
most exquisite sociability [exquisitissimae comitatis] and
charm for both of them, in order to avert suspicion.

(Suetonius, *Otho* 3.1)

I'm trying to score a cena at your
house, Maximus; I'm ashamed, but
I'm still trying.

(Martial, *Epigrams* 2.18.1)

cena Ancient Rome had no fine restaurants, so special dinners were either served at home for invited guests, shared by members of a tradesmen's guild (*collegium*) or a board of priests, or else given to the public by the state on special occasions. Since it was the main form of domestic entertainment, the *cena* developed a certain amount of ceremony: an egg was traditional to start, an apple at the end, for example. But it was always a time for relaxation. Neither togas nor shoes were worn. Still, manners were important. The bandits and brigands in Apuleius's novel the *Metamorphoses*, for example, dine without refinement (*incondite*): they grab from great piles of meat and bread, chugalug from huge goblets of wine, make loud jokes, sing at the top of their voices, and hurl joking insults. A true Roman *cena* is more civilized and leisurely, with witty and interesting conversation. Like the one that Otho gave for Nero and his mother the day before she was murdered, it must have *comitas*—good taste, elegance, graciousness, and friendliness.

Hangers-on, or "parasites" (*parasiti*), and witty men-about-town (*scurrae*) idled in the forum trying to land an invitation (*cenam captare*), and if invited they were expected to be clever and entertaining. The cruder hosts had a habit of serving such second-tier guests inferior food—a practice taken to absurd extremes by the unstable emperor Elegabalus. The *cenae* of all emperors were naturally a subject of intense interest. Bad emperors dined in the middle of the night on outrageous delicacies and humiliated their guests. Good ones ate moderately and showed their guests, of whatever status, a good time. Unlike the Greeks, the Roman sexes dined together, so it was also a place at which love might spark.

TLL 3.775-780. Apuleius: *Metamorphoses* 4.8.

AMOR: LOVE, PASSION; LOVE AFFAIR

> May amor burn him in deserted mountains.
> (Graffito from Pompeii, *CIL* 4.1645 = *CLE* 953)

Amor cannot be tortured out of
a person, but it can slip out.
(Publilius Syrus, *Sententiae* A 18)

> Unfortunate Dido drank in long draughts of amor.
> (Vergil, *Aeneid* 1.749)

An old amor pinches like a crab.
(Petronius, Satyricon 42)

> The minute the lover [qui amat] is struck by the
> arrow-like kisses of the one he adores, then without
> delay his money begins to slip and drip away.
> (Plautus, *Trinummus* 242–244)

When someone is dying of amor he kisses even the moles [on the beloved's cheek].
(Ut quisque amore quempiam deperit, eius etiam naevolos saviatur.)
(Proverb quoted by Fronto, *Letters* 2.42 ed. Haines)

> You produce evidence of no disgraceful parties, no amor,
> no reveling, no lust, no extravagant expenses.
> (Cicero, *Pro Murena* 13)

So now even slaves carry on love affairs [amant] here?
(Plautus, *Persa* 25)

amor In English one falls in or out of love or is smitten with it, it comes to town, it stinks, it is blind. In Latin one drinks it (like a poison), is wounded by it, struck with it like a weapon; it is a sickness or a disease, it snares or captures, flares up, tortures, bites the heart like a crab; one deserts it, puts it down, it slips out, one is "dying" from it. On the one hand, as these images suggest, *amor* was a domineering force. This aspect of love the Romans symbolized by the august goddess Venus. On the other, it was a pleasant luxury, an alluring diversion from the business of life. This aspect finds expression in Venus's mischievous son Cupid. In this guise *amor* was thought of as a traditional part of a well-to-do young man's life, frowned on by his elders, mainly because of the expense. Mistresses, parties, fine food, and musicians all cost money, and comic writers like Plautus loved to show young lovers outwitting their more frugal elders. Cicero, in the passage quoted above, defends his client Murena from the slander that he is a *saltator* ("dancer"): sane people only dance at the end of long and raucous parties, he argues, and the prosecution has shown none of that. No *amor*, no expensive parties, therefore no dancing: it was all a package. As an aristocratic pastime, *amor* is thus laughable among slaves: where would they get the money and the time? In Latin *amor* also has little or nothing to do with marriage. Inherently violent, unstable, and even poisonous, and harmful as well to the family fortune that marriage was meant in part to protect, *amor* would be out of place in that context.

TLL 1.1967–1973. R. O. A. M. Lyne, "Traditional Attitudes to Love, the Moral and Social Background," in *The Latin Love Poets: From Catullus to Horace* (Oxford: Oxford University Press, 1980) 1–18.

CORONA: A WREATH OR GARLAND WORN ON THE HEAD AS A TOKEN OF CELEBRATION OR VICTORY

Boy, bring me fragrant oil, and
coronae, and a cask of wine that dates
back to the Marsian War.
> (From a poem celebrating Augustus's
> victorious return from his Spanish war,
> 26–25 BC, Horace, *Odes* 3.14.17–18)

Why, Polla, do you send me a gift of
coronae that are fresh? I would rather
have roses you have worn and crushed.
> (Martial, *Epigrams* 11.89)

The legions placed a corona of grass on Decius, to signify
his rescuing them from a siege, and accompanied the gift
with their cheers .... Adorned with these insignia he
sacrificed a choice ox to Mars.
> (Livy, *Roman History* 7.37.2–3)

I would rather that the people wear coronae while giving thanks to the
gods of their own free will after a military success, than that they wear
wreaths on sale at the slave market after a military failure. [War captives
were traditionally sold into slavery *sub corona,* "wearing wreaths."]
> (Cato the Elder, *On Military Science* p.80 ed. Jordon)

Vincent, blessed martyr, make propitious the day of your triumph,
on which you receive a corona as the reward for your blood. This
day defeated the torturer and the judge, carried you out of this
world's darkness and delivered you in triumph to Christ. [The
Spanish martyr St. Vincent suffered in the persecutions of the early
fourth century.]
> (Prudentius, *Crowns of Martyrdom* 5.1–8)

Q.: Why do the dead wear coronae?
A.: To show that they have completed the contest of life.
> (From the anonymous *Dialogue of
> Hadrian and Epictetus* 25)

corona Flower wreaths—usually roses or myrtle—were put to dozens of uses by the ancient Romans. Supplying them was a reliable and profitable business. They were worn on the head by revelers at parties, by people in general at public celebrations like the triumph, and by victorious athletes or poets. They were held out by priests at temples, draped over cult statues, put on the door to announce the birth of a child, or put on an altar to celebrate a birthday. Any happy occasion was good enough excuse to take a bath, anoint the hair with a good-smelling oil, and put on a *corona*. The wearer of a *corona* was as likely as not to be drunk; Horace, who enjoyed a good drinking party, tells the story about a certain young man, out early after an all-night carouse, furtively slipping off his *corona* after running into a stern teacher unexpectedly.

Soldiers received various kinds of *coronae* (though not the kind made of flowers) as rewards. The *corona civica*, made of oak leaves, went to a citizen who had saved another citizen's life; the *corona obsidialis*, made of grass, was given to a commander who raised a siege (as with Decius in the passage quoted above); the *corona muralis* went to the man who first made it over the walls of an enemy city; the *corona castrensis* to the first to breach an enemy camp; and the *corona navalis* to the first armed man to board an enemy ship. The last three mentioned were made of gold, as was the greatest of all military decorations, the *corona triumphalis*, worn by the triumphing general.

It was the Roman soldiers who gave Jesus his *corona* of thorns, mocking his "triumph" in crucifixion. Early Christian authors adopted the symbolism of the *corona* but characteristically inverted it to serve their own purposes, so that his crucifixion was indeed depicted as his triumph. The Christian poet Prudentius wrote a whole book of poems on the "crownings" of the martyrs—that is, their victories in the midst of torture and death.

This grim symbolism came later, however. The primary meaning of the *corona* in pagan Latin was that of private indulgence and festive celebration. It is easy to forget, as well, the importance of the scents of perfumed oils and unguents in the Roman experience of *luxuria*. *Coronae* were part of this. The ode of Horace quoted above is typical on coupling the *corona* with fragrant oil or unguents, which would be worn on the hair and whose scent would mix with that of the flowers. That poem celebrates Augustus's successful return from battling with rebellious Spanish tribes, so it would be fair to say that for Horace, as for the Romans in general, the *corona* of flowers smelled like victory.

TLL 4.977–988. Horace: *Satires* 2.3.256–257.

CROCUS or CROCUM: A SAFFRON PERFUME MUCH LOVED BY THE ROMANS

The scent of an apple as a young girl bites it, the fragrance that comes from Corycian crocus *... the smell of fire pale with Eastern incense, of turf sprinkled lightly with summer rain, of a garland that has lain on hair wet with nard—this, Diadumenus, is the perfume of your kisses, cruel boy. What if you were to give them in their full-ness, unstintingly?* [The Corycian cave, really a crater in what is now southwestern Turkey, was a famous source of saffron.]

(Martial, *Epigrams* 3.65)

Like crocus, *sleep projects its fragrance from a distance and delights us from afar before it is near.*

(Fronto, *Letters* 1.96 ed. Haines)

And he ordered that crocum *be made to flow down over the steps of the theater.*

(SHA, *Hadrian* 19.6)

Today, whom do you think is wiser, the man who discovers how to shoot crocum *to an immense height through concealed pipes ... or the philosopher who demonstrates to himself and to others that nature's commands are neither harsh nor difficult?*

(Seneca, *Letters* 90.15)

The rewards for pious souls [in heaven] are fine scents, myrrh, aloe, and crocum, *whose scents waft in pleasant gardens and dispel the stench of sin.*

(Ambrose, *On Isaac* 5.48)

crocus or *crocum* The pleasures of perfumes—scented oils, unguents, incense—were not associated more strongly with one sex or the other. Some moralists disapproved of exotic unguents because they were expensive, imported luxuries, but both Roman men and women enjoyed them. The future emperor Otho is said to have schooled Nero in the art of perfuming the soles of the feet. "The practice of [pagan] cult stops without incense," says an early Christian writer, with only slight exaggeration. The religious use of unguents and incense attempted to reproduce the scent of the gods, while also communicating with them in the form of a burnt offering that would waft their way. Myrrh, cassia, balsam, frankincense, and nard were big business, and *unguentarii* and incense traders were important members of the Roman aristocracy.

In the atmosphere of private luxury, the most sensual odor was that of saffron. Celebrated by poets, sprayed in clouds over the theater and in temples, saffron delighted the Romans possibly more than any other scent. The self-indulgent emperor Elagabalus liked to swim in a pool scented with it, and the poet Martial, quoted above, compares it to the fragrance of his lover's kisses. This erotic herb had numerous medical uses as well and was also used in food, as it is today. And it was a natural candidate to be one of the scents that Christian writers included among the rewards of the righteous in heaven.

TLL 4.1215–1216. David S. Potter, "Odor and Power in the Roman Empire," in J. I. Porter, ed., *Construction of the Classical Body* (Ann Arbor: University of Michigan Press, 1999) 169–189. The soles of Nero's feet: Pliny the Elder, *Natural History* 13.22. The practice of cult stops: Arnobius, *Against the Pagans* 7.26. Elegabalus: *SHA, Elegabalus* 19.9.

ACROAMA: AN AFTER-DINNER ENTERTAINMENT OR ENTERTAINER

[The emperor Elagabalus] gave his male and female midgets, fools, singing male prostitutes, and all the acroamata and pantomime actors as a gift to the people; but he asked that those who were not of any use be assigned to individual cities for support, so the people would not be annoyed by the sight of them begging.

(SHA, Severus Alexander 34.2)

No one at his dinner parties heard any other acroama but a reader, which I personally think is the most pleasant of all. . . . The guests' minds were delighted no less than their bellies.

(Cornelius Nepos, Atticus 14.1)

He used to include either acroamata or actors, or even strolling players from the circus, and especially story-tellers [aretalogi].

(Suetonius, Augustus 74)

Trimalchio's two favorite spectacles in the whole world were acrobats and trumpeters. Other acroamata he considered mere trifles.

(Petronius, Satyricon 53)

acroama Wealthy Roman families supported a wide variety of actors, comedians, fools, witty dwarves, professional reciters of poetry, singers, and other entertainers. They performed at dinner parties, working either for tips or on the permanent staff as slaves. An *acroama* (which is a Greek word meaning any aural entertainment) was a standard element of any really good *cena* ("dinner party"). The highly cultured Atticus stuck to poetry recitations, but the emperor Augustus, known for his love of popular entertainment, brought in circus performers and *aretalogi,* tellers of fairy tales and miraculous stories about the gods. The summit of bad taste is the boorish Trimalchio in Petronius's novel the *Satyricon,* who likes only acrobats and trumpeters.

TLL 1.433.

SLAVERY

ingenuus
felix
ergastulum
cucullus
tortor

INGENUUS: NATIVE; FREEBORN; TYPICAL OF A FREEBORN PERSON, GENTLEMANLY, HONORABLE

But this hideous monster, who can endure him, or how? What is there in Antony but lust, cruelty, insolence, audacity? He is entirely a composite of these vices. Nothing in him is ingenuus, nothing moderate, there is no self-respect, no shame.

(Cicero, *Philippics* 3.28)

A man of honorable candor [ingenua veritas] admits his own ignorance.

(Aulus Gellius, *Attic Nights* 20.2.2)

The rose opens in spring, suffused with ingenuus blush on her virgin cheeks, and offers homage due in the temples of the gods.

(Columella, in a poetic section of his treatise *On Agriculture* 10.260–262)

My palate, Marcus, is just as ingenuus as yours.

(Martial to a rude host who served his guests inferior food, *Epigrams* 6.11.5–6) *ingenuus* Etymologically, *ingenuus* seems to be related to the past tense stem of the verb *gigno*, "to beget," and to mean "inborn" or "natural." The vapors at the resort of Baiae, for example, are called *ingenui*, "naturally occurring." But much more commonly it applies to people and means "freeborn." As the law codes define it, "the *ingenui* are those who were born from a free mother." If your mother is free, you are *ingenuus*, whatever the status of your father was.

When used not as a legal term but to describe people's actions, however, *ingenuus* outlined a loose code of conduct considered suitable for a free person, the violation of which made a person "slavish." Thus *ingenuus* comes to mean not just freeborn, but modest, possessing the sense of shame (*pudor*) appropriate for a freeborn person. It can also mean "honest": *ingenua veritas* is freeborn candor, and this is the meaning that has survived in the English derivative *ingenuous*—that is, honorably open, frank, and candid. Cicero says that it is more typical of an *ingenuus* to hate openly rather than keep his true opinion hidden. The *ingenuae artes* were the subjects considered suitable for a freeborn person, like grammar, geometry, rhetoric, and music. *Ingenuus* can mean handsome or beautiful, especially when applied to a woman's cheeks. It means "tender" as well. Ovid complains about sleeping outside his mistress's door, placing his *ingenuum corpus* on the hard ground. Finally *ingenuus* connotes an unwillingness to put up with harsh or insulting treatment, a lack of *patientia*. Thus the range of meanings for the word *ingenuus* gives us a kind of portrait of the ideal freeborn person as the Romans imagined him or her: modest, well-educated, sincere and candid, good-looking, tender, and proud. Conversely, the same word can yield a kind of photographic negative that suggests how slaves were viewed by the free: shameless, uneducated, ugly, physically tough and strong, and willing to take abuse. This impression is well backed up by other aspects of the written evidence.

Often *ingenuus*—and *liber* as well—is applied to certain personality traits and features. One has freeborn eyes, a freeborn face, hands, body, freeborn modesty, or a freeborn mind (*animus*). Interestingly, however, these words are rarely if ever applied to the blood. This is especially surprising given that the word *ingenuus* etymologically means "inborn." Though freedom could be inherited, it could also be achieved, and the Romans consistently see slave or free status as a matter of fortune, not inborn character, race, or nationality. If you were a slave, that was just your hard luck. The elder Seneca typifies this view. "No one is born free," he says, "and no one is born a slave; fortune coming after has placed these titles on each of us."

TLL 7.1543–1548. Keith Bradley, *Slavery and Society at Rome* (Cambridge: Cambridge University Press, 1994). Law codes: Marcian, in Justinian's *Digest of Roman Law* 1.5.5.2. Cicero: *On Friendship* 65. Ovid: *Amores* 3.11a.9–10. No one is born free: Seneca the Elder, *Controversiae* 7.6.18.

FELIX: FRUITFUL, PRODUCTIVE; BRINGING GOOD LUCK, LUCKY; FORTUNATE, SUCCESSFUL

[Here lies] Felix, freedman of Publius Clodius Pulcher. He was always pleasing to his own people. Athenais, freedwoman of Clodius Pulcher [set up the monument].
(An epitaph from Rome, first century BC, *CIL* 6.15735)

To the Di Manes of Felix, slave, a German by race. He lived 45 years. His fellow-slave Severus made [the monument] for one well deserving.
(From Rome, *CIL* 6.17861. On the *Di Manes*, see pages 234–235)

It is found in the official records that at the funeral of Felix, a charioteer of the Red team, one of his fans threw himself on the pyre.
(Pliny the Elder, *Natural History* 7.186)

felix A Finnish scholar has made a comprehensive collection of the names of slaves recorded in epitaphs, like those quoted above, from the city of Rome. The evidence starts in Republican times, when the inscriptional material begins to be available, and ends in late antiquity; in Christian epitaphs, designating the status of the deceased was no longer felt to be essential. Of the sample of approximately eight thousand known Roman slaves recorded with Latin names, by far the most common single name is "Lucky"—i.e., Felix. With its derivatives Felicissimus, Felicio, Felicitas and the like, it makes up approximately 8.3 percent of the total, 15.4 percent if we include the near-synonyms Faustus or Fausta ("fortunate") and Fortunatus or Fortunata. Add to that the fact that the single most common Greek slave name preserved in the same body of Roman evidence is Eutyches ("Lucky" again), and we get an interesting glimpse of the lack of empathy on the part of Roman masters. A slave, lucky? More of a misnomer it would be hard to imagine.

Of course it may be that this name was not used in the same way for slaves as it was for gladiators and charioteers, who often took the name Felix, or for free individuals, such as the famously fortunate General Sulla, who also took Felix as a cognomen. It might, in the case of slaves, mean not "fortunate," but "bringing luck"—i.e., to the master. In its most basic sense *felix* connotes agricultural fertility and prosperity. One can refer to fields and trees as *felix*—that is, fruitful or fertile. If so, it would jibe with the wide popularity of slave names such as Cerdus ("Profit"), Auctus ("Enriched"), Philargyrus ("Fond of Money") Victor ("Winner") and Nicephor ("Victory Bringer").

On the other hand, many popular slave names can be called "wish names" and seem to express the hopes of the owner for what the slave might be like: Hilaris ("Happy"), Fidus ("Trusty"), Vitalis ("Healthy"), Celer ("Swifty"). All of these names should probably be seen as words of good omen, intended to be auspicious when spoken aloud. But they carry a certain irony, especially given the Roman belief that slavery itself was not a matter of racial destiny but simply the worst kind of luck a person could have.

Another huge category of names is composed of Greek words. In fact, names derived from Greek outnumber Latin-based names in the evidence from the city of Rome by a factor of more than two to one. In American slavery it was typical for names to be given based on the place from which slaves were imported. The same principle could be at work in the Roman world, since major slave trading depots were located in Greece, at Delos, for example.

Yet the evidence for these names is largely inscriptions of imperial date, when few slaves were actually coming from Greek-speaking parts of the world, so the overwhelming preponderance of Greek names is still puzzling. One theory holds that the Greek names emphasize the slave's outsider status. These foreign, non-Roman names reinforce the social isolation and marginality of the slave in Roman society. Perhaps, but we need to keep in mind that Greece had also long been known to the Romans as the land of luxury, home of high culture, fine consumer goods, art, tapestries, food, and the good life in general. All of the Latin words for couch, for example, are Greek loan words (*scimpodion, sigma, stibadium, triclinium, reclinatorium*). It was pleasing somehow to see this kind of soft, luxurious stuff as non-Italian, an imported self-indulgence. Greek names for slaves marked slaves as an aspect of luxury and the good life, like fine furniture and art. Besides Eutychus, the most common Greek names for Roman slaves were Eros ("Desire"), Hermes (named after the messenger god), Onesimus ("Useful"), Chresimus ("Useful" again), and Epaphroditus (which could mean "Lovely" or "Favorite of Venus," or "Lucky," another synonym for *felix*).

American slave owners, traders, and shipmasters used a crude humor in drawing on ancient history and mythology for names (Caesar, Hannibal, Cato, Jupiter, Cromwell, Robin Hood). The Romans had anticipated this practice: Alexander was a favorite, as was Antiochus, and we also find Homerus, Draco, Solon, Leonidas, Socrates, Alcibiades, Plato, Attalus, Sulla, and Cleopatra. This could be sheer mockery, but the preponderance of Greek figures again suggests an association of domestic slavery with civilization, luxury, and culture.

Heikki Solin: *Die stadtrömischen Sklavennamen: Ein Namenbuch*, 3 vols. (Stuttgart, Germany: Franz Steiner, 1996). R. M. Miller and J. D. Smith, eds., *Dictionary of American Slavery* (Westport, Connecticut: Greenwood Press, 1988) s.v. names. One theory: Sandra Joshel: *Work, Identity and Legal Status at Rome: A Study of the Occupational Inscriptions* (Norman: University of Oklahoma Press, 1992) 191 n. 9.

ERGASTULUM: SLAVE PRISON AND WORKHOUSE

I do not like the flocks of slaves whose master does not even recognize them, nor the clangor of the ergastula in the spacious countryside.

(Vibius Gallus, from a practice speech indicting wealth, quoted by Seneca the Elder, *Controversiae* 2.1.26)

When we consider also the punishment for the various other crimes—the yoke, burning alive, the culleus, the hooks, and the precipices—who would not rather take the punishment doled out by Pythagoras and Empedocles? For even those who are supposed to be reincarnated as asses and mules, to be punished with servile labor, how pleased they will be when they consider the alternatives: the mines, the ergastula, the public works crews, and even the prisons.

(Tertullian, arguing against the philosophical doctrine of reincarnation into animals as punishment, *On the Soul* 33)

If you must pollute the seats of high office with servile crime, then go, unlock the leg irons and let the consul stride forth, open up the ergastulum and let him don the robes of Romulus.

(From an invective against Eutropius, minister to the emperor Arcadius and the first eunuch ever to become consul, AD 399. Claudian, *Against Eutropius* 1.26–28)

ergastulum The vocabulary and the mental categories of slavery had a pervasive impact on Roman thinking and affected ancient philosophy and religion in important ways. Greco-Roman philosophical ethics laid a heavy emphasis on emotional self-control. The philosopher was to be a rational being, striving to live a life that was well-examined, self-aware, and in accordance with a rational conception of nature. His emotions therefore had to be reasoned, moderate, and appropriate. Any excess of anger, lust, or fear could endanger the mental equilibrium without which a truly good and happy life would be impossible. The more philosophically oriented of Roman writers, such as Cicero, Horace, and Seneca, turned many variations on this theme. All employed the imagery of slavery to make obedience to the passions as shameful as possible.

Seneca puts it succinctly: "No one is free who serves the body" (*Nemo est liber qui corpori servit*). Elsewhere, "To serve oneself is the worst kind of slavery" (*Sibi servire, gavissima est servitus*), and on anger he says, "A man cannot even be called free if he is captive to his anger." The only truly free man is the wise man, he who is subject to no man's authority and slave to no appetite. The moral slavery of the man without self-control is brought across most pointedly in one of Horace's *Satires*, in which he portrays his own slave Davus as talking back to him on the Saturnalia, when slaves were given more freedom to speak. Giving his master a good taste of his own medicine, Davus chastises Horace for not living up to his own philosophical principles. Davus calls his master *fugitivus et erro* ("runaway slave and a vagabond"), because he cannot be alone with himself; he runs from his problems and his responsibilities by sleeping and drinking. This is part of what these philosophers mean: caring only for your own bodily needs and comforts leaves no room for true philosophical reflection and commitment.

The pagan philosophers deployed the language of slavery to shame people into self-mastery. Christian Latin authors, taking their cue from St. Paul as well as from certain passages of the Old Testament, proclaimed their slavery to God as a point of pride, indeed the key to true freedom. Though there are some analogies in the cult of Isis, the Christian emphasis on submission and willing slavery is something new and different from what we find in pagan authors, for whom slavery is always a shameful, degrading thing. At the same time as the believer gloried in his slavery to God, the sinner was thought of as enslaved to sin, or to the flesh, or to lust, and here the Christian authors echo pagan philosophical ideas.

The phrases *servus dei* and *ancilla dei* to refer to believing Christians are very common. We also find variations using other words for slave: *famulus dei, vicarius dei,* etc. The church fathers go further, however, beyond these almost unthinking figures of speech, and expand the symbolic and metaphorical potential of all the trappings of slavery. Take the example of the *ergastulum*. The *ergastulum* was a prison house where slaves worked in gangs, chained. It could be a quarry, or a chain-gang doing field work, but usually it means a rural workshop, above or underground. A farming manual recommends that they be built underground with skylights high enough to be out of reach. They must have been a fairly common sight (and sound, according to Vibius Gallus, quoted above) in rural Italy in ancient times, common enough at any rate to be a source of metaphor in religious thought. Tertullian compares demons to rebellious *ergastula* workers who constantly threaten to break out and attack us. Augustine refers to the pagan gods as jailors who chain us up in wretched *ergastula*. Ambrose says that our souls are constantly straining to escape the *ergastulum* of the flesh.

TLL 5.756–758. William Fitzgerald, *Slavery and the Roman Literary Imagination* (Cambridge: Cambridge University Press, 2000). No one is free who serves the body: Seneca, *Letters* 92.33. To serve oneself: Seneca, *Natural Questions* 3 pref. 17. Captive to his anger: Seneca, *On Anger* 3.4.4. Slave of no appetite: Cicero, *De finibus* 3.75. Vagabond and runaway: Horace, *Satires* 2.7.113. Metaphor in religious thought: Tertullian, *Apology* 27.7; Augustine, *City of God* 12.27; Ambrose, *On the Death of his Brother Satyrus* 2.20.

CUCULLUS or CUCULLA: A ROUGH HOODED JACKET WORN BY SLAVES AND TRAVELERS AND BY ARISTOCRATS IN DISGUISE (LATER, BY MONKS)

[The owner] should keep his slaves groomed and dressed more for utility than for style, and have them carefully protected from wind, cold, and rain. All these can be kept out by animal skins with sleeves, by stitched rag-coats, or by cucullus-coats. If so, no weather is so intolerable that some kind of work cannot be done outside.

(Columella, *On Agriculture* 1.8.9)

When the wife had ascertained that her husband was asleep, this imperial whore dared to don the night-time cucullus, to prefer a mat to her bed in the palace—she used to leave, accompanied by no more than one slave girl.

(Juvenal on Messalina, wife of the emperor Claudius; *Satires* 6.116–119)

They say [the emperor Lucius Verus] used to play dice all night, a vice he had picked up in Syria, and that he used to wander at night through the taverns and whorehouses, his head covered by a cucullus like a common traveler, and drink with commoners, pick fights, concealing his identity, and that often he returned home with a black eye after being recognized in some tavern.

(SHA, *Lucius Verus* 4.6, referring to a period in the 160s)

For monks a cuculla and a tunic are sufficient: a wooly cuculla in winter, a plain one in the summer.

(From the monastic manual, *The Rule of Benedict* 35)

cucullus or *cuculla* The spooky hooded capes worn by medieval monks in the movies and by the likes of Yoda and Obi-Wan Kenobi in the *Star Wars* series have their ultimate origin in the utilitarian work coat usually worn by Roman slaves. Dress is the most important and visible indicator of social status, and just as the toga was the preeminent sign of the Roman citizen, so the *cucullus* was indicative of a slave or other insignificant person who needed to be outside in bad weather. So an emperor, or his wife, wearing a *cucullus* is just the kind of sleazy detail picked up on (or fabricated) by the more sensational imperial biographies contained in the *Historia Augusta*. It was proverbial that well-to-do adulterers who did not wish to be recognized put it on. Hence the satirist Juvenal imagines a woman ordering her sleeping lover to "hurry up and put on your *cucullus*"—that is, come over as soon as possible. Monks adopted the trappings of humility for more noble reasons. They were, after all, supposed to be slaves of God, so the symbolic connotations of the *cucullus* were just right for their purposes. Jerome prescribed that the *cuculli* should bear the insignia of the monastery. From this monkish use the hooded cape has come to suggest for us solemnity, humility, and learning.

TLL 4.1280–1281. Hurry up: Juvenal, *Satires* 6.236. Jerome: translation of the Greek monastic manual *The Rule of Pachomius* 99.

TORTOR: TORTURER

I bet you are a real man. I bet. Do you admit it? Or do I have to
take the servant girls to the shop of the tortor?
(Question asked of an effeminate *cinaedus* suspected of being in fact
an adulterer, Juvenal, *Satires* 6.Oxf. 28–29)

We ought to choose a place to live that is healthy not
just for the body, but also for the character. Just as I
should not like to live among the tortores, neither
for that matter would I live at a café.
(Seneca, apparently referring to a neighborhood where
torturers had their shops, *Letters* 51.4)

What need is there of a tortor? What fact do you wish to determine?
Whether [the defendant] killed the man? He did kill him. Whether
he was justified or not? But that has nothing to do with the tortor.
The rack we use to seek information only on questions of fact;
questions of justification belong in the courts.

(Cicero, *Pro Milone* 57)

His body was stretched out on the rack ... whips were aided by
fire .... Still he denied. But what the hateful tortor sought he
found in the end: that we were the informers.
(False information elicited under torture, from a speech in a
hypothetical legal case, Calpurnius Flaccus, *Declamations* 7)

tortor Slaves were routinely tortured in connection with criminal or quasi-criminal investigations about which they were thought to have information, on the assumption that if they were not tortured they would lie. Yet there was a nagging awareness that torture too produces lies. An edict on this subject was issued by the emperor Augustus, who came down in favor of torture in cases of serious crimes, because such crimes "cannot be discovered or investigated without the torture of slaves, and I consider this a most effective way of finding the truth." This belief in the truthfulness of torture-induced testimony was held also by the ancient Greeks, one of whose words for torture is *basanos*, "touchstone," the substance on which pure gold leaves a yellow streak; the plural *basanoi*, meant confessions by torture.

Augustus's was a relatively humane ruling, insofar as it recognized the seriousness of torture. Satirists portray cruel masters, male and female, who on slight pretexts hauled disobedient slaves to the shop of the torturer. Themselves slaves owned by the state, *tortores* worked freelance for private individuals as well as for the state in official contexts. Juvenal, in a satire directed against upper-class women, claims that "there are some women who pay the torturers an annual salary" (as opposed to paying by the job), an exaggeration that would not be satiric unless there was a grain of truth to it.

The words *tortor* and *tormenta* ("torture") derive from the verb *torqueo*, to twist. A *tortor* is literally "one who twists or tightens" the ropes on the rack. It seems to be a translation of analogous words in Greek, where *strebloun* means to "twist or tighten," and *strebloterion* is the rack. Torture is not mentioned in early Roman law codes or attributed to early Roman institutions, so it may be that its routine use on slaves should be considered one of the less-heralded borrowings of the Romans from Greek civilization. Despite the etymology of the word, *tortores* had standard equipment that included not just the rack (*eculeus*), but whips, pitch, candles, wax, and hot iron plates for burning the flesh. There is some evidence for more exotic methods, such as one using vinegar, but in general the ancients were far less inventive in this regard than the modern technological age has been.

Roman torture of slaves is occasionally spoken of as punitive, but in the majority of known cases it was intended to elicit information, as Cicero assumes in the passage quoted here. This is reflected interestingly in the language, for in legal contexts *quaestio*, "interrogation," is shorthand for *quaestio per tormenta*. The word for torture that Augustus uses in the edict just quoted is *quaestio*. Interrogation and torture were thus strictly synonymous, such that one legal text has to specify that in a particular context, "by *quaestio* we mean not just torture [*tormenta*] but all kinds of question-asking and defense." Another cautions that *quaestio* should be applied so that the slave survives, either for innocence or, if guilty, for punishment.

RE 2nd ser., 6.1775–1794, s.v. "tormenta." F. Hinard and J. C. Dumont, *Libitina* (Paris: Boccard, 2003) 89–95. Augustus's edict: quoted in Justinian's *Digest of Roman Law* 48.18.8. Juvenal: *Satires* 6.480. Not just torture: Ulpian, in Justinian's *Digest of Roman Law* 29.5.1.25. So that the slave survives: Ulpian, in Justinian's *Digest of Roman Law* 48.18.7pr.

CRIME AND PUNISHMENT

flagitium

infamia

crux

culleus parricidae

stigma

FLAGITIUM: HUE AND CRY; A LOUD PUBLIC DISPLAY OF DISAPPROVAL OUTSIDE A PERSON'S HOUSE; DISGRACE, DISHONOR; A DISGRACEFUL ACT

If anyone has committed slander or composed a song or poem which brings shame or flagitium upon another [the penalty shall be death].

(*The Law of the XII Tables* 8.1)

In military parlance flagitium *is something worthy of noisy, violent reproach [increpatio].*

(Donatus, Commentary on Terence, *Eunuch* 382)

What lust has not touched your eyes, what crime has not touched your hands, what flagitium has not touched your entire body?

(Cicero, *Against Catiline* 1.13)

In the same year [AD 58] Nero, moved by the loud demands [flagitationibus] of the people accusing the excessive zeal of the tax-collectors, considered whether he should order all indirect taxes abolished, and so make a lovely gift to the human race. [The plan was dropped.]

(Tacitus, *Annals* 13.50.1)

I came to Carthage, and all around me hissed a cauldron of illicit loves [flagitiosorum amorum].

(Augustine, *Confessions* 3.1)

flagitium Loud public chanting of abuse is a venerable tradition in pre-modern, pre-police societies, an aspect of necessary judicial self-help known as *charivari*, or "rough music." A person denied his due, instead of resorting to legal means, confronted the malefactor, waylaying him in public or standing at his front door, if possible with a crowd of supporters. He then shouted a demand for satisfaction at him in abusive terms, in hope of publicly shaming him into compliance. The Roman word for this procedure was *flagitium*, or *flagitatio*, and it is the favored technique, for example, of the moneylenders in Roman comedy when trying to collect a debt. One of these characters, at the end of his patience, starts chanting, "I want my interest, give me my interest, give up the interest! Are you going to give me the interest right now?" A poet, addressing a woman who will not return some of his writing tablets, imagines collecting all of his nastiest verses and standing outside of her house and delivering this serenade: "filthy slut, give me back my little notebooks; give me back, filthy slut, my little notebooks," and, when that doesn't work, "good and chaste woman, give me back the notebooks." The goal was to produce shame and public disgrace.

In a law dating to the fifth century BC (quoted above), chanted slander that results in public disgrace is to be punished by *death*. A harsh law, no doubt, and one written to protect the rich and socially prominent, whose social existence could be threatened by defamation. By comparison, the Anglo-Saxons sometimes punished slander by excision of the tongue. After this early period the law of libel moderated, and the practice of *charivari* seems to have become more rare. The word *flagitium* lived on, however, as a key moral term for any disgraceful act, something that is worthy of public outcry. In particular, it had a special military application for desertion or cowardice. Orators, by contrast, usually imply something sexual, a nod perhaps to the old *charivari* tradition which often fixed on family and sexual misdeeds. The ire of the Christian apologists was especially directed at the *flagitia* portrayed in the Roman theater, such as the adulteries and rapes committed by the gods in mythological tales. Tertullian, that ancient ally of all critics of sex and violence on television, asks rhetorically, "Why is it right to permit people to watch that which it is an outrage [*flagitium*] to actually do?"

While the noun *flagitium* lost its association with public ambush and entered a purely moral realm, the related verb *flagitare* always retained the idea of loud, importunate demands. Organized shouting was an important way for the common people of Rome to make their wishes known to the upper orders. Crowds might chant in the theater to demand official action against grain speculators, or (as they demanded from Nero) relief from tax collectors, or from a famine; they chanted to demand the blood of criminals, Christians, or (if a Christian crowd) heretics. The church father Lactantius claims that theater crowds chanted for courtesans to strip, whereupon they danced to the spectators's immoral satisfaction. The Roman crowd, whether shaming or shameless, was always vocal. The rough music of their shouting lives on now only in the relatively rare English verb *flagitate*, "to demand earnestly," and the slightly more common adjective *flagitious*, "extremely wicked, criminal, or villainous," as in Gibbon's comment on a certain immoral but Christian king of Armenia: "his faith is pure, though his manners are flagitious."

TLL 6.837–843. Wilfried Nippel, *Public Order in Ancient Rome* (Cambridge: Cambridge University Press, 1995) 39–46. Moneylenders: Plautus, *Mostellaria* 603–604. Filthy slut: Catullus 42.11–12, 24. In the theater: Tertullian, *On Spectacles* 17; Lactantius, *Divine Institutes* 1.20.10. Edward Gibbon: *The Decline and Fall of the Roman Empire* ch. 32, vol. 2 p. 224 in the Modern Library edition.

INFAMIA: BAD REPUTATION, ILL FAME, DISGRACE; OFFICIAL DISGRACE (INVOLVING THE LOSS OF CERTAIN RIGHTS)

Even death ... is easier to bear than dishonor
and infamia.
(From an anonymous rhetorical treatise of the first
century BC, *Rhetorica ad Herennium* 3.4.9)

He is branded with infamia *who is discharged from the army*
dishonorably by his commander ... he who appears on stage as
an actor or a reciter, he who works as a pimp, he who has been
judged to have acted in a public trial when motivated by
slander or collaboration with the other side, he who has been
convicted of theft, forcible robbery, or defamation ....
(Julian, in Justinian's *Digest of Roman Law* 3.2.1)

But what does infamia *matter, so long as the money is safe? Marius*
the exile starts drinking at four o'clock and lives high, despite the anger
of the gods. But you, victorious province, you weep.
(Juvenal, on the corrupt governor of Africa who, though
convicted of fleecing his province, managed to find
a comfortable exile in Marseille; *Satires* 1.48–50)

There exist men whose lust and infamia *cause*
them neither shame nor disgust.
(Cicero, prosecuting another corrupt governor,
Againt Verres 1.1.35)

infamia What we would now consider white-collar crime—official corruption, legal collusion, fraud—was not called "toga crime" by the Romans, though the label would have been fitting. Just as today, the crimes committed and the consequences suffered by the rich, well-connected, and politically powerful differed substantially from those of the lower classes. In an influential edict, the emperor Hadrian specified separate punishment scales for upper-class and lower-class offenders. Not only were all men not equal before the law, but the differential penalty system was a cornerstone of imperial jurisprudence. While the *humiliores* ("humbler" persons) might be sent to hard labor in the mines, thrown to the beasts, burnt alive, or crucified, the worst that the *honestiores* ("more honorable" persons) had to fear was usually exile, a fine, or *infamia*, a kind of formalized dishonor involving certain legal disabilities and restrictions.

The word usually refers to the strong public criticism (*fama* is "what people say") that results from some generally known misdeed, often committed by a public official or member of a group, such as the Senate or a jury. It can mean "scandal," and it is often coupled with other shame words, like *invidia, turpitudo,* and *dedecus* ("odium," "shamefulness," "dishonor"). One "burns" (*flagrat*) with *infamia*, and punishing the crime of one senator, say, could "extinguish" the *infamia* suffered by the whole order. Formal *infamia*, as it appears in the later law codes, deprived a man for moral reasons of the right of appearance in court as an advocate or of being represented by another; it excluded him from legal tutorship and denied him the right to obtain public office or to be an accuser in a criminal trial. Legal *infamia* could originate either in the practice of a dishonorable profession, such as acting or pimping (a combination revealing of Roman attitudes toward the theater). Bankruptcy, dishonorable discharge from the army, simultaneous betrothal to two persons, and other breeches of trust in contractual relationships could also lead to a person being declared officially *infamis*. Thus, while as a penalty it was a far cry from being fed to the beasts, *infamia* did effectively put an end to a man's public career and make him, at a stroke, into a second-class citizen.

The use of this shame word as the name for an official punishment reveals the important role played by public opinion in Roman notions of justice. Like the *nota censoria*, *infamia* and other penalties inflicted on the upper classes were directed exactly at scolding the delinquent in public so as to bring dishonor upon him. Modern corporate and celebrity criminals cannot, unfortunately, be punished with "disgrace" and sent to an island. The dishonorable discharge of the military justice system, however, does retain the Roman blending of moral and legal terminology.

TLL 7.1337–1339. P. Garnsey, *Social Status and Legal Privilege in the Roman Empire* (Oxford: Oxford University Press, 1976) 185–187. J.F. Gardner, *Being a Roman Citizen* (New York: Routledge, 1993) 110–154.

CRUX: A WOODEN FRAME ON WHICH CRIMINALS WERE EXPOSED TO DIE; DEATH BY THE CROSS, CRUCIFIXION

Julius Caesar, whose virtues procured him access to heaven, was traveling to Asia Minor as a young man and still a private citizen, when he was captured by pirates around the island of Pharmacusa, and provided a ransom for himself of fifty talents. Fortune thus willed that the brightest star of the world be bought for such a sum from a pirate galley. So what reason do we have to complain about Fortune if she spares not even her fellow divinities? But divine power avenged its own injury: for he immediately captured the pirates and nailed them to cruces. *[Caesar was twenty-six at the time.]*

(Valerius Maximus, *Memorable Doings and Sayings* 6.9.15)

*But it was a further trick of Fortune, meant to torment [*cruciare*] me even more, that this delightful child preferred me to his nurses, to the grandmother who raised him, to all those who win over children of that age.*

(Quintilian, after the death of his five-year-old son, whose mother had also died, *On the Orator's Education* 6 pref. 8)

He who envies the happy tortures himself. (Sese excruciat, qui beatis invidet.*)*

(Apuleius, *Anechomenos* or *The Patient Sufferer* 3)

You deny that any [of the philosophers] practices what he preaches, or lives up to the example of his own speeches. Why not, when their words are heroic, towering, and transcend all the stormy disturbances of human life? While they attempt to un-nail themselves from their cruces *(*cruces *upon which each of you critics nail your own selves) they are crucified nonetheless and hang, each on his own post [*stipes*]. These men, who punish themselves, are torn apart by as many* cruces *as they have desires. But their malicious critics dispense elegant abuse to others: I would believe that they had the time for this, were they not spitting on the spectators from their own cross-beams [*patibulum*].*

(Seneca, *On the Happy Life* 19)

*I hate, and I love. Perhaps you ask why? I do not know, but I feel it happening, and I am in agony [*excrucior*].*

(Catullus, probably talking about his feelings for his mistress Lesbia, poem 85)

crux The Romans were not the only ancient people to engage in *crux*, but they certainly perfected its horrific combination of torture, public humiliation, and execution. As a prelude, the man condemned, commonly a slave or bandit/pirate/revolutionary (the three things being hard to separate in Roman thinking, and covered under the word *latro*), was bound to a wooden apparatus with a fork (the *furca*). He was then made to carry this around the neighborhood, earning him the nickname *furcifer* (a common insult in Roman comedy, usually translated "gallows bird"). He was often beaten in addition, but this was only preparatory to the crucifixion proper, in which he was stripped of clothing and bound fast with outstretched arms to a crossbeam (*patibulum*) or nailed firmly to it through the wrists. The crossbeam was then raised up and attached to a high post (*stipes*), and his feet were nailed to the upright shaft. Over the criminal's head was placed a notice stating his name and crime. Exhaustion, heart failure, or shock after suffering the additional torment of *crurifragium* (the breaking of the legs with an iron bar) seem to have been the most frequent proximate causes of death. Humans were not the only creatures to suffer in this way. A dog was ritually crucified annually near the temple of Iuventus in Rome, because the watchdogs had failed to give an alarm to warn of the ascent of the Capitoline by the attacking Gauls in 380 BC.

Apart from its literal use for an apparatus of execution, *crux* suited the rough colloquial Latin of curse and insult: colloquial are the expression *mala crux*, for anything that torments one, a plague or annoyance, and the related curse *i in malam crucem*, roughly, "go and be hanged" (literally, "go into an evil crucifixion"). Crucified criminals were said to "feed the crows on the cross" (*"pascere corvos in cruce"*), hence the colorful and alliterative insult "morsel from the cross, food for crows' (*"crucis offla, corvorum cibaria"*). Most pervasive, however, is the way that the cross entered the vocabulary of emotion. When a Roman wanted to explain an intense feeling, whether envy, the torment of sexual longing, the grief of bereavement, or even the agony of not being able to do one's duty, he said *excrucior*: "I am being thoroughly crucified." The philosopher's first job was to quench the desires that disturb the mind. Hence Seneca, quoted above, vividly speaks of these human and so imperfect philosophers as being crucified by their desires and the carping critics of the philosophers as "spitting on spectators from the cross."

Crucifixion itself was outlawed in the fourth century by the first Christian emperor, Constantine. The pure use of the *furca* was put in its place, in which the criminal simply hung by the neck from the wooden fork until he was dead. But for obvious reasons *crux* and its cognates had a bright future in Christian Latin, which produced such postclassical formations as *crucifixio* ("crucifixion"—classical Latin made do with the simple *crux*), *crucifer* ("cross carrier" of Christ), and the insulting epithet put in the mouth of a Jewish critic, *crucicola* ("cross worshipper"). The English word *crucial* derives not from classical or Christian but from modern scientific Latin. Francis Bacon used the phrase *instantia crucis* (instance of the cross), and Newton spoke of the *experimentum crucis*, (the "experiment of the cross") a metaphor from the crux or finger post at a crossroads. The "crucial" experiment is that which decides between rival hypotheses and determines the road we are to follow next.

P. Garnsey, *Social Status and Legal Privilege in the Roman Empire* (Oxford: Oxford University Press, 1970) 126–129. Crucifixion of dogs: Pliny the Elder, *Natural History* 29.14.57. Insults: *Otto* 95, s.v. *corvus* 3. Replacement of *crux* by *furca*: Justinian's *Digest of Roman Law* 48.19.38.2. Christian vocabulary: A. Blaise, *Dictionnaire Latin-Français des Auteurs Chrétiens* (repr. Turnhout: Brepols, 1993) 231. Crucial: C. T. Onions, ed., *Oxford Dictionary of English Etymology* (Oxford: Clarendon, 1966) 231, s.v. "crucial."

CULLEUS PARRICIDAE: THE SACK OF PATRICIDE: A LEATHER BAG IN WHICH THOSE WHO KILLED THEIR FATHERS WERE TIED UP AND HURLED INTO THE SEA

According to ancestral custom the punishment for patricide is as follows: the culprit is whipped with switches, then sewn into a culleus with a dog, a rooster, a snake and a monkey; then the culleus is thrown into the deep sea. That is how it is done if the sea is near. Otherwise, he is thrown to the beasts, as in the enactment of the emperor Hadrian.

(Herennius Modestinus, in Justinian's *Digest of Roman Law* 48.9.9)

[The emperor Claudius] sewed more men into the culleus in five years than history says were sewn up in all previous centuries. We saw more cullei than crucifixions.

(Seneca, *On Clemency* 1.23)

The postponement of my punishment was unpleasant: waiting for it seemed worse than suffering it. I kept imagining the culleus, the snake, the deep.

(From a practice speech on legal issues surrounding patricide, Seneca the Elder, *Controversiae* 5.4)

Jupiter should have been chopped in half and divided between two cullei [i.e., for murdering his father, Saturn, and marrying his sister, Juno].

(Tertullian, *Ad nationes* 2.13.16)

Augustus dispensed justice not only with care but also with extreme mildness. Even if a defendant was manifestly guilty of patricide, to avoid the man's being sewn up into a culleus—a punishment inflicted on those who confess—he is said to have asked, "Surely you did not kill your father . . . ?"

(Suetonius, *Augustus* 33.1)

culleus parricidae Cullei were commonly used to transport wine in bulk (a *culleus* was equal to about 144.5 gallons), and so they would have been readily available. The punishment, described in the quote from *Digest of Roman Law* above, was a horrific one, even by Roman standards. A nautical equivalent of the live burial that was inflicted on unchaste Vestal virgins, the method similarly avoided polluting the earth by traditional interment. It was meant to deter what they considered the most horrific of crimes—the killing of one's father—and according to legend it worked extremely well. Plutarch claims that there was no patricide in Rome for the first six hundred years of its existence, until after the Hannibalic War. Whether or not this is true, the *culleus* treatment was a rare and exemplary punishment, recalling the good old days of ancestral severity and employed in historical times only by the sternest of judges and on men who openly confessed to the crime. The emperor Augustus tried to avoid it; Claudius, the ultra-traditionalist, brought it back. It seems to have been more talked about than inflicted. Probably most convicted patricides suffered not this exotic treatment (where would you get a ready supply of monkeys?) but the other one envisioned by the law codes—simple exposure to the beasts in the arena. Still, the lingering specter is a sign of the special importance placed on obedience and loyalty to the father in Roman culture.

TLL 4.1289–1290. *RE* 4.1744–1748. Plutarch: *Romulus* 22.4.

STIGMA: A MARK OF INFAMY TATTOOED WITH A HOT NEEDLE ON RUNAWAY SLAVES, CRIMINALS, AND PRISONERS OF WAR

[Caligula] condemned many men of the upper class to be disfigured with the marks of stigmata and to labor in the mines, or on repairing the roads, or to [be killed by] the beasts [in the arena].

(Suetonius, *Caligula* 27.3)

In so far as we have mentioned drastic and caustic medications, we shall set down the method for removing stigmata. This calamity unexpectedly befalls many people who do not deserve it, such as the financial administrator of Calvisius Sabinus, who, after suffering shipwreck, was put in a slave work-prison. Tryphon freed him [from the tattoo]... after he had been disappointed by many other doctors. [There follows a recipe for tattoo removal. Calvisius Sabinus was consul in AD 26.]

(Scribonius Largus, *Compositiones* 231)

The Scots take their name in their native language (Picti) from the fact that their bodies are tattooed (picto corpore), because they are marked with the stigma of various designs by means of iron needles dipped in ink.

(Isidore of Seville, *Etymologies* 9.2.103)

A man who [like St. Paul] took more than his share of beatings, was thrown into prison frequently, was flogged three times, once stoned, and all the rest of the things written in his catalogue of glory, such a man carries the stigmata of Lord Jesus on his body. And he who perhaps wears out his body and subjects it to servitude, lest while preaching to others he be found to be a hypocrite, he carries the stigmata of Lord Jesus in his body.

(Jerome, *Commentary on Paul's Letter to the Galatians* 3.6.17) *stigma* *Stigma* derives from the Greek word that refers to the actual process of tattooing (*stizein*, "to prick") and is related to the English *sting*, *stick*, and *stitch*. The ancient method involved pricking the skin with needles, wiping away the blood, and rubbing in first the juice of a leek, then the ink preparation. Disobedient slaves and criminals condemned to the mines or hard labor would permanently bear on their foreheads or faces the name of their crime. The exact Latin texts of penal tattoos are unfortunately not recorded, but a Greek example read "Stop me, I'm a runaway." A typical one in Latin was probably FVG, for *fugitivus* ("runaway").

Only barbarians like the Scots and Thracians engaged in decorative tattooing. Indeed it was not practiced in modern Europe until fairly recently. (The word *tattoo* is of Tahitian origin and was introduced to English by Captain Cook in 1769.) Since in the Greco-Roman world it was primarily a form of punishment, not self-expression, *stigma* early on took the meaning "stain, mark of infamy." Julius Caesar, for example, admitted that the obscene verses with which the poet Catullus had attacked his henchman Mamurra had "placed perpetual *stigmata*" on him. In this broader sense, *stigma* might refer to any physical mark of disgrace, like a scar or a brand.

In a key sentence at the end of St. Paul's letter to the Galatians (6.17), he says that he "bears the marks of Jesus" on his body. These *stigmata* seem to refer to all the scars and marks that Jesus received as a result of his ill-treatment at the hands of the soldiers, the welts from the whipping, etc. But Paul also regards his own *stigmata* as a kind of figurative tattoo imposed on him as a slave of Christ. Out of the commentary on this difficult passage (such as the words of Jerome quoted above) grew the medieval use of the word *stigmata* for marks received on the body by participation in Jesus' suffering, either by self-laceration or (in the later Middle Ages) by mystic transmission.

C. P. Jones, "Stigma: Tattooing and Branding in Graeco-Roman Antiquity," *Journal of Roman Studies* 77 (1987) 130–155. Stop me, I'm a runaway: from a scholion on Aeschines 2.83, quoted by Jones, "Stigma," 148. Placed perpetual *stigmata*: Suetonius, *Julius Caesar* 73.

RELIGION AND MAGIC

auspicium

paganus

fascinum

(ars) magica

AUSPICIUM: AN OMEN DERIVED FROM BIRDS

But an *auspicium* is the flight of birds which declare that whatever one has begun should be done or abandoned; the word comes from the "observation of birds," as it were, "bird-watching" [avispicium].

(Servius, Commentary on Vergil, *Aeneid* 3.374)

Gaius Marius made the temple of Honor and Virtue lower in height than the other temples so that the augurs would not force him to tear it down, if by chance it got in the way of the taking of the public auspicia.

(Pompeius Festus, *On the Meaning of Words* 516, p. 466 ed. Lindsay)

Varro gave the signal to advance. Paulus was hesitating on his own account, and when the chickens did not indicate a favorable *auspicium*, he ordered this message to be relayed to his colleague, who was already taking his standards out through the gate. Varro was furious at this. However, the recent disaster of Flaminius and the famous naval disaster of the consul Claudius in the first Punic War filled his mind with religious anxiety.

(Livy, *Roman History* 22.42.8–9)

The omen belongs to the observer.
(Auspicium observantis est.)
(Seneca, *Natural Questions* 2.32.6.)

Christ shone forth and appeared as a herald of great news, carrying a fine auspicium and a message of salvation for believers.

(Arnobius, *Against the Pagans* 1.65)

When we take the auspices [auspiciamus] at home, it is my solemn obligation to pay honor to the immortal gods. If one of the slaves or servant women farts under his cloak, and I do not perceive it, as far as I am concerned it creates no religious fault.

(Cato the Elder, *Speeches* 18.1, p. 47 ed. Jordan)

auspicium The practice of using birds and other animals to predict the future is not unique to the ancient Romans. But augury and auspice-taking did have a particularly important role in Roman life that has left its imprint on Latin and, by extension, on English as well. A person in authority, before beginning an important action, such as a battle, needed to ascertain whether the time was right. With the help of an augur skilled in the arts of divination he consulted the birds, their flight patterns or songs or feeding behavior, which when properly observed contained signs of divine approval or disapproval, and thus of future success or failure. A general, for example, brought with him on campaign a type of augur called a *pullarius*, the keeper of the sacred chickens (*pulli*), whose job it was to see if the chickens would eat before a contemplated attack. Only if they ate greedily and food fell from their beaks and struck the ground could the attack safely begin. In a famous case referred to by Livy above, an impatient naval commander named Appius Claudius disregarded the chickens, saying allegedly as he threw them overboard, "If they will not eat, let them drink." He proceeded to lose the battle and the whole fleet, providing a powerful warning to those who would discount the chickens. Later, Appius's sister was fined for suggesting another such expedition as a solution for overcrowding in Rome (the Claudii were a notoriously haughty clan).

Silence and proper procedure were essential. Cato's flatulent slaves could potentially invalidate the ceremony, but not if the official observer did not perceive it. As Seneca puts it, "The omen belongs to the observer." To be meaningful, an omen must both occur and be recognized by the right person. In war, the right to take the auspices resided solely with the commanding general, who thus had not only *imperium*, legal power to command, but also *auspicium*, the right to take auspices. Assuming the omens were favorable, this was a concrete demonstration of divine approval. Lucius Mummius, the looter of Corinth, boasted on a victory monument that it had been done under his "leadership, auspices, and authority," and this was a kind of formula. Victories won by subordinates were won "under the auspices" of the supreme commander, who retained much of the credit.

The practice of consulting the auspices and augurs at the beginning of any important enterprise, including weddings, led to the use of *auspicium* to mean simply "omen" or "beginning." This usage remained current in Christian Latin among authors (like Arnobius, quoted above), who did not believe at all in the efficacy of aviary divination. The English word *auspicious* and the phrases "to augur well" and "under the auspices of" ultimately derive from this custom.

TLL 2.1542–1549. M. Beard, J. North, and S. Price, *Religions of Rome* (Cambridge: Cambridge University Press, 1998) 1.21–28. Appius Claudius: Suetonius, *Tiberius* 2.2. His sister: Livy, *Roman History*, epitome of Book 19. Lucius Mummius's victory monument: *CIL* 1.541.

PAGANUS: PERTAINING TO A VILLAGE OR HAMLET, RUSTIC; CIVILIAN, NON-MILITARY; HEATHEN, NON-CHRISTIAN

In this style there is no urbane charm but a rustic simplicity [pagana simplicitas].
> (Sidonius Apollinaris, on his own style of letter writing, *Letters* 8.16.3)

Just as a well-trained army desires battle, a poorly-trained one fears it. We should keep in mind that, in battle, experience does more good than strength; take away training in the use of weapons, and there is no difference between a soldier and a paganus.
> (Vegetius, *Epitome of Military Science* 2.23)

Today you are a paganus; how do you know whether tomorrow you will be a Christian?
> (Augustine, *Sermons* 71.87)

The pagani sit and count the years, they listen to their frenzied prophesiers who say "Someday there will be no Christians," and they have their idols to worship, just as before.
> (Augustine, *Commentaries on the Psalms* 1.40.1)

paganus The use of *paganus* to refer to non-Christians is a late development, not common, at least in written sources, until the end of the fourth century AD. Before that time the usual term was "the nations": *nationes*, *gentes*, or *gentiles*. These words had a long and literate history, stemming ultimately from the biblical Hebrew *goyim* ("non-Jewish peoples") by way of its Greek translation *ethnici*, which Latin authors encountered in Greek translations of the Hebrew Bible, and in the Greek of the New Testament itself. *Paganus*, by contrast, seems to be slang or lower-class usage and may have begun as a joke. It came into currency in the lifetime of St. Augustine (AD 354–430) who refers in a letter to "unbelievers, whom we have been accustomed to call *gentiles* or, in the term now commonly used, *pagani*." Augustine's contemporaries Jerome and Ambrose, more attached to classical norms of writing, never use the newer term. Augustine himself usually prefers *gentiles,* except in the sermons, which were aimed at a popular audience. When addressing (and trying to convert) non-Christians, by contrast, he consistently avoids *paganus,* which shows it had an insulting tone.

A *paganus* was originally the inhabitant of a *pagus,* or village. Some scholars see the religious usage as derived from, and retaining the flavor of, its early meaning: "rustic, hick." This etymology was current at the time, and there is some historical support, since it seems that non-Christian beliefs hung on longer in rural areas than in cities. Also very plausible, however, is the derivation from another sense that would have been common in spoken Latin of the later empire: "civilian." In the rough language of the Roman soldier, "peasant" was anybody who did not belong to their own privileged and powerful caste, and eventually *paganus* became a fairly neutral, even legal, term for anyone not in the army. Christian Latin took many of its favorite metaphors and terms from military parlance, and if this is the true derivation, then originally *paganus* was a colorful and derisive term for all those civilians who were not "soldiers of Christ" (*milites Christi*).

Whether early Christians adopted *paganus* to describe their opponents because it meant "rube" or "outsider," it is no coincidence that the word became popular in the later fourth century, when Christianity was decidedly on the ascendant. If "the nations" reflects the perspective of a numerically small but distinct chosen people in the midst of a bewildering variety of earthly powers, *paganus* comes from an era in which Christians were on top and could ridicule a foe they no longer needed to fear.

It is ironic, etymologically speaking, that many people today try to revive "pagan" religions. *Paganus* was never meant to describe a coherent set of religious beliefs, just the heinous errors of unbelievers. In Christian Latin the adjective is seldom used to describe some particular religious practice; rather we hear of pagan insanity, blindness, and cruelty, pagan foolishness, mendacity, and perfidy. As with so many religious terms, ancient and modern, *paganus* comes from a particular doctrinal perspective that it implicitly promotes by its very use.

The key evidence is collected by *TLL* 10.78–84. See OCD[3] s.v. "pagan, paganism," and James J. O'Donnell, "Paganus," *Classical Folia* 31 (1977) 163–169. Augustine: *Letters* 184.5. Etymology current at the time: Orosius, *Histories against the Pagans* 1, prologue 9.

FASCINUM: FASCINATION, BEWITCHMENT; AN EMBLEM (TYPICALLY PHALLIC) USED FOR PROTECTION AGAINST BEWITCHMENT

There is also something fearsome among the pagans, which they call fascinum, the unhappy result of excessive glory and praise. We [Christians] sometimes put this down to the devil, since he hates everything good; at other times we put it down to God, for he is the judge of arrogance, exalting the humble and humbling the exalted.

> (Tertullian, arguing that women should be veiled to protect them from the evil eye. *On the Veiling of Virgins* 15)

When an animal has been bewitched [fascinatum] it is sad, weighed down and emaciated, and, unless you take action to help it, becomes diseased.

> (Vegetius, *Mulomedicina* 2.138)

He wrote fascinum for the virile member, because the ugliness of this member is often applied to protect things from bewitchment.

> (Porphyrio, Commentary on Horace, *Epodes* 8.18)

Women also often persuade each other that they should apply to their sick children, as a fascinum, something that is not appropriate to the Catholic faith.

> (Caesarius of Arles, *Sermons* 184.4)

And we see that in gardens and the forum they dedicate statues resembling satyrs [i.e., with large erect phalluses], simply to combat malicious bewitchment [contra invidentium effascinationes].

> (Pliny the Elder, *Natural History* 19.50)

The fascinum is the guardian not just of infants but of generals as well ... it protects the chariot of the triumphator, dangling beneath it as an antidote to envy.

> (Pliny the Elder, *Natural History* 28.39)

fascinum Children especially needed to be protected from the evil eye with amulets and phrases of good omen, a custom that was treated as merely a colorful superstition by educated Roman writers. The use of an image of the phallus for this purpose is known from a few literary references, but the true magnitude of the practice becomes clear from archaeology. Small circular amulets made from deer horn and engraved with a phallus and testicles are commonly unearthed on military sites in the northern part of the empire, and they were often worn by soldiers. Visitors to Pompeii may notice a large erect member engraved on a wall panel at a street corner or on a paving stone. The Naples museum houses a dazzling collection of phallic artifacts from Pompeii and Herculaneum: wind chimes, lamps, brooches, rings, and other jewelry; architectural ones that protrude gargoyle-like from walls, little toy ones made of clay and endowed with wings, eyes, and feet.

Fascinare means to bewitch. Catullus in one of his love poems jokes nervously about ill wishers who might count the kisses he gives to his beloved and thus be able to "fascinate" the lovers with an evil, envious spell. A shepherd in one of Vergil's poems looks at his lambs, all skin and bones, and concludes, "some eye or other is bewitching them [*fascinat*]"—to which the commentator Servius adds "[the shepherd] obliquely indicates that he has a handsome flock, since it was worth afflicting with the evil eye [*fascinari*]." Any unusual felicity or success was felt to be subject to the unspecific but powerful force of envy [*invidia*]. That is why everyone from soldiers to infants to triumphing generals needed a *fascinum*, a remedy against the evil eye, an antidote, something that would make the evil wisher look away. By far the preferred image for this purpose was the male member. The Latin language itself reflects this widespread practice, in that one term for penis, with no magical significance attached, is *fascinum*.

TLL 6.300–301. *RE* 6.2009–2014. Catullus: 7.12. Vergil: *Eclogues* 3.102-103 and Servius, Commentary on Vergil, *Eclogues* 3.103.

(ARS) MAGICA: MAGIC

They are to be punished by death who kill men with hateful arts, whether with poisons or with magicians' whisperings [susurris magicis].

(From an introductory law textbook of AD 533, Justinian's *Institutes* 4.18.5)

The ars magica—if in fact it is an art, and not a sham perpetrated by all the greatest liars...

(Curtius Rufus, *History of Alexander* 7.4.8)

Ordinary usage considers that man to be a proper Magus who, by speaking with the immortal gods, can accomplish whatever he wishes by certain amazingly powerful incantations.

(Apuleius, *Apology* 26)

When the doorposts are touched everywhere with [hyena's blood], they say that the arts of the Magi are made ineffective, that they cannot evoke the gods, nor speak with them, whether they attempt to use a lamp, a bowl, water, a globe, or any other type.... The flesh or bones of a man when found inside the stomach of a killed hyena are said to relieve gout by fumigation. ... Excrement or bones voided when the animal is killed have power against magical attacks [magicae insidiae].

(Pliny the Elder, *Natural History* 28.104–105)

(ars) magica We speak of magic tricks, magic moments, and magic numbers, of cleaning products that work like magic, as though magic, if it existed, would be fun, exciting, and useful. This is an indication of the steep decline in belief in magic since the spread of rationalistic and scientific explanations of the natural world. Latin writers speak rather of magic terror (*magici terrores*), secret magical attacks (*magicae insidiae*), or magic crimes (*magica maleficia*). Ordinary people throughout the ancient world (as in many quarters of the modern one) relied heavily on magical means for healing, predicting the future, harming their enemies, and helping their friends. Names for practitioners and salesmen of these arts are numerous: *augures, haruspices, sortilegi, mathematici, harioli, vates, Chaldaei, divinatores, caragi, praecantatores*. The Magi were dis-

tinguished among this crew in that they could claim ancestry and lore handed down from an ancient clan of arch-priests given royal honor by the Persian kings. Their prestige helped them win out, linguistically speaking, and give their name to the entire panoply of spells, potions, and techniques of divination: the *ars magica*.

Still, in Greek (from which the Latin term derives) *magus* could mean either Persian high priest, or "quack, charlatan." The figure of the Magus always possessed a dual reputation. On the one hand he commanded a respect tied to ancient Eastern wisdom and occult knowledge. Among the events announcing the birth of Jesus was the arrival of three Magi, vaguely "from the East," announcing that astronomical observation had shown them that the king of the Jews had been born. On the other hand, the Magus could be seen as an imposter playing on the curiosity and credulity of the uneducated. One such "pseudo-prophet Magus" (the Jew Elymas) is shown up and temporarily blinded by St. Paul in the book of Acts. It is revealing of the Roman attitude to the Magi that Elymas happened to be found in the retinue of the Roman governor of Cyprus at the time. *Magia* can be a term of abuse for foreign religious humbug, like *mumbo-jumbo*, but the art itself was taken seriously enough to attract both highly placed adherents and scholarly attention from the likes of Pliny the Elder, who discusses their lore at length.

The Roman authorities were originally quite permissive with regard to magical practices, intervening only in cases where magic was used maliciously—e.g., for homicide, in which case it was called *veneficium*, a term which also covered poisoning. But some time in the second century AD *magia* itself became a crime, and during the disastrous third century very harsh penalties began to be applied, including crucifixion, throwing to the beasts, and, for actual Magi, burning alive. Hysterical laws against magic grew hand in hand with the persecution of Christianity. Both types of persecution were signs of a wider political and military crisis and the resulting concern with religious uniformity. The attitude of Christian leaders, once they came into positions of influence, was complex. They needed to defend the miracles of Jesus and the apostles, while casting all other sorts of supernatural feats as works of the devil. If the church thundered against magical beliefs, that was because they were wicked, not untrue. A bishop delivered a sermon on the subject in the 530s: "But perhaps someone says, 'What should we do if omens themselves and magicians [*caragi*] or diviners [*divini*] often announce the truth to us?' On this matter the scriptures warn and advise us: even if they speak the truth to you, do not believe them . . . . Again you say: 'Sometimes many would run the risk of death from snake bite or from some other illness, if there were no enchanters [*praecantatores*].' It is true, dear brothers, that God permits this to the Devil . . . ." Notice he does not claim that magic is ineffective, only wicked.

James B. Rives, "Magic in Roman Law: The Reconstruction of a Crime," *Classical Antiquity* 22 (2003) 313–339. Jan N. Bremmer, "The Birth of the Term 'Magic,'" *Zeitschrift für Papyrologie und Epigrafik* 126 (1999) 1–12. Ramsay MacMullen, *Enemies of the Roman Order* (Cambridge, MA: Harvard University Press, 1966) 95–127. Magi from the East: *Matthew* 2.1. Paul and the Magus: *Acts* 13.6–12. Harsh sanctions: *The Opinions of Paulus* 5.23 (ca. AD 300). Sermon: Caesarius of Arles, *Sermons* 54.3.

MADNESS

phreneticus
furor
bacchor

PHRENETICUS: ONE SUFFERING FROM AN ACUTE AND FEVERISH DELIRIUM, A LUNATIC

Phrenetici *seem to be helped by a warm sheep's lung tied around the head. For who could bear to administer the brain of a mouse to be taken in water, or the ash of a weasel ... to a delirious person, even if the medicine were sound?*
(Pliny the Elder, *Natural History* 30.95)

When the phreneticus *laughs, the sane cry for him.*
(Augustine, *Sermons* 99, PL 38.599)

Mania *can be discerned and distinguished from* phrensis, *since in those suffering from mania we see neither crocodismus, a sort of plucking of the threads from the covers, nor carphologia, a sort of picking of small pieces of straw from the walls; but* phrenentici *always do this.*
(Caelius Aurelianus, *On Acute Diseases* 1.48)

He asked for idols to be made for himself, and in honor of those very idols he began to prance and sing, and twist his limbs in various dances like a phreneticus.
(Caesarius of Arles, *Sermons* 16.3)

phreneticus Some words for madness derive directly from the names of particular deities, suggesting the old belief that it is the gods who cause people to act irrationally: *cerritus*, literally "possessed by Ceres," or *bacchor*, "to rave like a worshipper of Bacchus." Others are general and not religious, like *insania*, "lack of (mental) health," and *furor* ("rage"). *Delirium* (a raving frenzy) is a typically Roman agricultural metaphor: *deliro* means to deviate from the furrows while plowing—as we would say, to "go off the rails." Still others derive from the jargon of Greek doctors, who developed a typology of mental illnesses, which they saw not as divine interventions but physiological conditions, diseases with organic causes that had to be treated by medical means. Many of the Greek terms (which do not correspond to modern diagnoses in any systematic way) were adopted by Latin-speaking medical writers and have subsequently made their way into English. *Coma* (Latin *coma*) is from the Greek medical word for "deep sleep." *Lethargy* (Latin *lethargia*) is from Greek, meaning "drowsiness" or "lethargy."

The adjective *melancholy* (Latin *melancholicus*) is from Greek, meaning "having black bile." *Mania* (Latin *mania*) is from the Greek term designating various kinds of altered mental states, including prophetic inspiration, erotic desire, and a specific medical syndrome involving the chronic impairment of reason, but without fever. The acute, feverish form of *mania* was *phrenitis*, the adjectival form being *phreneticus*. These Latinized Greek medical terms provide the origin both of the obsolete English medical term *phrenitis*, which was current into the nineteenth century and meant "brain fever," as well as of the more common English words *frenetic*, *frenzy*, and *frantic*.

In Latin *phreneticus* has a distinctly medical ring. But its ultimate origin is nontechnical. The names of diseases are generally pre-scientific popular terms, and *phrenitis* seems to go back to a folk belief connecting psychic activity with the heart or midriff (Greek *phrenes*). Nevertheless, ancient doctors locate it clearly and exclusively in the head (hence Pliny's suggested remedy: tying warm sheep's lung around the temples). They define it as an acute attack of mental derangement (*alienatio*, "alienation" from the self) accompanied by fever, small and rapid pulse, and as Caelius Aurelianus insists, worried movements of the fingers. Other possible symptoms include unaccountable laughter, singing, or dancing; in some cases sadness, silence, murmuring, crying, or muttering; fits of rage and shouting, seeking to hide in fear, speaking to those not present or to the dead, sleeplessness, fixed gaze without blinking or else constant blinking, and "sometimes he puts his hands before his eyes as if seeking to catch or remove some object which he thinks has been stuck in his eye or is flying in front of him."

The recommended treatments run the gamut from sleep (sometimes induced by soporific unguents), to cabbage juice, music, bloodletting and cupping, baths, prayer, and the more exotic prescriptions discussed by Pliny in the passage quoted above. But the usual fate of the *phreneticus* seems to have been to be tied up. Caelius, a humane and sensitive physician, disapproves of this and says that if he has to use ropes to restrain the insane, he winds wool around them so as not to hurt the patient. Phrenetics, however, were well known for attacking their doctors. Even Caelius suggests that, when moistening the lips of a phrenetic, one should take care not to be bitten. In his sermons and scriptural commentaries St. Augustine often takes the *phreneticus* as a metaphor for the violently insane nonbelievers who lash out at the doctor, Christ, despite the fact that he only has their best interests at heart. "Let us be healed, then, brothers . . . let us not rage against him like *phrenetici*, nor turn away from him like *lethargici*," (roughly, "the depressed"). Those suffering from *lethargia* are prodded awake by family members, he says, lest in deep sleep they die, while *phrenetici* are bound—"yet both are loved." The ubiquity of binding these unfortunates comes through in an offhand comment in a sermon by Gregory the Great, that a Pharisee is refuted by his own argument, "like a *phreneticus* who provides the rope with which to tie him up."

TLL 10.2054–2057. I. E. Drabkin, "Remarks on Ancient Psychopathology," *Isis* 46 (1955) 223–234. C. Gill, "Ancient Psychotherapy," *Journal of the History of Ideas* 46 (1985) 307–325. Sometimes he puts his hands before his eyes: Caelius Aurelianus, *On Acute Diseases* 1.36. Let us be healed: Augustine, *Sermons* 87, *PL* 38.538. Both are loved: Augustine, *Commentary on Psalm* 34, 2.13, in *Corpus Christianorum, Series Latina*, vol. 38. Gregory the Great: *Homilies on the Gospels* 2.33.4.

FUROR: MADNESS, INSANITY, FRENZY, RAGE

 Furor: a lover's unsoundness of mind, which comes from potions which are customarily given to men by their wives to increase their love.

(From a late antique glossary, *CGL* 6.478)

And just as often in a great crowd a seditious disturbance arises, and the lowly mob rages in their minds, and now torches and rocks fly—furor provides the weapons; but then if by chance they see a man whose devotion and services to the state carry weight, they grow quiet and strain to hear.

(Vergil, in a simile describing the quieting of the waves after a storm, *Aeneid* 1.148–152)

They seized the property of Roman citizens, slaughtered some, sold others into slavery. As things were going down hill Convictolitavis gave them a push, urging the common people on to furor, *so that when the crimes had been done they would be too ashamed to revert to sanity* [sanitas].

(Julius Caesar, speaking of a revolt of 52 BC in Gergovia, near modern Limoges in France; *Gallic War* 7.42)

Be silent, Furor! *Bite your tongue, you wicked dog, and eat your words with your own mangled mouth.*

(Prudentius, addressing the Manichean heresy, personified as "Madness," *Apotheosis* 979–980)

furor Furor is a nontechnical word that differs from its close synonym *insania* mainly by being more violent and intense. Cicero defines it as "a blindness of the mind toward everything" (*mentis ad omnia caecitas*), whereas *insania* is the sickness of a mind that lacks tranquility and constancy, the hallmarks of *sanitas* or mental health. A rabid dog attacks with burning *furor*. A young man's grief at the death of his sister is so intense that he contracts a fever, "drenched in noxious *furor*." *Furor* provides improvised weapons to a rioting mob, makes a gentle poet strike his mistress, inspires the frenzied prophecies of a priestess, or the ravings of a heretic. It makes a promising young man abandon a public career to write poems about a woman of dubious virtue. It makes soldiers fight not for booty or desire for plunder, but in pure rage. Personified by a tragic poet, "*Furor*, the waster of life, exhausts the war god."

Like the English words *madness* and *insanity*, *furor* gets applied to all kinds of actions that are not strictly insane but which the speaker considers ill advised in the extreme: enthusiasm for the amphitheater, according to a Christian moralist, a passion for expensive Greek vases, according to a pagan one. We commonly see the description *furor* applied to violent rage, grief, and erotic obsession. But the most distinctive Roman extension of the concept lies in the political realm, where it means "enthusiasm for political change." *Furor*, especially in the late Republic and early Principate, becomes a code word for any behavior that challenges the established order, be it the populist agitation of tribunes of the *plebs*, Gallic resistance to Roman domination (as in the passage of Caesar quoted above), mutiny by the soldiers or by a mob of commoners, or the open and doomed resistance to the emperor on the part of a refractory senator. All these are "insanity." To return to obedience, as the crowd does in Vergil's simile at the sight of an idealized elite statesman, is to return to "sanity": *sanitas*.

TLL 6.1629–1638. *RE* 7.380–382. Tragedian: an anonymous fragment in O. Ribbeck, *Tragicorum Romanorum Fragmenta* (2nd ed., Leipzig: Teubner 1871) p. 240. Cicero: *Tusculan Disputations* 3.11.

BACCHOR: TO CELEBRATE THE RITES OF BACCHUS; TO RAVE, RANT, OR RUN WILD

This vile man was raising a ruckus with
his raving [bacchabundus]; he kept
opening a letter and protesting loudly
to the people, "Apuleius is a wizard..."
(Apuleius, *Apology* 82)

You guys are hatching a secret plot [bacchanal facitis]
in the wine cellar. I'm going right now and getting the
master from the forum.
(Plautus, *Miles Gloriosus* 857–858)

The Bacchanalia, a nocturnal rite of Greek origin, and the
nursery of all kinds of wickedness, had turned into a conspiracy
of very large proportions. It was investigated and suppressed
with the punishment of many.
(Livy, *Roman History*, epitome of Book 39)

But how many days you reveled [perbacchatus es]
disgustingly in that villa! There was drinking beginning
at the third hour of the day, dice playing, vomiting.
(Cicero, *Philippics* 2.104)

Even if a slave has on occasion gone into a frenzy
[bacchatus sit] at a sanctuary and given oracular
responses, still, if he is not currently doing it, he is
not to be considered defective.
(Vivianus, in Justinan's *Digest of Roman
Law* 21.1.1.10)

bacchor Bacchus was the god of wine. Some forms of his worship notoriously involved ecstatic rituals in secret settings, something viewed with great suspicion by the Roman authorities. Since they were secret, we do not know very much about the rites themselves. But clearly they were noisy and exotic and involved some kind of special religious association. A famous crackdown on the practice by the Senate in 186 BC was severe but, in the long run, ineffective: the rites continued to be celebrated out of the public eye for hundreds of years. By extension, the verb *bacchor* and its variants came to be used for all people who rave wildly (poets, partiers, politicians); a *bacchanal* could be any secret plot or cabal. The verb sometimes retains its religious feeling ("to be possessed by divine frenzy," as in the "defective" slaves discussed by the jurist Vivianus), but often it means simply "to have a wild party."

TLL 2.1663–1664. Roy Porter, *A Brief History of Madness* (Oxford: Oxford University Press, 2002) 10–33.

INSULTS

homo novus
latro
carnifex
cinaedus

HOMO NOVUS: "NEW MAN," THE FIRST IN HIS FAMILY TO REACH POLITICAL DISTINCTION, "UPSTART"

In the seeking of elected office nobility has promoted certain utterly disgraceful characters over those who are energetic but new [novi]. And not without reason, for sacred is the memory of great and virtuous deeds.

(Seneca, *On Benefits* 4.30.1)

It was this information in particular that made people eager to have the consulship entrusted to Marcus Tullius Cicero. For hitherto most of the nobility was seething with jealousy [invidia], and they thought that the consulship was practically polluted if a homo novus got it, however outstanding his merits.

(Sallust, referring to the panic in Rome when the conspiracy of Catiline was uncovered by Cicero. *The War with Catiline* 23.6)

I was the first homo novus you elected consul in a very long time, practically in living memory, and that place which the nobility had kept under guard and barricaded in every possible way, you broke it open under my leadership, and you declared your intention that in the future it should be accessible to merit [virtus].

(Cicero, *On the Agrarian Law* 2.3)

homo novus In the Roman Republic it was quite possible to break into public life and become a minor senator, given a lot of money, oratorical or military talent, and the right connections. This was how the elite invigorated and also protected itself—by absorbing men of talent and energy from outside. Potential troublemakers were brought into the fold. But to rise from outside the Senate to the highest office, the consulship, to give one's name to the year, this was extraordinary and provoked extreme resentment among the great old families who, by the late Republic, had ruled Rome for centuries. The classic cases of such rocket-like upward mobility were the famous general Marius and Cicero the orator (both coincidentally from the same town of Arpinum). Their ancestors had been nothing at Rome. Both men were highly gifted, both found patrons among the aristocracy early on, both rose to be consul in the midst of public emergency, and both endured ceaseless abuse and hostility from their noble competitors. The usual term for this malice is *invidia*, a kind of jealousy or ill will that borders on the evil eye.

Marius, who superceded the aristocratic but ineffective general Metellus, made a point of rubbing his success in the face of the nobles whenever he got the chance. The historian Sallust gives him an immortal speech before the people, in which he speaks for the claims of all new men, ridiculing the nobles's sloth, addiction to luxury, and sense of entitlement, contrasting his own self-made *labor* and *industria*. Marius represented to Sallust, and Cicero represented to himself, true *virtus* of the kind that made Rome great, an ideal disgraced by the degenerate elite with no interests beyond their books, dinner parties, and gardens. Cicero coined the term *piscinarii*, "fishpond fanciers," to refer to such men, and in letters he speaks of their implacable *invidia* toward himself.

Once they became established, however, most new men made no effort to reform the system, but became its defenders and sought recognition equal to that accorded their social superiors. Cicero himself, though he was never fully accepted during his lifetime, became the Senate's foremost defender and theorist, identifying completely with its conservative values. It was his tireless advocacy for the Senate and opposition to the radical populism of Caesar and Antony that eventually got him killed, his severed head displayed on the rostra, and his golden tongue pinned to the roof of his mouth by a needle.

Despite the admiration that certain authors like Sallust felt for the energy of some new men, the Latin *novus* has none of the pleasant associations of the word "new" in English. As Ronald Syme puts it, "Lacking any perception of the dogma of progress—for it had not yet been invented—the Romans regarded novelty with distrust and aversion. The word *novus* had an evil ring." In matters political and aesthetic it almost always has a tone of distaste, like *modern* when spoken by a conservative curmudgeon. The "new poets" (*poetae novi*) were an eccentric avant-garde who rejected the classics; "to be eager for new things" (*rebus novis studere*) is to be a wild-eyed revolutionary, ready for chaos and probably intent on installing a monarchy; and to seek "new tables" (*novae tabulae*) was to advocate a total abolition of debts. A new man might be ridiculed as a "lodger" in Rome (*inquilinus*), or said to have recently "risen from the muck" (*emergere ex sordibus*). An anonymous later invective against Cicero, in addition to implying a history on Cicero's part of male prostitution and incest between Cicero and his daughter, and harping on his supposedly ill-gotten wealth, calls him *reperticius . . . civis* ("new-found citizen"), which suggests he had just walked in off the street and may possibly be of servile roots. Another epithet, *homo novus Arpinas*, carries extra disdain because it mentions his origin in an Italian town, not from the city proper. And the best is *Romulus Arpinas*, something like "The George Washington of Dubuque." In a day when small town origins and a working-class background are the ultimate badges of authenticity in politics, it takes some imagination to hear the word *novus* with its original sneer.

T. P. Wiseman, *New Men in the Roman Senate* (Oxford: Oxford University Press, 1971).
Sallust: *The War with Jugurtha* 85. Piscinarii: Cicero, *Letters to Atticus* 1.19.6, 1.20.3.
Ronald Syme: *The Roman Revolution* (Oxford: Oxford University Press, 1939) 315.
Anonymous invective against Cicero: ps.-Sallust, *Invectiva in M. Tullium Ciceronem* 1.3.4.

LATRO: OUTLAW, BRIGAND, BANDIT, DESPERADO

[In memory of] Julius Timotheus who lived twenty-eight years, more or less. He led a blameless life. He was deceived by latrones, along with seven foster children [alumni]. Otacilia Narcisa [set this up] for her sweet husband.

 (An epitaph found near Rome, along the via Portuensis, *ILS* 8505)

The traveler is not always killed by the latro; sometimes the bandit is killed by the traveler.

 (Cicero, *Pro Milone* 55)

Shall we endure the disgusting, fiendish despotism of this foul latro?

 (Cicero, on Marc Antony, December 44 BC;
 Philippics 3.29)

As for that latro, I will pass over his hateful name. For I detest that hero of the gymnasium, who brought the consulship into his family before even his colony had obtained the full rights of Roman citizenship.

 (The Emperor Claudius, in a speech circa AD 48, on his
 erstwhile advisor, the former consul Valerius Asiaticus
 of Vienne in Gaul; *ILS* 212, col. 2, lines 15–16)

latro Latrones were land-based pirates who lived in caves and survived by plunder taken from travelers, whom they often killed. They were a serious threat all around the Roman empire, and the importance of this word in the Latin vocabulary serves as a reminder of the very limited policing capabilities of the Roman state, which left untouched large swaths of what was supposedly part of the *pax Romana*. Brigands seem to have been a serious worry in the mind of anybody who traveled outside a city. Several proverbs concerned their conduct: "If they don't kill you, they say they gave you life," and "The bandit ignores the naked man"—i.e., because he has nothing to steal. A popular children's game was "little robbers" (*latrunculi*), played with statuettes of bandits and soldiers. A late antique elementary schoolbook, not unlike the American "Dick and Jane" series of early readers, contains the following stereotyped scene: "The accused brigand is produced. He is questioned as befits his deeds. He is tortured. The interrogator strikes him, his chest is thrashed, he is strung up . . . ."

Legally speaking, a *latro* was anyone who posed a violent threat to public order, and the term might include various types of thieves, kidnappers, temple robbers, and rebels. They usually operated in bands and had charismatic leaders, so the word lent itself to political use, making an excellent slur against political opponents, revolutionaries, and in the Christian era, heretics. Insofar as it took in various anti-state actors with a variety of motives and methods, it resembles certain aspects of the English word *terrorist*. Though the *latro* does not act to inspire fear per se, as does the terrorist, both terms imply an abandonment of the norms of civilized society and a subversion of the whole social order. Like the terrorist, the Roman *latro* was denied ordinary legal protections accorded to citizen defendants. Both words designate men who are not precisely common criminals but who operate outside the framework of states and governments and represent a violent threat to them, and thus provoke extreme measures. In the Roman case, governors were expected to prosecute "wars" on organized brigands and, if necessary, made use of vigilante gangs as well as regular soldiers.

In its debased use as a political slur, *latro* is one of the linguistic symptoms of the collapse of the Roman Republic, coming into particularly intense use during episodes of civil war, such as that which followed the death of Julius Caesar. This kind of hyperbole became the norm under the Principate. The senator and historian Tacitus notes with disgust the habit of historians of referring to men of the caliber of Brutus and Cassius as *latrones*, just to please the emperor. It so happens that we possess the inscribed text of a speech before the Senate given by the emperor Claudius, in which he uses this very term to refer to one of his advisors, a former consul, whom he had forced to commit suicide. For Tacitus this kind of abuse of language, and the silent acceptance of it by the senatorial class, was among the bitterest pills of autocracy.

TLL 7.1013–1018. Brent D. Shaw, "Bandits in the Roman Empire," *Past and Present* 105 (1984) 3–52. Proverbs about *latrones: TLL* 7.1016.12–18; Otto 247, s.v. *nudus* 3. Elementary schoolbook: a manuscript in Vienna, transcribed and discussed by A. C. Dionisotti, "From Ausonius' Schooldays? A Schoolbook and Its Relatives," *Journal of Roman Studies* 72 (1982) 83–125, section 75, p. 105. Tacitus: *Annals* 4.34.

CARNIFEX: A SLAVE SERVING AS EXECUTIONER OR TORTURER OF OTHER SLAVES; "BUTCHER," "SCUMBAG"

If anyone wishes to have a slave, male or female, punished privately, he who wishes to have the punishment inflicted shall have it done as follows: the contractor will provide the posts, chains, ropes for the floggers and the floggers themselves; the person having the punishment inflicted is to pay four sesterces to each of the workers who carry the fork, to the floggers, and the same amount for the carnifex.

(From a mortuary law of the late Augustan period, the *Lex Libitinae Puteolana*, AE 1971 no. 88, column II, lines 8–10)

If any woman would even so much as touch him, shouldn't we suppose that she would also lick the asshole of a sickly carnifex?

(From a poem directed at an anonymous target, Catullus 97.11–12)

You carnifex, don't I know you? Get out of my sight. What business is this of yours? . . . I'll take this staff right now and—

(Lines spoken by Jupiter in Plautus's comedy *Amphitryo* 518–20)

That slave [who connives at his mistress's love affairs] is in favor, he has the whole household on a string, and does not feel the lash; he is powerful. The rest, a wretched mob, lie at his feet. . . . Yet once in a while the mistress should also invent quarrels with you, pretend to cry, and call you carnifex.

(Advice given by Ovid to a slave charged with watching a young woman; *Amores* 2.2.29–36)

carnifex The *carnifices* were publicly owned slaves who served as executioners and/or head torturers, both on behalf of the state and for private individuals who contracted for their services. They also cared for the instruments of torture and disposed of corpses. Such was the revulsion felt for them that laws prohibited them from dwelling inside the city. They did their grim work at Rome just outside the Esquiline gate. The *carnifex* is so called because he takes a man and makes him into meat (*carnes ex homine faciunt*).

Though not really obscene, *carnifex* could be an insult of great power, especially when applied to free citizens. It combines, in various proportions, the imputation of brutality, physical pollution, and servile social status. During the late Republic, a nobody, the son of an ex-slave named Helvius Mancia, was once ridiculed in public by the great general and popular hero Pompey the Great. Helvius had brought an accusation against another man in front of the censor, and Pompey quipped that Helvius, who was very old, had come back from the underworld to make the charge. Helvius did not deny it but said that during his sojourn among the dead he had run into some of Pompey's old victims from his days as a henchman of Sulla in the civil wars, decades earlier: Gnaeus Domitius Ahenobarbus, Marcus Brutus, Gnaeus Carbo—distinguished men. "All were complaining in one voice that without judicial sentence they had perished thanks to you, the *adulescentulus carnifex*." This last phrase is variously translated as "the stripling executioner" [Pompey had been in his early twenties at the time, with no official position], or better, "the boy butcher." It was a nasty epithet that stuck to Pompey down the historical tradition.

Part of the shock value of this remark came from the public setting and the extreme social distance between Helvius and Pompey. It was a notable example of free speech (*libertas*), the kind of thing not destined to happen again in the days of the emperors, at least outside the bitter pages of historians. In the language of comedy, by contrast, where terms of abuse are common, *carnifex* is weakened by repetition, and the same was probably true in everyday private speech. In the passage from Plautus quoted here it means little more than "scum," spoken to a meddling servant (in this case the god Mercury). When Ovid imagines an aristocratic lady calling her slave minder *carnifex* in a fit of temper, it might be translated as "you brute."

J. Bodel, "Dealing with the dead: undertakers, executioners and potter's fields in ancient Rome," in V. Hope and E. Marshall, eds., *Death and Disease in the Ancient City* (London: Routledge, 2000) 128–151, esp. 144–145. Men into meat: Donatus, Commentary on Terence, *Hecyra* 441. Helvius Mancia and Pompey: Valerius Maximus, *Memorable Deeds and Sayings* 6.2.8. See R. Syme, *The Roman Revolution* (Oxford: Oxford University Press, 1939) 26–27.

CINAEDUS: MALE PROSTITUTE OR SLAVE CONCUBINE

A man who is dressed with scented oils every day in front of a mirror, whose eyebrows are shaved, who walks around with a thinned beard and hair plucked from the under parts of his thighs, who reclines at dinner-parties like a boy, wearing a long-sleeved tunic with his lover, one who is not only full of wine but full of men—who would doubt that he has done what cinaedi are accustomed to do?

> (Scipio Africanus Minor, on a certain Sulpicius Gallus probably during the former's censorship, 142 BC. *Speeches* fr. 17 ed. Malcovati = Aulus Gellius, *Attic Nights* 6.12)

You should laugh, Sextillus, at the man who called you a cinaedus, and stick out your middle finger.

> (Martial, *Epigrams* 2.28.1–2)

Thanks to that beating, I'm softer
than any cinaedus.

> (Plautus, *Aulularia* 422)

No soft cinaedus can dance
as well as I do.

> (Plautus, *Miles Gloriosus* 668)

I received your letter in which you complain about how tiresome you found that dinner party, even though it was splendidly appointed, because comedians, cinaedi, and fools were strolling among the diners.

> (Pliny the Younger, *Letters* 9.17.1)

Free-born maidens and boys are entering the dancing schools,
right alongside the cinaedi!

> (Scipio Africanus Minor, 129 BC. *Speeches* fr. 34 ed. Malcovati = Macrobius, *Saturnalia* 3.14.6.)

cinaedus Just as English speakers, in more decorous times, used to take some of their words for sexual things from French (*affaire, liaison*), so the Romans took many such words from Greek. *Cinaedus* is a Greek loan word that refers to a male prostitute or slave concubine, such as was kept by well-to-do Roman men whose tastes ran in that direction. These latter-day Ganymedes were not all young. According to the sources, they liked to keep their beards meticulously groomed and generally dressed and acted in an effeminate way. They curled their hair and learned to dance well (one late etymology derives *cinaedus* from the Greek roots meaning "rump shaker"). Pliny, in the passage quoted above, attests that they might entertain guests at a *cena* by acting and talking amusingly feminine, a practice about which he tries to be open-minded. It was a position of some privilege for a slave, no doubt, though for us it inevitably evokes uncomfortable comparisons with men's prison sexuality. The satirist Martial imagines (freelance?) *cinaedi* becoming rich off of gifts from wealthy lovers. He also hints at the huge prices paid for them.

Not that the practice of keeping *cinaedi* was widely accepted; in fact the word is usually an insult applied to any male considered "soft," a category that might include those who were well groomed, trimmed their body hair, and smelled nice. The Romans generally viewed effeminate men with a mixture of horror and fascination. The poet Catullus hurls the insult frequently, as did graffiti artists from Pompeii in terms too obscene to be quoted here.

TLL 3.1059. I. Opelt, *Die lateinische Schimpfwörter* (Heidelberg: Winter, 1965). Rump shaker: *CGL* 6.212. Pliny the Younger: *Letters* 9.17.1. Martial: *Epigrams* 12.16. Catullus: poems 16, 25, 33, and 57. Graffiti: *CIL* 4.1825.

VIRTUES

mores

    virtus

        pietas

            decus

                humanitas

MORES: MORAL CHARACTER, HABITS, ETHICS, WAY OF LIFE

It is likely that [in primitive times] many people died for lack of help against disease; still, for the most part they had good health because of their good mores, which inactivity and luxury had not yet spoiled.

(Celsus, *On Medicine* pref. 4)

His own mores create the destiny for each man.
[Sui cuique mores fingunt fortunam hominibus.]
(Anonymous, quoted by Cornelius Nepos, *Atticus* 11.6)

The good fortune of the empire changed along with its mores.
(Sallust, *The War with Catiline* 2.5)

Neither marriage nor lineage makes a mater familias, but good mores.
(Ulpian, in Justinian's *Digest of Roman Law* 50.16.46.1)

Let him first learn mores, then eloquence; it is useless to learn the second without the first.
(Pliny the Younger, giving advice to Corellia Hispulla about the education of her son, *Letters* 3.3.7)

If there was any slipping in public mores due to laziness or bad habits, he undertook to reform them.
(Suetonius, *Tiberius* 33)

mores A *mos* is a custom or practice, a way of doing something. It was the *mos* of the Spartans, for example, to have two kings. The plural *mores* refers rather to the character of a person, a community, or a generation, its behavior in respect to right and wrong, its morals. For a Roman to have good *mores* typically meant that he or she was honest, self-controlled, modest, and energetic. To have bad *mores* was to be self-indulgent, addicted to luxury, wasteful, vain, greedy, dishonest, ungrateful, or lazy. When it comes to *mores*, the ancestors, it was generally agreed, reigned supreme. The advice was often given, "live by ancient *mores*" (*moribus vivito antiquis* or *vive moribus praeteritis*). The ancestors' cultivation of good, frugal, disciplined *mores* in fact accounted for their success in creating and governing the empire. "Rome stands on the *mores* of its men," says an often quoted line by the poet Ennius. Contemporary *mores*, despite a few good examples, tended to be lax (*dissoluti*), distorted and erroneous (*depravati*), or ruined, reckless, and wild (*perditi*); *mores* had an inexorable tendency to slip (*labare*) from the severe standards of earlier days. Unlike the English notion of "character," then, *mores* was very closely tied to a sense of tradition and historical continuity.

Also unlike our "ethics" or "morals," *mores* was less a matter for private and religious reflection than for public discussion and even governmental action. The high office of censor was charged primarily with overseeing the *mores* of the community, and while censors rarely exercised their power, they did on occasion expel members of the Senate for moral turpitude. One of the chief duties of the Roman emperor was to improve *mores* both by personal example and by punishing malefactors. In a well-known fable of Aesop, the frogs ask Zeus for a king because they are "distressed at their own anarchy." In the Latin version by Phaedrus, significantly they ask for a king "to forcibly restrain their lax *mores*"—leaders were responsible for keeping people in line, morally speaking. Indeed the battle to preserve good *mores* was carried on in public constantly and on many levels: in the education of the young, in oratory, in poetry and art, in history writing, etc., as though constant sandbagging was necessary to protect against an over-flowing river of decadence.

The remark by the Roman doctor Celsus quoted above is revealing both because he equates good health in primitive times with good *mores* and also because he identifies the causes of the decline: inactivity and luxury (*desidia* and *luxuria*). These are the same causes by which the historian Sallust explained the fall of the Republic. Cicero associates a decline in *mores* with increasingly lascivious music. So, much as they enjoyed the improving comforts of urban life, the financial benefits of empire, and the increasing refinement of the arts, one of the main ways of understanding these changes was not progress, but moral decline.

Donald Earl, *The Moral and Political Tradition of Rome* (Ithaca, NY: Cornell University Press, 1967). Phaedrus: *Fables* 2.1.12. Sallust: *Histories* frag.1.16. Cicero: *De Legibus* 2.38.

VIRTUS: MANLINESS, COURAGE, EXCELLENCE, VIRTUE, GOODNESS

You will find virtus in a temple, in the forum, in the Senate house, standing before the walls, dusty and sun-burnt, with calloused hands; voluptas [pleasure] you will often find hiding and taking the shade around the baths and saunas and the places that fear the aedile*—soft and enervated, dripping with wines and unguents, pale, or else artificially colored, and embalmed with make-up.

(Seneca, *On the Happy Life* 7.3)

---

*The *aedile* was an official charged with keeping public order.

Virtus aims at what is difficult.
(Tendit in ardua virtus.)
(Ovid, *Letters from the
Black Sea* 2.2.111)

Virtus, however, is active, and your God,
who does nothing, has no part in virtus.
(Cicero, referring to the Epicureans, *On the
Nature of the Gods* 1.110)

Lucius Cornelius Scipio Barbatus, son of Gnaeus, a brave man
and wise, whose fine form quite matched his virtus; he was
aedile, consul, and censor among you; he took Taurasia,
Cisauna, and Samnium; he overcame all the Lucanian land
and brought hostages from them.
(Epitaph inscribed on the tomb of the consul of 298 BC, *ILS* 1)

To the one who wore the honored cap of Jupiter's high priest:
Death caused everything of yours to be short-lived, your honor,
good reputation, and virtus, your glory and your talents. If you
had but been allowed long life in which to enjoy them, it would
have been very easy for you to surpass by great deeds the glory
of your ancestors. Wherefore, O Publius Cornelius Scipio, son of
Publius, joyfully does Earth take you to her bosom.
(Epitaph on the tomb of the son of the general Scipio Africanus,
around 170 BC; *ILS* 4)

virtus At the heart of Roman aristocratic life was competition and the pursuit of personal preeminence in the service of the *res publica*. Expectations were high on members of prominent families, who were goaded to equal or surpass not just their contemporaries but the deeds of their own distinguished ancestors, either in war as military officers, or in peace as holders of elected office. They were urged, in other words, to display *virtus*, the quality most admired in Roman tradition. Etymologically, *virtus* connotes manly vigor (*vir* = man), resolution, valor, and steadfastness. Yet certain standards of conduct are implied, not just raw, manly courage. Those praised for *virtus* gained wealth and office by honest means, they did not misuse their privileges, they dealt justly with Rome's allies, they helped their friends, and they pursued justice.

Philosophically trained thinkers interpreted *virtus* as primarily moral excellence, like Plato's *arête*. Yet energetic activity and competition were always central to the Roman versions of the concept. The Stoic philosopher Seneca, an exponent of the school most congenial to traditional Roman thinking, says, "Without an adversary, *virtus* withers" (*marcet sine adversario virtus*). As the metaphor of withering suggests, *virtus* implies strength and growth. When applied to plants it means "mature vigor."

It could also be said to shine. A historian says of Julius Caesar, "He longed for a great command, an army, a new war, in which his *virtus* could shine forth [*enitescere*]." Caesar found one in the command that gave him an opportunity to conquer the area of modern France, Belgium, and Holland in about ten years and add it to the Empire of the Roman people. His contemporary, Crassus, also looking for an arena in which to display *virtus*, was lead even further afield, in an attempt to conquer the Parthian empire. He died in northern Syria with his legions, seventy miles across the Euphrates. It was in part this hunger for the display of *virtus* that took Roman generals further and further in search of fresh conquests. The admiration for *virtus* made such military adventurism acceptable. In a sense, *virtus* of the traditional aristocratic type was both the engine that drove the creation of the Roman empire and the cause of its over-expansion and eventual collapse.

Donald Earl, "Political Terminology in Plautus," *Historia* 9 (1960) 235–243. H. Roloff, "*Maiores* bei Cicero," in H. Oppermann, ed., *Römische Wertbegriffe* (Darmstadt, Germany: Wissenschaftliche Buchgesellschaft, 1967) 274–322. Carlin A. Barton, *Roman Honor: The Fire in the Bones* (Berkeley: University of California Press, 2001) 34–87. *Virtus* withers: Seneca, *On Providence* 2.4. His *virtus* could shine forth: Sallust, *The War with Catiline* 54.4.

PIETAS: DEVOTION, LOYALTY, DUTIFULNESS; PIETY; PITY

*The gods favor the cause of dutifulness and pietas,
through which qualities the Roman people has come
to such a summit of power.*

(Lines spoken by Quintus Marcius Philippus,
the consul of 168 BC, to his troops,
in Livy, *Roman History* 44.1.11)

*Here is the reward for pietas, these are the gifts of a devoted
husband in return for good deeds. I, Marcellina, was much loved.
What you see is what my husband Aelius could give, mindful
even after death of our love.*

(Epitaph of a woman from Sarmizegethusa in Dacia,
modern Romania, *CIL* 3.1537 = *CLE* 597)

*Praiseworthy is that last will and testament
written by pietas, good faith, and respect, in
which every relation is thanked in proportion
to the service of each.*

(Pliny the Younger, *Letters* 8.18.7)

*We had a king, Aeneas; no man was more just in doing his duty
in pietas, and none greater in warfare.*

(Lines spoken by Ilioneus, one of Aeneas's men, who thinks
he might be dead, in Vergil, *Aeneid* 1.545)

*Bear witness, Philippi, battlefield white with scattered bones:
this was the task, this was pietas, this was the ABC of Caesar
[Augustus]: to avenge his father in just warfare.*

(Ovid, *Fasti* 3.707–710)

pietas Latin *pietas* leads both to English *piety* and to *pity*, but only by a circuitous route. The original Roman concept is broader than either of these, taking in devotion to family, gods, and fatherland and attentiveness to one's precise duties toward each. It was seen by the Romans themselves as the quintessentially Roman virtue. It also tends to be the most obnoxious of Roman virtues to modern observers, first because it seems to stress a sense of obligation in religion and family affairs, as opposed to sincere belief, emotion, and affection; second, because it celebrates duty toward authority figures over personal freedom of expression; and third, because the Romans were forever crowing about how much they embodied it. "I am *pius* Aeneas," says the hero of Rome's national epic, in a line that has annoyed generations. "O gods, give me this in exchange for my *pietas*," prays Catullus. "You have earned that felicity, most excellent of emperors, by your *pietas*." "As for me, I will pay to my father the debt of *pietas* I owe to my country." Even when the emotion is unmistakably heartfelt, the language of owing, paying, earning, and of self-praise tends to engulf Roman *pietas* and stifle it. Nowhere else does the Roman reputation as stiff, authoritarian, and pompous seem so well deserved.

Just what did one have to do to be considered *pius*? The obligations of *pietas* toward the gods included just prayers (*iustae preces*, prayers for things that are good and right, not, say, that your neighbor's sheep get mange), offerings of incense and animal sacrifice, and the building and adornment of temples. In the case of family, one had to tend to (*colere*) relatives, even difficult ones, keep a grateful attitude toward one's parents, and be generous toward one's children and siblings. The most important obligations, however, centered around death: the proper burial of relatives, obedience to the terms of wills, the proper writing of wills to reward and thank family members, and the avenging of wrongs against family, even after death.

Obedience to authority is part, but not the most important aspect, of Roman *pietas*. More often the emphasis was on reciprocal care and support. A father or mother can display *pietas* toward a son, as well as vice versa, and it encompasses compassion as well as duty. Aeneas saves his father Anchises by carrying him out of the burning city of Troy on his back, and after Anchises dies in Sicily, Aeneas takes great trouble to arrange an elaborate funeral. In this, and in his preservation of the gods of Troy during his long journey to Italy, Aeneas is the model of *pietas*. Another famous instance involved a poor woman who kept her mother alive when the mother was starving on death row, much to the puzzlement of her jailer. She had been surreptitiously breast-feeding her. This woman was actually contravening state authority to help her parent but became celebrated also as a model of *pietas*. The legend was part of the story behind the founding of a temple in Rome to *Pietas* itself, who was also conceived of as a goddess. *Pietas* demanded that family members care for and nurture one another, no matter what. The principle was general and even applied in slave families. As a jurist explains, "Usually slaves who are not sick are returned [to the seller] with sick slaves, if they cannot be separated without great inconvenience or offending against the demands of family affection [*rationem pietatis*]."

In Christian Latin, *pietas* undergoes several important changes. It now has as a central element the confession of faith (*pietatis professio* or *confessio*), not just the performance of proper ritual action and prayer, as in the pagan variety of *pietas* toward the gods. It also demands an attitude of humility and obedience to God more complete even than that of a Roman son to his father. "This is the worship of God," says Augustine, "this is true religion, this is right *pietas*, this the service [*servitus*] owed to God." The pervasive reciprocity of Roman *pietas* gives way to a more unidirectional "service" model. Indeed, Christian *pietas* sometimes involved breaking the reciprocal family ties so sanctified by Roman *pietas* in favor of complete devotion to the one God. In a letter St. Jerome urges his friend Heliodorus to become a monk, even if he has to trample his resisting father underfoot as he leaves the house. "In these matters to be cruel is a type of *pietas*," he argues. More drastic still is the advice Jesus gave to a disciple who wanted to go and bury his father before continuing on with him: "Follow me, and leave the dead to bury their dead." A Latin commentary explains what this shocking neglect of the first duty of *pietas* means: "Hatred toward one's own is *pietas* towards God." Gradually *pietas* lost its broad application to family bonds and narrowed in conception to refer only to the worshipper's relationship with God; in other words, it came to mean "piety."

Another important distinction between Christian piety and pagan *pietas* is that the latter allows for, even demands, the pursuit of vendettas. The eighteen-year-old Octavian (future emperor Augustus) took his adoption in the will of Julius Caesar as a pretext to raise a private army and hunt down his killers, taking de facto control of the government while he did so. The remarkable thing is not just that he had the audacity to embark on civil war, but that the justification of righteous vengeance in the name of *pietas* was accepted, even celebrated, by his supporters. What Ovid says explicitly above, Vergil had implied. The emphasis on Aeneas's *pietas* and his prowess in war in the *Aeneid* is in part an oblique compliment to the early career of his own patron, Augustus.

The more pacific Christian ideal of *pietas* is memorably put by Lactantius, in a passage where he excoriates the warlike *pietas* of Aeneas as empty, if it involves killing. "At this point someone will say, What then is piety? Where is it? What is it like? It exists where people know nothing of war, live in concord with all, are friendly even to enemies, love all men like brothers, know how to curb their anger and how to soothe all strong emotions with a tranquillizing control." In later Latin *pietas* drifts even further into gentleness and comes to signify "pity." Old French *pite* and *pitie* retain both meanings, "piety" and "pity," as Italian *pietá* does to this day.

TLL 10.2086–2105. *RE* 20.1221–1232. R. P. Saller, *Patriarchy, Property and Death in the Roman Family* (Cambridge: Cambridge University Press, 1994) 102–112. I am *pius* Aeneas: Vergil, *Aeneid* 1.378. Catullus's prayer: 76.26. Most excellent emperors: *Panegyrici Latini* 11.18.5. The debt of *pietas*: Livy, *Roman History* 23.9.10. Jurist: Ulpian, in Justinian's *Digest of Roman Law* 37.15.1.1. This is the worship of God: Augustine, *City of God* 10.3. To be cruel is a type of *pietas*: Jerome, *Letters* 14.2. Leave the dead to bury their dead: *Matthew* 8.22. Hatred toward one's own: Jerome, *Commentary on Matthew* 1.10.37. What then is piety?: Lactantius, *Divine Institutes* 5.10.10, trans. Bowen.

DECUS: THAT WHICH ADORNS OR BEAUTIFIES; DISTINCTION, HONOR, GLORY

He returned to poetry and improvised a little elegy to the subject of hair: "O Hair, sole decus of the human form, you have fallen out, and grim winter has despoiled the verdant crop of your pate . . . ."
(Petronius, *Satyricon* 109)

Diana, shining decus of heaven . . . .
(Horace, *Carmen Saeculare* 2)

[Military discipline is] the chief decus and mainstay of the Roman empire.
(Valerius Maximus, *Memorable Deeds and Sayings* 2.7 pref.)

We were born for decus and for freedom. Let us either hold on to these, or die with dignity.
(Cicero, *Philippics* 3.36)

True decus lies in virtue, which is made manifest in great services done for the good of the state.
(Cicero, *Letters to His Friends* 10.12.5)

decus Romans of all stations were peculiarly conscious of personal honor, and Latin has several words for it, each with a different nuance. *Dignitas* and *honor* suggest official distinction, *honestas* and *fides* an honorable moral integrity, *pudor* means an honorable sense of shame, *existimatio* and *fama* describe honorable reputation, and *virtus* is the honor won by great deeds. The notable thing about the Roman conception of honor as *decus* is its aesthetic nature. *Decus* combines, in various proportions, the ideas of beauty, dignity, and public recognition (compare the English derivatives *decorous*, of attractive and proper behavior, and *decoration*, a beautiful feature to be seen in public). It is a type of honor based not on a code of conduct or a personal ethical compass but on the possession of a jewel-like preeminence in one's sphere. Cato the Younger was the *maximum decus* of his family, just as the playwright Plautus was the *decus* of the Latin language, and the moon the *decus* of the night. It is a quality immediately perceptible and, like any form of beauty, dependent on the perception of others for its existence.

TLL 5.235–248. Cato the Younger: Valerius Maximus, *Memorable Deeds and Sayings* 3.4.6. Plautus: Aulus Gellius, *Attic Nights* 19.8.6. The moon: Apuleius, *On the God of Socrates* 1.14.

HUMANITAS: KINDNESS, PITY, SYMPATHY; CIVILIZATION, REFINEMENT, CULTURE, CHARM

The general public's humanitas performed some sort of funeral rites for the corpse of one unknown to them.

> (From a practice legal speech, ps.-Quintilian, *Major Declamations* 6.3)

In these premises of Aurelia Faustiniana is the bath, where you can bathe in the manner of the city, and where every civilized refinement [humanitas] is available.

> (Inscription from Ficulea, *ILS* 5720)

Humanitas forbids arrogance towards associates, and it forbids greed. In words, deeds, and feelings, it shows itself gentle and courteous to all men.

> (Seneca, *Letters* 88.30)

Those who fashioned the Latin vocabulary and have used it properly intended humanitas to mean not what most people think—which is expressed by the Greeks as philanthropia and signifies ... a certain benevolence toward people in general—rather, they referred to as humanitas more or less what the Greeks call paideia, and which we call learning, and education in the good arts.

> (Aulus Gellius, *Attic Nights* 13.17)

No doubt the famous Scipio, a most learned and humane man, did not appreciate [Greek vases]; but you, without any education, without humanitas, without talent, without knowledge of literature, no doubt you appreciate and judge them!

> (Cicero, *Against Verres* 2.4.98)

So exquisite was the humanitas of Crassus, that when they had bathed and sat down to dinner, all the bitterness of that earlier discussion had vanished.

> (Cicero, *On the Orator* 1.27)

humanitas As an ethical virtue, *humanitas* is a disposition toward compassion and sympathy for others. It was particularly admired in the powerful: generals, judges, provincial governors, and emperors. "[Pompey] is a man of such *humanitas* that it is difficult to say whether the enemy fears his courage when fighting against him as much as they love his mercy after they have been conquered." "Caesar, those who dare to speak before you are ignorant of your greatness; those who do not dare are ignorant of your *humanitas*." The emperor Constantius was addressed not as, say, "your highness," but "your *humanitas*." If you were a conquered enemy, a provincial, or an imperial subject, you hoped for *humanitas* from those in power, but you took what you got. In ordinary people, *humanitas* is the quality that makes one bury a dead stranger, take in a guest or traveler, give money to a beggar, cry in grief, reject a suitor without arrogance, or treat an animal well. We do small favors not for a man, but for humanity, says Seneca (*non homini sed humanitati*)—that is, on principle, not expecting any return. Kindness, above all, is what it means to be "human" in Latin.

As an aspect of luxury, *humanitas* was urban refinement and comfort, such as that advertised for the country baths of Aurelia Faustiniana, and which allowed one to rise above the beasts and enjoy life a bit. It was what Nero had in mind when, after the completion of his vast new palace complex, the construction of which demolished whole neighborhoods in the center of Rome, he said that at last he could begin to live like a human being (*quasi hominem*).

The notions of human sympathy and cultured refinement are joined in a peculiar development of the language in the first century BC associated with Cicero and his contemporaries. Here *humanitas* connotes not, or not only, the Greek term *philanthropia*— a benevolent attitude toward people in general—but also the Greek *paideia*, liberal education. Education in the arts, Cicero believed, leads to both aesthetic refinement and to personal charm and ethical sensitivity. As a cultural attainment, *humanitas* involves a broad knowledge of history, law, philosophy, literature, and the arts. It is the virtue that allows one to diffuse even the most awkward situations with interesting conversation, to adorn a persuasive speech with effective illustrations, to act courteously in the face of insult, to win over a difficult audience with personal ease and charm, to settle a question with an amusing and apposite remark, to write a beguiling letter, or to quarrel in a manner considerate of others' feelings.

The idea that broad education in literature, philosophy, and the arts is the key to *humanitas*, to "living like a human being," is closely associated with Cicero (especially his treatise on the ideal orator). For some reason this educational definition of *humanitas* is not picked up by later generations of Roman authors, apart from some scholars like Gellius, quoted above. In subsequent centuries the word usually means simply "kindness." Perhaps the notion that literary culture makes one humane seemed naïve given the sins of the highly literate Roman aristocracy. The emperor Tiberius, for example, had extremely refined literary tastes but was also known for having people thrown off the cliffs near his seaside villa on Capri. As Seneca points out just after the passage quoted on *humanitas*, virtue has no necessary relationship to educational level.

At the center of the word is the hopeful idea that ethics and education and leadership might not be separate. When the emperor Valentinian fell ill in AD 367, the Gauls in attendance on him held a clandestine meeting and nominated as his successor the master of records, Rusticus Julianus, a man, according to the contemporary historian Ammianus, whose bestial thirst for human blood verged on madness. Luckily the emperor revived, and the plan to install Rusticus (whose name aptly enough means "boor") was thwarted. Ammianus then writes a speech which gives the virtue of *humanitas* a civic turn. Valentinian is commending his chosen successor, his young son Gratian, to the troops: "Because he has been educated from the beginning of his youth in *humanitas* and the studies of ingenious disciplines, he will weigh with impartial judgment the merits of deeds done rightly, or the opposite. He will act in such a way that good men will know that they are appreciated. . . . He will risk his life for the companions of his labors and, what is the first and highest form of loyalty, he will know how to love the Republic as he loves the house of his father and grandfather." This Ciceronian dream of *humanitas*, in which literary and philosophical education makes us both better people and better citizens, was a powerful inspiration to Petrarch, Erasmus, and the other scholars whose devotion to classical learning shaped the European Renaissance. They have been given the name "humanists" in homage to it.

TLL 6.3.3075–3083 collects the evidence. See *RE* Suppl. 5.282–310. Greg Woolf, *Becoming Roman: The Origins of Provincial Civilization in Gaul* (Cambridge: Cambridge University Press, 1998) 54–60. Paul Veyne, "*Humanitas*: Romans and Non-Romans," in Andrea Giardina, ed., *The Romans* (Chicago: University of Chicago Press, 1993) 342–369. Pompey's *humanitas*: Cicero, *On the Manilian Law* 42. Those who dare to speak: remark by Q. Varius Geminus, the orator and friend of Augustus, quoted by Seneca the Elder, *Controversiae* 6.8. Constantius: *TLL* 6.3081, lines 66–67. Small favors: Seneca, *On Benefits* 4.29.3. Live like a human being: Suetonius, *Nero* 31.2. Valentinian and Gratian: Ammianus Marcellinus, *The Later Roman Empire* 27.6.

FINAL MOMENTS

iudicium (supremum)

mors voluntaria

(di) manes

monumentum

IUDICIUM (SUPREMUM): FINAL JUDGMENT, WILL, TESTAMENT

In the last analysis the iudicia of the dead
must be protected.

(From a practice speech, ps.-Quintilian, *Minor
Delcamations* 374.9)

[Augustus] weighed the suprema iudicia of his friends with
the utmost persnicketiness, and he did not conceal his grief
when mentioned too briefly or with insufficient honor, nor his
joy if someone spoke of him with gratitude and devotion.

(Suetonius, *Augustus* 66.4)

I wish, Rufinus, that you had not gotten in the way of [your brother's]
suprema iudicia. What thanks he would have rendered to me in his
will! . . . . I would rather produce that recent will of your brother,
imperfect though it is, in which he mentions me with the utmost
dutifulness and honor. But Rufinus prevented that will from being
drawn up or completed, due to his shame at losing his inheritance.

(Apuleius, in a speech defending himself against
a capital charge, *Apology* 96–97)

iudicium (supremum) The main Latin word for will is *testamentum*, which derives from the verb *testor*, "to affirm solemnly before witnesses" (a witness was a *testis*, his evidence *testimonium*). *Voluntas* ("wish," "desire," "will") was also used, as was *tabulae* ("tablets"). But the most idiomatic and Roman way of referring to a will was "final judgment," *iudicium supremum* (= *ultimum, postremum, novissimum*), or sometimes simply *iudicium* alone. The Roman will was not the private, family affair of today, but a public document, read before an audience of interested onlookers, its terms quickly repeated around town. Contemporary letters from those outside Rome show a keen interest in the subject of recent wills. Testators themselves used wills not only to dispose of property but as an opportunity to comment on other people's characters, and to reveal their real feelings about people, even those not in the immediate family. Since the writer was now past caring, the gloves came off and real opinions were aired. The Romans, said one Greek critic of Roman upper-class artificiality, tell the truth but once in their lives, in their wills.

These judgments, precisely because they were so honest and uncompromising, could make or break reputations. "How respectfully and loyally he tends to his friends," reads a letter of recommendation, "you can deduce from the *suprema iudicia* of many men." Cicero boasts of the number of people who continued to mention him in their wills, even when he was in exile. Adverse comment could be explicit. "We must not approve of parents who injure their own children in their wills," says a jurist, "which many do, ill-naturedly passing judgment on their own blood, corrupted by the wiles and incitements of stepmothers." Simple omission was also an effective way of damaging someone's reputation. The emperor Tiberius was humiliated when the wealthy and prominent Iunia (sister of Brutus and widow of Cassius, the assassins of Caesar) named almost every leading citizen of Rome with honor but omitted to mention him at all. Finally, for real malefactors, it was customary to leave the bequest of a rope (with or without a nail) with which to hang themselves.

TLL 7.610. Edward Champlin, *Final Judgments: Duty and Emotion in Roman Wills*, 200 BC–AD 250 (Berkeley: University of California Press, 1991). Greek critic: Lucian, *Nigrinus* 30. Letter of recommendation: Pliny the Younger, *Letters* 7.31.5. Cicero: *On His Own House* 85. Jurist: Gaius, in Justinian's *Digest of Roman Law* 5.2.4. Tiberius omitted from Junia's will: Tacitus, *Annals* 3.76. Rope and nail: Martial, *Epigrams* 4.70; CIL 6.12649: *Atimeto lib(erto), cuius dolo filiam amisi, restem et clavom unde sibi collum alliget.*

MORS VOLUNTARIA: VOLUNTARY DEATH, SUICIDE

I omit the murders; I pass over the acts of lust, of which we have the most distressing evidence: it is agreed that maidens of most noble families have thrown themselves into wells, and avoided through mors voluntaria *their inevitable disgrace.*

(Cicero, cataloguing the crimes of Lucius Piso, governor of Macedonia in 56 BC, *On the Consular Provinces* 6)

Love reason! Love of this will arm you against the greatest hardships. Love of their young impels wild beasts to rush into the spears of hunters; desire for glory has endowed many young minds with contempt for enemy swords and fire; the mere appearance and semblance of courage has impelled some men to mors voluntaria. *How much stronger than all these is reason, how much more constant.*

(Seneca, *Letters* 74.21)

mors voluntaria Latin has no word for suicide; that is, no single word refers to the deliberate act of self-homicide. Many circumlocutions existed, however, among which "voluntary death" was the closest thing to a technical term. The English word "suicide" *appears* to be based on a Latin word *suicidium*, combining *sui* ("self") with *occidere* ("to kill"). But in reality there is no such Latin word. *Suicide* is a pseudo-Latin coinage, apparently invented twice, first in the twelfth century (when it did not catch on), then again independently in the seventeenth (when it did). Latin pronouns were not used as prefixes, so by rights *suicidium* should mean "killing of a pig" (*sus, suis*), which it in fact does mean in one medieval text.

Lack of a term did not, of course, prevent some ancient Romans from killing themselves, nor Latin authors from discussing the concept, and in several famous instances spectacular suicides changed Roman history. Lucretia was a Roman noble woman of the regal period who was raped by Sextus Tarquinius, the son of the last Roman king. After binding her husband Collatinus to vengeance, and despite being innocent herself of any crime, Lucretia stabbed herself, an act romanticized by later historians and poets as the ultimate defense of her chastity. According to tradition, outrage over the incident sparked a revolt that put an end to the monarchy itself. Lucretia was treated as a paragon of chastity, proof that remaining sexually pure could be more important to a Roman woman than life itself. It was an extreme example of suicide motivated not by private despair but by honor and shame, and the story was told and re-told by authors who stressed the Roman attachment to a sense of personal honor. Anthropologists would say that Lucretia's act relates to an ethical system based not on guilt, which requires intent, but on pollution, which can be contracted regardless of any criminal intent. The young Macedonian women who Cicero says threw themselves into wells after being raped by the Roman governor Piso acted in a similar fashion.

A case on the male side involved Cato the Younger, the politician and devotee of Stoic philosophy who was an inflexible partisan of the old Republican system of government and an implacable opponent of Julius Caesar, whose rise to power he rightly saw as dooming that system. Defeated in the civil war against Caesar, he chose to fall on his sword rather than live on under the tyrant. This was another "honor" suicide. Caesar likely would have let him live, as he did other prominent opponents, such as Brutus and Cassius. Cato advised his friends and even his own son to make peace with Caesar. But Cato held himself to a higher standard. The night before he killed himself, he read Plato's work on the immortality of the soul twice before falling asleep. Cato's calm, philosophical fortitude was an inspiration to later generations of Roman nobles, and quite a few killed themselves rather than live under (or be executed by) tyrannical emperors. They did so in spectacular Catonian fashion, so as to bring maximum ill will to the emperor: not alone in private misery, but like Socrates, surrounded by grieving friends, discoursing on philosophy and dictating their last words. The fashion for such "brave" political suicides at Rome was powerfully set by the example of Cato. Seneca criticizes this wastage more than once ("the mere appearance and semblance of courage"), but when the time came, and he was falsely implicated in a conspiracy against his old student, the emperor Nero, Seneca opened his veins, as did his wife, who insisted on following him.

The traditional Roman admiration for honor suicide and its moral/philosophical justification are attacked at length by St. Augustine, who argues that an innocent person who kills him or herself is simply a murderer, nothing more. In taking aim at the moral authority of Lucretia and Cato, he avoids the neutral-sounding phrase *mors voluntaria*, which emphasizes moral autonomy, and harps again and again on the verbal phrase *se occidere*, "to murder oneself." This phraseology employs the same verb used in the Latin version of the sixth commandment, "thou shalt not kill" (*non occides*). In sharp contrast to Christian and medieval discussions of the topic, pagan Roman documents that record suicides rarely carry a hint that the act itself might be blameworthy. The terms they use for it are euphemistic: "to take oneself away" (*se auferre*), "to bring violence to oneself" (*vim sibi afferre*), "to decide on oneself" (*de se statuere*). Christian authors, influenced by the prohibition of suicide elaborated by Augustine and others, tend to use pejorative terms such as *se ipsum occidere* and *ad mortem festinare* ("to hasten to death").

The lack of a single agreed-upon term is perhaps not so surprising, given the unpleasant, even taboo, nature of the subject. Better to speak in euphemisms, expressions that do not quite hit the nail on the head, rather than look at the terrible deed for what it really is; vagueness eases both the justification of suicide and the avoidance of the topic altogether. From that perspective the problem was not too few words to talk about suicide but too many.

Alexander Murray, *Suicide in the Middle Ages,* two of three vols. published so far (Oxford: Oxford University Press, 1998, 2000). Miriam Griffin, "Philosophy, Cato, and Roman Suicide," article in two parts, *Greece and Rome* 33 (1986) 64–77 and 192–202. Seneca: *Letters* 74.21. Augustine: *City of God* 1.17–25.

(DI) MANES: THE SPIRITS OF THE DEAD, CONCEIVED OF AS UNDERWORLD GODS

Sacred to the Di Manes. C. Julius Felix lies here. He lived 82 years, 7 months. His dear wife made [the monument]. Poor Felix, you were deprived of life too soon, and undeservedly. You should have lived—you could have lived—to a hundred. If the Manes exist, may the earth be light upon you.

(Epitaph from Ammaedara in modern Tunisia, *CIL* 8 Suppl. 11594 = *CLE* 1328)

Do not disturb the Di Manes; so may another man not disturb yours.

(Epitaph, *CIL* 6.13383)

And [the orator Argentarius] used to swear "by the Manes of my teacher Cestius," while Cestius was still alive. [The hostility was mutual. Cestius called Argentarius "my ape."]

(Seneca the Elder, *Controversiae* 9.3.12)

Life is good, life is bad, but death has neither quality. If you are wise consider what is more advantageous. But because there are Manes, may the earth be light upon you. Tittia Lucilla lived 14 years 5 months, of which time she spent scarcely 18 months, up to the day of her death, with her husband.

(Epitaph of a young bride, put up by her husband, Fabius Exsuperantius, *CIL* 8 Suppl. 11665 = *CLE* 1497)

(di) manes In contrast to the ancient Chinese or Egyptians, the Romans held out no hope whatsoever for a decent time in the afterlife. The underworld was a gloomy place, often referred to as *tenebrae*—the shadows. "Live a good life, friend," urges one epitaph, "Why? After death there will be no laughter, no play, nor any pleasure." Other epitaphs concurred. "Live day to day, hour to hour, for no possession is sure." "While I lived I drank with pleasure; drink also, you who are still alive." "Aged 18, I lived as well as I could, pleasing to my parent [only one] and to all my friends. I urge you, play and have fun, for here there is the utmost seriousness [*severitas*]." Still, it was commonly believed that *something* survived of a person after death, and that something was given the name *Di Manes*. Etymologically, it derives from the archaic word *manis*, meaning "good," so that *Di Manes* were the "good gods." Thus it is a euphemism of a kind that the subject of death naturally attracts. In English we refer to a dead person as "the late" so-and-so, or

say that someone has "passed away," or "gone to a better place," a practice that perhaps originated with the magical belief that to speak the word "death" was to invite it.

Di Manes is one of those phrases that gives translators pain. Not exactly "ghost" (manes don't haunt, typically, and they dwell in the lower world, not ours; one epitaph calls them secreti—hidden); nor quite "soul," which would endow these shadowy beings with too much individuality. And since manes is a generalizing plural (never singular) and can be used to refer to the undifferentiated mass of the dead, as well as the post-mortem being of a single individual, it is often not clear whether we are dealing with a group of underworld gods or one dead person's spirit. As for the Di part, most translators simply omit it. Are they in fact gods? Yes, in the sense that they received cult worship—gifts like dedicatory inscriptions, liquid and food offerings (sometimes through pipes leading into the ground) at certain occasions, and being invoked with prayers; no, in that they had no temples and lacked mythology, indeed any substantial individuality. The Romans themselves seem to have held various views about their nature and activities.

We also have an unusual number of expressions of skepticism or outright disbelief in the existence of the manes. "That the manes exist," asserts one poet, "not even boys believe, unless they have yet to pay to get into the baths" (i.e., are too young to bathe themselves). Tombs, even the ones ostensibly sacred to the Di Manes, sometimes raise doubt ("If the manes exist . . .") or find it necessary to assert their existence ("Since the manes exist," respect the tomb, etc.). Yet D.M.S. (dis manibus sacrum, "sacred to the Di Manes") continues to appear, even on many Christian and Jewish graves, well into late antiquity. Curse tablets addressed to them directly have been found thrown into wells all over the empire.

Skepticism and belief appear side by side in a practice speech written on a hypo-thetical legal case involving a woman who keeps seeing her dead son in her dreams. Her husband consults a sorcerer, who casts a spell on the tomb, whereupon the mother stops seeing her son. The mother then (in an unlikely turn typical of the genre) sues the father for cruel treatment. The father argues in defense that the manes do not exist, and that everything perishes with the body. The response by the wife's counsel fills in some of the emotional background behind the simple D.M.S. of the gravestones. Asserting that the souls of the dead remember their former incarnation, he says, "Hence the manes come forth when called upon [evocatos], hence they take on body and face and whatever else we see [in dreams]; that is why they appear as beloved images to those near and dear, and why occasionally they serve as oracles to warn us with nocturnal advice, why they sense the offerings we send to them, and perceive the honors we pay their tombs. I ask you, is it not better to believe this when a son dies?"

TLL 8.293–299. "Seize the day" epitaphs: CLE 186, 185, 243, 85. Not even boys believe: Juvenal, Satires 2.149–152. Practice speech: ps.-Quintilian, Major Declamations 10.16–17.

MONUMENTUM: TOMB; MEMORIAL; (ESPECIALLY PLURAL) A WRITTEN WORK, HISTORICAL ACCOUNT, HISTORY

Tomb monumenta are placed along the road for this reason, to remind [admonere] passersby that the deceased existed and that they too are mortal. From that, all the other things which are written or made for memory's sake are called monumenta.

(Varro, *On the Latin Language* 6.49)

All Greece has decorated his bravery ... with monumenta: sculpture, statues, honorary inscriptions, histories, and other things.

(Cato the Elder, on Leonidas, the hero of the battle of Thermopylae in 480 BC; *Origines* 4.7 = Aulus Gellius, *Attic Nights* 3.7.19)

What makes acquaintance with history particularly healthy and fruitful is that you can look at instructive examples set out, as it were, on a conspicuous monumentum; from it you can take for yourself and for your Republic things to emulate, and from the same source other things, disgraceful in conception and outcome, to avoid.

(Livy, *Roman History* pref. 10)

I have completed a monumentum more lasting than bronze, higher than the royal mass of the pyramids.

(Horace, referring to his three-book collection of *Odes; Odes* 3.30.1–2) *monumentum* The Romans placed great importance on grave markers and monuments, not just as a dignity due to the dead but as the only sure way to perpetuate the memory of one's life and deeds among the living. Pity for those who did not have one was surpassed only by fear of not having one oneself. The many thousands of epitaphs that survive represent a veritable literary genre, and they belonged to people of all social classes.

A grave *monumentum* is something that, as Varro says, both reminds and admonishes (two senses of *admonere*), calling to mind the past and cautioning the living that they too are mortal. "You are a human being: stop and consider my tomb. As a young man I set out to get what I could use. I did injury to no one, and did favors for a great many. Hurry up and live well: you are on your way here," reads the monument of a freedman and pig merchant. Don't have a noble life or famous deeds to boast of? Try humor: "Stranger, pause and, if you don't mind, read this. Don't get indigestion. Take my advice, drink hot beverages. We all must die. Farewell."

The concern to have a memorable epitaph or monument is part of the wider cultural tendency toward monumentalization—seize the day, but build for the ages—that partly explains why so many Roman buildings still stand, roads and aqueducts are still in use, tombs are still seen, and poems are still read. But unlike Pharaonic Egypt, not only rulers and officials could have a piece of immortality in this dimension. Everyone from emperors to slaves received monuments with formal epitaphs. A formulaic abbreviation on many of them reads *H.M.H.N.S.* (*hoc monumentum heredes non sequetur*), "this *monumentum* will not follow the heirs"—i.e. "not to be removed." Roman pagans did not have cemeteries per se. (The word *coemeterium* is a third-century Christian coinage, based on the Greek *koimaterion*, meaning "dormitory," the idea being that the departed is not truly dead but only asleep, awaiting the resurrection.) The traditional Roman *monumentum* is placed not near a church or temple but along a road leading into town, like the many still visible along the Appian Way south of Rome. The point was maximum visibility.

In a wider sense a *monumentum* can be anything that recalls the past and makes us consider the present, including a statue, sculpture, or written document, in particular histories. While the Greek term *historia* connotes research or enquiry, *monumenta* as a word for historical writing presents a much more Roman conception of the craft: not just the recording of information for its own sake (as if the mere collection of facts were sufficient) but public memory of important deeds as a call to virtue, achievement, and reflection. It is fitting that Livy, the great exponent of this kind of historical writing, imagines his ideal reader as the passing viewer of a roadside *monumentum*, drawing from history examples to emulate and avoid, both for himself and for his Republic.

Freedman and pig merchant: *CLE* 83 = *CIL* 9.2128.
Hot beverages: *CLE* 118 = *CIL* 10.5371.

ACKNOWLEDGMENTS

I AM GRATEFUL to Dickinson College, especially the Research and Development Committee, the Roberts Fund, and the Central Pennsylvania Consortium (which includes Dickinson, Franklin & Marshall, and Gettysburg Colleges) for financial support that helped in completing this book. I would like to thank my friends and colleagues at Dickinson, Leon Fitts, Marc Mastrangelo, and Mark Wardecker, who read and commented on the manuscript at various stages, and saved me from many blunders. Invaluable help in fact checking and copy-editing came from David Hewett and Anthony Moore, respectively, and in both cases the assistance went well beyond those tasks. The mistakes remaining are all mine. I feel a great debt of gratitude to the, if not anonymous, at least relatively unsung makers of the *Thesaurus Linguae Latinae* and *Oxford Latin Dictionary*, and the database maestros who gave us the Packard Humanities Institute Latin disk and the CETEDOC library of Christian Latin texts on CD-ROM. Without those tools a project like this would be far more difficult. Thanks also to Barbara McDonald, Tanya Shohov, John and Christopher Roberts, Andrew Fenton, Jeffrey Wood, Tina Maresco, Sandy Gority, Monica Bentley, William Thayer; and most of all to Peter and Paula Francese, to whom this book is lovingly dedicated.

SUGGESTIONS FOR FURTHER READING

TEXTS:

The most frequently cited authors in this book are all available in convenient bilingual editions in the Loeb Classical Library, published by Harvard University Press. In many, though not all, cases the translations in the Penguin Classics and Oxford World Classics series are more readable. They are usually less expensive, too, though they lack Latin texts. I single out David West's beautiful and accurate prose translation of the *Aeneid* in the Penguin series, the Loeb of Martial by the late D. R. Shackleton Bailey, and the translation of Suetonius by Catherine Edwards in the Oxford World Classics series, with its helpful notes. Good translations of some late antique texts, such as Lactantius' *Divine Institutes*, are starting to appear in the important series Liverpool Translated Texts for Historians.

LATIN:

Andrew Keller and Stephanie Russell, *Learn to Read Latin*. New Haven: Yale University Press, 2006.

L.R. Palmer, *The Latin Language*. London: Faber and Faber, 1954.

Jószef Herman, *Vulgar Latin*, trans. Roger Wright. University Park, PA: University of Pennsylvania Press, 2000.

ROMAN HISTORY:

Michael H. Crawford, *The Roman Republic*, 2nd ed. Cambridge, MA: Harvard University Press, 1993.

C. M. Wells, *The Roman Empire*, 2nd ed. Cambridge, MA: Harvard University Press, 1995.

Pat Southern, *The Roman Empire from Severus to Constantine*. London: Routledge, 2001.

Stephen Mitchell, *A History of the Later Roman Empire, AD 284–641*. Oxford: Blackwell, 2007.

ROMAN DAILY LIFE:

Jo-Ann Shelton, *As the Romans Did*, 2nd ed. New York: Oxford University Press, 1998.

Lesley and Roy Adkins, *Handbook to Life in Ancient Rome*. New York: Facts on File, 1994.

Paul Veyne, ed. *A History of Private Life, vol. 1, From Pagan Rome to Byzantium*. Trans. A. Goldhammer. Cambridge, MA: Harvard University Press, 1987.

Index of Authors Quoted

All dates are AD, unless otherwise noted. The dates are drawn mainly from *OCD*, third edition, and Fritz Graf, ed., *Einleitung in die Lateinische Philologie* (Stuttgart and Leipzig: Teubner, 1997), where further details, such as the complete original forms of the authors' names, can be found. Conventional modern names are used here. Anonymous works are listed by the title of the work and spurious or doubtful works under the names of their supposed authors, with the prefix *ps-* (pseudo).

AUTHORS / WORKS	DATES	PAGES
AE	*see abbreviations*	98, 212
The African War (*Bellum Africum*)	composed 47–40 BC	126
Ambrose	appr. 335 to appr. 397	19, 48, 84, 92, 103, 154, 162, 171
Ammianus Marcellinus	appr. 333 to after 395	63, 102, 143, 154, 228
Apuleius	appr. 125 to after 170	26, 62, 76, 78, 144, 157, 182, 196, 204, 225, 230
Arnobius	early fourth century	63, 163, 190
Asconius	9 BC–AD 76	70, 90, 122
Augustine	354–430	18, 40, 41, 42, 44, 63, 66, 68, 85, 108, 120, 147, 171, 178, 192, 193, 200, 201, 224, 233
Augustus	63 BC–AD 14	31, 175, 184
Aulus Gellius	appr. 130 to appr. 180	48, 49, 64, 106, 166, 214, 225, 226, 236
Ausonius	appr. 310–393 or 394	147
Benedict	appr. 480 to appr. 550	172
Caelius Aurelianus	fifth century?	200, 201
Caesarius of Arles	470–542	68, 194, 197, 200
Calpurnius Flaccus	imperial period	51, 174
Cassiodorus	appr. 490 to appr. 583	77, 97
Cato the Elder	234–149 BC	75, 80, 85, 86, 106, 120, 130, 160, 190, 236
Catullus	appr. 85 to appr. 55 BC	48, 89, 96, 179, 182, 194, 212, 215, 224
Celsus	early first century	152, 218
Cestius Pius	Augustan period	32
CGL	*see abbreviations*	102, 202, 215
Cicero	106–43 BC	18, 26, 27, 38, 44, 48, 56, 58, 60, 64, 74, 77, 85, 86, 87, 99, 110, 111, 114, 115, 118, 119, 129, 122, 128, 130, 135, 140, 144, 153, 158, 166, 167, 171, 174, 178, 180, 203, 204, 208, 209, 210, 219, 220, 225, 226, 231, 232

Authors / Works	Dates	Pages
CIL	*see abbreviations*	16, 30, 34, 39, 52, 68, 96, 97, 98, 119, 126, 131, 158, 168, 191, 215, 222, 231, 234
Claudian	died before 404	39, 170
CLE	*see abbreviations*	30, 39, 131, 158, 222, 234, 235, 237
Codex Justinianus	promulgated 529	74
Columella	first century	18, 74, 77, 153, 166, 172
Cornelius Nepos	100 to after 27 BC	28, 156, 218
Curtius Rufus	first century AD	58, 196
Cyprian of Carthage	appr. 200–258	77
The Dialogue of Hadrian and Epictetus	second to third century	65, 100, 102, 160
Donatus	fourth century	178, 213
Ennius	239–169 BC	140
Fronto	appr. 100 to appr. 167	91, 130, 140, 158, 162
Gaius	second century	231
Germanicus	15 BC–AD 19	148, 150
Gregory the Great	appr. 540–604	44, 77, 201
Gregory of Tours	appr. 538 to appr. 594	80
Horace	65–8 BC	32, 39, 48, 50, 52, 55, 56, 60, 62, 63, 81, 110, 142, 147, 155, 160, 161, 171, 225, 236
ps.-Hyginus, *On Camp Fortifications*	second century	33, 132
ILS	*see abbreviations*	58, 66, 90, 108, 112, 134, 156, 210, 220, 226
Isidore of Seville	appr. 570–636	16, 19, 31, 40, 44, 78, 186
Jerome	345 or 348–420	20, 32, 35, 40, 58, 63, 66, 68, 102, 143, 154, 173, 186, 224
Josephus	37 or 38 to after 97	138
Julius Caesar	100–44 BC	26, 30, 50, 75, 100, 106, 128, 202
Justinian's *Digest of Roman Law*	promulgated 533	119, 125, 132, 140, 167, 175, 180, 183, 184, 204, 218, 224, 231
Justinian's *Institutes*	promulgated 533	196
Juvenal	appr. 60 to appr. 130	57, 80, 98, 135, 148, 172, 173, 174, 175, 180, 235
Lactantius	appr. 250 to appr. 325	19, 48, 118, 120, 197, 224
Laus Pisonis	first century AD	56
Law of the Twelve Tables	promulgated fifth century BC	178
Livy	59 BC–AD 17	26, 56, 66, 80, 114, 118, 123, 132, 138, 146, 160, 190, 191, 204, 222, 224, 236
Lucian	appr. 120 to after 180	103, 231

Index of Latin Words

Note: Featured terms are capitalized.